The
Secret Treachery
of Words

The
Secret Treachery
of Words

Feminism

and Modernism

in America

Elizabeth Francis

University of Minnesota Press
Minneapolis • London

Parts of chapter 1 originally appeared in "From Event to Monument: Feminism, Modernism, and Isadora Duncan," *American Studies* 35, no. 1 (April 1994): 25–47; copyright Mid-America American Studies Association; reprinted with permission. Parts of chapter 4 previously appeared as "A Real Life, Fissured: Josephine Herbst's Sense of History," introduction to Josephine Herbst, *The Starched Blue Sky of Spain and Other Memoirs* (Boston: Northeastern University Press, 1999); used with the permission of Northeastern University Press.

Published by the University of Minnesota Press
111 Third Avenue South, Suite 290
Minneapolis, MN 55401-2520
http://www.upress.umn.edu

Library of Congress Cataloging-in-Publication Data

Francis, Elizabeth, 1959
    The secret treachery of words : feminism and modernism in America / Elizabeth Francis.
        p.   cm.
    Includes bibliographical references and index.
    ISBN 0-8166-3327-4 (HC : alk. paper) — ISBN 0-8166-3328-2 (PB : alk. paper)
    1. Feminism—United States.   2. Feminist criticism—United States.
    3. Modernism (Literature)—United States.   I. Title.
    HQ1426 .F797 2002
    305.42'0973—dc21
                                                                    2001005641

Printed in the United States of America on acid-free paper

The University of Minnesota is an equal-opportunity educator and employer.

12 11 10 09 08 07 06 05 04 03 02   10 9 8 7 6 5 4 3 2 1

Contents

Acknowledgments

I am grateful to many people for their ideas, criticism, and support as I wrote this book. My mentor at Brown University, Mari Jo Buhle, encouraged me to push the boundaries of women's history. Also at Brown, Ellen Rooney helped me to create a theoretically informed history and Mary Gluck inspired me to look at modernism in new ways. John L. Thomas shaped my approach to intellectual portraiture.

The creative insights and painstaking criticisms of Chris Amirault helped me immeasurably.

I owe a special debt to Gail Bederman, who has the rare gift of being both challenging and supportive. I could not have finished this without her. I also was privileged to be a member of groups of gifted women scholars whose conversations and insights I have valued greatly, including Jane Gerhard, Ruth Feldstein, and Melani McAlister; and Carolyn Dean, Gretchen Schultz, and Tamar Katz. At an earlier stage, Linda Grasso, Mary Louise Roberts, and Donna Penn made very insightful comments.

I'm also grateful to my former editor, William Murphy, and my current editor, Richard Morrison, at the University of Minnesota Press and to the readers of the manuscript for the press, especially Daniel J. Singal, who made helpful, generous, but incisive recommendations.

Finally, I thank my parents, Don and Ruth Francis, whose quest to live beautifully I cherish, and my daughter Lulu, who has taught me so much about the power of words.

Introduction

The Enmeshment of
Feminism and Modernism

Feminism faced a crisis after American women won the right to vote in 1920. Though feminists continued to launch major initiatives for women, feminism itself seemed to be out of step with the times and to have lost its cultural power. Some feminists confronted the crisis by associating feminism explicitly with modernism, then dominating the arts and all sorts of cultural expression. The journalist Dorothy Dunbar Bromley, for instance, proclaimed that a modernist style would do for feminism what it had done for art: make it new. This infusion of modernism created a new figure for feminism altogether, a figure Bromley called "Feminist—New Style." Drinking in the excitement of the Jazz Age, Bromley wrote:

> She aspires to understand the meaning of the twentieth century as she sees it expressed in the skyscrapers, the rapid pace of city life, the expressionistic drama, the abstract conception of art, the new music; the Joycian novel. She is acutely conscious that she is being carried along in the current of these sweeping forces, that she and her sex are in the vanguard of change.[1]

Bromley's "Feminist—New Style" was hypothetical; "she" stood for the author and yet was more abstract and general than just one person, suggesting that any modern, urbane woman could adopt the new style of feminism.

Through this abstraction, Bromley linked the vanguard of sex to avant-garde culture, which in her characterization was resonant with stereotypical descriptions of modern life in 1927. Indeed, modernism's critical stance toward "the modern" was no longer critical at all; characteristically, modernist genres of artistic media were simply compatible with the growing skyline and hustle and bustle of the city. As evoked here, modernism wasn't a set of high art forms to be admired, either—it was a style, a set of associations, touchstones of contemporary cachet. For example, instead of citing *Ulysses*, Bromley named a novelistic *style* after its famous author James Joyce. Though this list that connected feminism to avant-garde culture was suspiciously vague and associational, it did not lack power. Rather, for Bromley it represented a "sweeping force" of "change," and its power lay precisely in this gesture to the abstract, general, and categorical. By riding this force, feminists could gain membership in modern culture, and they could connect themselves to vibrant strands of cultural activity. Through modernism, feminists would be able to assume historical agency in a period in which their status was in doubt.

The relationship of feminism to modernism that Bromley referenced is one among many that needs more interpretation—of its historical complexities as well as the contemporary critical disputes it has engendered. Historians, literary critics, and cultural theorists have addressed the connection between them, but their differing views have led to contention rather than consensus. Some have argued that feminism was a claim to female modernism, while others have argued that modernism's pervasive themes of fear and hatred of women made such a claim impossible. Other scholars have revealed modernist contempt for women in mass culture, on one hand, and the traces of radical social practices such as feminism in modernist writing on the other.[2]

As these contrasting positions indicate, feminism and modernism were entangled with each other at formal, analytical, and cultural levels. Bromley's evocative description of "Feminist—New Style" suggests that we do not have to take these entanglements as a critical dead end. As Bromley implied and this book asserts, the figure of the feminist modernist allows us to understand this entanglement. Rather than a narrative history of groups, genres, or institutions, this book focuses on how individuals attempted to break away from the Victorian past and discovered new opportunities as well as new constraints in modern culture. *The Secret Treachery of Words* explores modernism and feminism as lived cultural practices and positions that changed over time. Writers, artists, and critics saw in feminism not only a liberal idea about equal rights for women but also a force of liberation in avant-garde art, cultural radical-ism, and revolutionary politics. Their essays, performances, and auto-biographies traced the possibilities and conflicts of this engagement. Looking at how people figured themselves and others as feminist mod-ernists allows us to draw an imaginative view of gender and cultural practice in the early twentieth century.

The popular statement "Feminist—New Style" reveals many of the problems of interpreting feminism and modernism together. Bromley's celebration of women's ability to consume modernism was by no means shared by modernists at the time, nor by the critics who established the canon of high modernism, nor by the cultural theorists who attacked the effects of mass culture under capitalism. Bromley's essay reflected the dy-namics of consumerist appropriation and popularization that critics as different from each other as Clement Greenberg and Theodor Adorno have seen as the death knell of any rebellious and experimental culture. Published in *Harper's,* the essay, with its implied middlebrow reader-ship, mediated modernism and its other—mass culture—and thus could never really be part of the vanguard it claimed to be included in. Authen-tic modernism, in distinction, was hostile to mass culture because mass culture always flattened formal innovation into something palatable and yet tantalizing to bourgeois taste.[3] The essay's tone was glib and enthusi-astic and also appropriated experimentation as consumable style. In this view, to read Joyce or, worse, a novel that used some of the stylistic inno-vations of the master modernist was to consume modernism rather than to produce it. To read such a novel was to make a fashion statement, like wearing a new hat. Essays like Bromley's turned what had been revolu-tionary into an embarrassment.

The modernist critique of consumerist appropriation was deeply in-flected by gender, the attribution of differences between men and women in the field of culture. Andreas Huyssen, in his groundbreaking essay, "Mass Culture as Woman: Modernism's Other," argues that modernists expressed an adversarial view of capitalism and bourgeois life by de-spising the new culture of consumption that had developed in the mid-nineteenth century and by the 1920s was a solid pillar of mass culture. Nothing exemplified this loathing more than the modernist's hatred of sentimentality, itself symbolized by the habits and sensibilities of middle-class women, who rapidly became the targets of the new institutions of consumer capitalism. Modernists attacked the effects of mass culture by condemning the qualities of susceptibility and weakness attributed to women consumers. Huyssen insightfully reveals the extent to which such condemnations actually cloaked modernists' own identifications with women's habits of novel-reading and desires to revel in the sensuous, seductive world of commodities displayed in new public spaces such as department stores. Through this anxious identification and yet fear of contamination, a politics of gender in modernism unfolded: in order to become an artist, the modernist had to purge himself of his contamination by mass culture, and he did so by attacking its symbolic target, "woman." While this argument explains much about the representation of women in modernist texts, it creates an analogy that is too neat and tight: modernism is to mass culture as masculinity is to femininity. In this view, modernism was an inherently masculinist enterprise, a worldview in which women modernists, if they were anything, were a significant absence. Into this system, Bromley introduced a significant twist: Feminist—New Style was a consumer, yes, but she consumed modernism, not mass culture.

In the context of feminist thought from the mid-1920s to the early 1930s, Bromley's enthusiasm was a counterpoint to a more general ambivalence and malaise. Bromley's references to modern culture were common, but her point of view was not shared by all postsuffrage feminists. The "vanguard of change" that Feminist—New Style claimed to be actually referred to a large problem in feminist thought, a problem that extended from the meaning of consumer capitalism to many of the other changes that made women modern, including wage-earning, political rights, psychological consciousness, and sexual behavior and beliefs.

On one hand, "change" and "women" seemed to go hand in hand: women had won the vote, reformed conditions for many working women, expanded their educational opportunities, and forged new standards of sexual behavior. Many believed that these developments constituted progress of the most dramatic sort for women. But the actual discussion of modern womanhood by feminists in the 1920s raised objections to the narrative of change as one that simply and only led to progress. Though Bromley glossed over these issues, other feminists focused on problems that "change" had not solved or had created in its wake. The changes themselves appeared to have effected a crisis for feminism. Did women still need feminism? What was its role and purpose? Even though women had won the vote, feminists' sense of political and cultural unity *as* women was shattered. Feminists' anxiety could be heard particularly in discussions of the implications of modern culture for women.[4] The younger generation seemed to have little interest in carrying on the political torch their foremothers had borne so long. Instead, they reveled in new styles, youth-oriented activities, and the pleasures and sensations made possible by consumer capitalism.

In surveying the proliferation of commodities and the expansion of leisure activities that became the defining characteristics of mass culture, some feminists wondered whether the new culture would really change the structural or psychological basis of women's lives. For example, psychologist Lorine Pruette addressed the problem of change and progress in her study *Women and Leisure: A Study of Social Waste* (1924):

> Women have, in the last few hundred years, gone on small adventures. . . . They have adventured forth against political conservatism and gained for themselves votes. . . . They have, small adventurers moving cautiously, . . . gained certain rights over their own bodies . . . over their own children . . . over their own property. [But] women have not gained for themselves the right to select their own activities, they have not the right to their own energies, they have not the choice of their own vocations.[5]

Pruette's rhetoric reflected a sense of political alienation: it reduced woman suffrage, surely one of the most important and hard-won achievements of the women's movement, to a "small adventure." At the same time, this reduction made room for Pruette's point that women's individual psychology had not caught up to their material achievements, a point that also reflected a sense of alienation from modern culture. Pruette's feminist critique, then, sought to define politics through psychology and the dynamics of consumption. The link was necessary in order to account for what was happening in modern culture: the more women engaged in a quest for sexual and stylistic pleasure, the more they tended to become ensnared in economic dependency on men and to leave aside their other aspirations. Unlike Bromley, who believed that the consumption of modernism would invigorate feminism, feminists like Pruette feared that consumer revelry itself, not what was consumed, had impeded the development of women's independence and had taken the edge off women's desires for total—psychological as well as political and economic—transformation.

Historians of feminism have interpreted this anxiety in terms of an incompatibility between feminism and modern culture after 1920. According to Rayna Rapp and Ellen Ross, "[A] dramatic transformation of American culture, fusing sex, love, and consumerism, made the all-female organizations of the feminists seem stuffy and outmoded."[6] In this literature, Bromley's feminism has been characterized as inauthentic: she capitulated to style and consumerism, and she defied the sisterhood that could bind women together in a common cause and thus sustain feminism. Certainly, Bromley's text supported such a reading: "Feminist— New Style professes no loyalty to women *en masse,* although she staunchly believes in individual women." Bromley's disloyalty to "women" was at the heart of the crisis for feminism, according to many historians; without a shared definition of womanhood, feminism was left with an individualism bereft of political and social moorings. This new individualism among women is one of the key factors blamed for destroying the women's movement after 1920. Susan Ware, who included "Feminist—New Style" in her excellent documentary history, *Modern American Women,* has summed up this conclusion: Bromley was representative of an optimistic but misguided generation for whom "the women's movement was no longer necessary."[7]

While this critique has illuminated central problems for American feminism, it nevertheless has separated "feminism" from modern culture. The changes in sexuality and the representation of gender difference wrought by both modernism and mass culture worked to undermine feminism, producing the tendency to see feminism in opposition to modern culture. The interpretation of the history of feminism as separatist and residual thus has produced a similar position as that of modernist critics. Here, Bromley was complicitous with both the forces that worked to derail the experimental and therefore potentially disruptive power of modernism and with the forces that tore apart women's solidarity with each other. She had two strikes against her: writing as a middle-class consumer, she appropriated a stance that contributed to the massification of modernism; writing in the new mode of feminism, she betrayed the ideals of an earlier feminist sisterhood.

Both conclusions have rushed too quickly past an important point: despite all the problems, modern culture was the crucible for feminism. Rita Felski has persuasively argued that interpretations that place feminist concerns outside the "logic of the modern" are limited by the ways in which they can't account for "their own inevitable enmeshment within the categories they seek to transcend."[8] These limitations have real effects: placing feminism in opposition to modern culture has obscured an important area of women's activities in the early twentieth century. This book responds to Felski's criticism by engaging the "inevitable enmeshment" of feminism and modernism as people lived and defined these categories, as their contemporaries saw them, and how they have been understood in history.

The Secret Treachery of Words argues that changing gender relations and the discourse of women's emancipation were central to modernist interrogations of modern culture. Reciprocally, some of the boldest and most far-reaching efforts to create and reinvent feminism can be seen in the style and practice of modernism. The ties between feminism and modernism that Bromley described as indicative of 1927 had actually been established earlier. For example, the elements that Bromley listed in her evocation of "Feminist—New Style" characterized the emergence of feminism in the 1910s, defining women's emancipation as part of modern culture. "Feminist—New Style," then, was a popular instance of a longer connection between feminist thought and practice and modernist ideas, style, and language. The Bromley moment was one that symptomatically documented a crisis, suggesting the need to go both backwards to the beginnings of the link between feminism and modernism, and forwards to the fate of the connection in the thirties.

Affiliation with modernism was central to feminism over a thirty-year period. As Nancy Cott and Mari Jo Buhle have shown, when the term *feminism* first began to be widely used in the 1910s, it was part of an American Left that blended cultural radicalism with activism in established social movements, including labor, socialism, and progressive reform.[9] By the end of the decade, *feminism* had become an accepted term for beliefs in and movements for women's emancipation. In both Left and popular accounts, feminism reflected and advocated major changes in the organization of gender and sexuality in American life. It encompassed a wide variety of issues, including women's demanding the vote, widening the availability of birth control, redesigning the home and the very structure of domesticity, experimenting with dress reform and new fashions, and pursuing nontraditional careers. Feminism was a key word in the discourse of sexual freedom that characterized the transformation of American culture in the early twentieth century; feminists both advocated women's independence from men and claimed a new agency for women as desiring, sexual subjects. Feminism—its utopian possibilities and the cultural anxieties it produced—also was extensively addressed by both women and men in the world of the arts, literature, and ideas in a variety of contexts, from political radicalism to avant-garde art.

Though there were many attempts to define feminism within a coherent agenda for social and political change, its *meaning* was consistent with a modernist spirit or ethos that was highly individualized. Marie Jenney Howe, for example, started the famous feminist group called Heterodoxy, composed of women intellectuals, professionals, scholars, and artists, a group that defined by its very composition a sense of expanded possibility for women in urban, modern life.[10] Howe's definition of feminism, published in an essay for a socialist publication in 1914, referred to progressive issues advanced and symbolized by feminism, such as higher education, occupational advancement, and middle-class women's enlarged presence in public life. Most important, though, she emphasized the meaning of feminism as an awakening *consciousness* in women:

> No one movement is feminism. No one organization is feminism. All woman movements and organizations taken together form a part of feminism. But feminism means more than these. . . . Feminism is not limited to any one cause or reform. It strives for equal rights, equal laws, equal opportunity, equal wages, equal standards, and a whole new world of human equality. But feminism means more than a changed world. It means a changed psychology, the creation of a new consciousness in women.[11]

In its roominess and elasticity, Howe's definition insisted on goals more far-reaching than those encompassed by a traditionally defined political agenda, even as it emphasized a subjective, psychological transformation as distinctive to feminism.

The emphasis on change and newness exemplified by Howe's statement led feminists to insist on their modern qualities and to try to remove any taint of the Victorian past. One of the central gestures of feminist discourse was to *proclaim* a break from the past, including disaffiliation from an earlier generation of women activists, with history, with an older model for womanhood, and with previous legitimations of women's cultural activity and public identity. Women's writing, performance, and thought in the early twentieth century often rejected older, residual definitions of womanhood, in order to make claims for the revolutionary potential of who they were and what they did. This tendency to proclaim a break with the past made feminism part of and productive of modernism. The British writer Virginia Woolf's famous statement both symbolized and enacted the gesture: "[O]n or about December, 1910, human character changed."[12] This kind of bold, definitive claim was made over and over in a wide variety of modernist contexts. For Woolf and for many other writers, artists, and thinkers, the arrival of the New Woman was part of what had *changed* in human character.

Despite many feminists' insistence that they represented newness and change, modernists often symbolically associated women with a past they were attempting to escape. The perception of feminism in modernism must be interpreted within the history of modernism's efforts for self-expression over and against a repressive older culture. This history often ignored women's contemporary activism or associated them with older, especially Victorian, models of repression. Modernist contempt for women influenced their perception of feminism: they often connected feminism to the history of women's activism in the nineteenth-century antislavery and temperance movements. On the one hand, such a link reveals how firmly established was the belief that cultural change was connected to social reform. On the other hand, it ignores women modernists' self-understanding as breaking with the past and much of what womanhood had meant in the nineteenth century. Militant women remained connected to a nineteenth-century tradition, which in a modernist history was tantamount to either being hopelessly old-fashioned or the enemy to be destroyed.

Feminists were thus connected to Victorianism, even though significant areas of their efforts and contributions were dedicated to the production of modernism. This irony is key to sorting through important recent interpretations of women's relation to modernism in literary analysis, cultural history, and gender history. As historian Christina Simmons has written in her discussion of the formation of modern sexuality, "The myth of Victorian repression constituted a response to . . . forms of women's power. . . . [R]evisionists proclaimed a modernist liberation from a repressive Victorian past, and subsequent historiography has tended to accept that frame of reference."[13] In this "subsequent historiography," women are seen as having a negative relation to modernism; they embodied the culture of Victorianism, including sentimentality and repression.

Ann Douglas's recent cultural history of modernism, *Terrible Honesty: Mongrel Manhattan in the 1920s,* makes the association of women with a repressive Victorianism the very basis of interpretation. While innovative in its synthesis of white and black thought in the formation of a distinct, independent, and ultimately hegemonic American modernism, Douglas's study makes this argument through the symbolic opposition of the "Victorian matriarch." Women, understood to be inherently connected to Victorianism, were what modernists had to rebel against. Indeed, Douglas argues that American intellectuals created modernism as a symbolic act of matricide, a killing-off of the Victorian mother, who came to represent everything culturally retrograde or dishonest, including moralism, a sentimental religion, sexual repression, and racism. "The moderns aimed to ridicule and overturn everything the matriarch had championed." Where women reformers had feminized American culture and represented a "block to modernity," modernists masculinized it.[14]

Through such interpretations, the opposition between self-expression and repression was gendered, with women representing the forces of repression and men the power of self-expression. This gendered opposition erases the extent to which self-expression was something feminist modernists embraced.

The critique of female sentimentality as a model for women's activism was linked to the devastating attack on sentimental literature that the modernist movement launched. Women and men from the 1910s through the 1930s understood the shift in style associated with modernism as a renunciation of genteel, bourgeois culture and of its moral hypocrisies and inhibitions, which they claimed were covered over by the language of sentimentality. With the rise of realism, naturalism, and stream-of-consciousness in literature as much as the new styles of political activism in the Progressive Era and the bohemian renaissance, sentimentality became a pejorative associated with repressive aspects of Victorian cultural practices. Modernists were dedicated to dismantling the style of sentimentality in favor of language stripped of cliché, platitude, and moralistic pieties. The rejection of sentimentality has held powerful sway over literary history; the modernist evaluation accounts for much of the ideology of what today constitutes "literature" itself.

Recent feminist revisions of literary modernism have attempted to turn the Victorian negative into a positive, showing continuity between the "sensational designs" of nineteenth-century literature and modernist women's writing. Suzanne Clark, in her important book *Sentimental Modernism: Women Writers and the Revolution of the Word,* invents what she calls a "sentimental modernism," arguing that part of the reason women writers have been excluded from the modernist canon is that they held onto the rhetoric of sentimentality and thus were marginal to the rise of modernism as a reified literary, formalized category. "[T]he revolt against the sentimental, after its three or so decades of ascendancy, effectively buried that tradition. Women writers found themselves gradually cut off from the very past that might nurture them."[15] Here, modernist women's history is a narrative of orphaned daughters, bereft of the legacy of the novelists and activists who used sentimental language to inspire moral outrage and to legitimate their public presence as published writers and speechmakers. Such a narrative is ultimately reassuring because it implies that we can restore that legacy.

As with all stories about generations, there was conflict and contestation. Modernist women were often explicitly critical of their foremothers, and they attacked sentimental language and gestures. These acts could be seen as ripping feminism from the sheltering arms of its nineteenth-century precursors. An alternative interpretation suggests that modernist feminists were themselves looking for a way out: out of the logic of sentimentality, its necessity for women's public identity, and the seemingly indissoluble link between maternalism and politics. This desire to escape from a form of expression rooted in an ideology of motherhood often led to generational confrontations between modernist feminists and the older guard of reformers and agitators. The editor Margaret Anderson, as we shall see in chapter 2, staged the confrontation over and over again, most strikingly in her friendship with the great anarchist activist and orator Emma Goldman.

The rhetoric that women could and should break their historical shackles often provoked disunity among women instead of encouraging a harmonious sisterhood. Goldman, for example, sharply attacked the politics of the suffrage movement and the reformist orthodoxies of "women's emancipation" in the 1910s through an attack on history. "Emancipation should make it possible for woman to be human in the truest sense.... [A]ll artificial barriers should be broken, and the road towards greater freedom cleared of every trace of centuries of submission and slavery." Goldman criticized the suffragist argument that women voters would purify American politics and the common belief among reformers that work would liberate poor women from dependency: to her, these seeming efforts at emancipation were simply new forms of social regulation and class bias. Her critique of the "narrow respectabilities" among women activists led her to formulate one of the great aphorisms of modern feminism: "Now, woman is confronted with the necessity of emancipating herself from emancipation if she really desires to be free."[16]

In their embrace of change in modern life, even if it meant confronting some hard issues, political radicals such as Goldman had a lot in common with women artists and writers. According to Carolyn Burke, a poet like Mina Loy took up feminism as she "abandoned the chaperonage of the late Victorian sensibility."[17] Influenced by the Italian futurists in the 1910s, Loy also defined feminism as a break from the past, declaring in a "Feminist Manifesto" in 1914:

> Women, if you want to realize yourselves ... all your pet illusions must be unmasked. The lies of centuries have got to be discarded. Are you prepared for the WRENCH? There is no half-measure, no scratching on the surface of the rubbish heap of tradition. Nothing short of Absolute Demolition will bring about reform.[18]

Loy's program for "Absolute Demolition" was both fascinating and incoherent, calling for "the surgical destruction of virginity" as the only way to end the ideology of women's moral purity. Yet Loy also exhorted women to stop lamenting their state of inequality and to enhance the qualities that made them different from men. Loy's extreme program borrowed heavily from futurist motifs, and her rhetoric echoed the explosive phrasing and imagery of Marinetti and others. Placed in the context of feminist discourse, it retains its shock value even today—like the manifestos of second-wave feminists in the late 1960s and early 1970s, there were no soothing tones, no sentimental gestures to smooth the way for the reader to accept a changing role for women.

Taken as a whole, statements by and about feminists in diverse contexts all tended to make a break with the Victorian vocabulary associated with the term *woman,* especially words like *mother, domesticity,* and *tradition.* Feminists also tried to change the ideology purveyed through those terms, even when that meant criticizing the social movements of women in the present and the past. Feminists defined their positions against some efforts to regulate sexuality and to enact social reform because these movements originating in the nineteenth century defined women in terms of motherhood and beliefs in women's innate moral superiority, which tied women to the past rather than freeing them from it.[19] Cultural radicals also had long criticized the exclusionary and oppressive effects of these reform efforts, especially for working-class, immigrant, and nonwhite women.[20] Feminist modernists were distinctive because they linked these social critiques to a critique of the forms of representation, in language, in visual culture, and in narrative that bound women to particular ideologies and, therefore, to conventional understandings of what women were.

The critical gestures by feminist modernists, such as Howe's proclaiming a new consciousness, Loy's advocating "Absolute Demolition," or Goldman's testy critique of the tendency of "emancipation" to produce its opposite, are exciting and compelling. But such gestures have been impossible to sustain; to proclaim that an individual, a group, a practice, or a philosophy broke from the past was to deny the fundamental state of being part of history, of being embedded within it, whether one saw that as a form of nightmarish entrapment or enriching continuity. One can particularly see the stakes of and effects of this failure to recognize the tenacious hold of history in the gender politics of modernism.

The title of this book, *The Secret Treachery of Words,* is taken from Maxwell Bodenheim's review of Margaret Anderson's autobiography in

1930, taken up in chapter 2. The phrase also describes the subject of this book as a whole. It suggests that the feminist modernist belief in the explosive, revolutionary potential of language to represent changing social relations and to express a new subjectivity for women also contained a hidden dimension that limited such transgressions. This dimension, the treacherous waters of historical representation, has had important implications for understanding feminism in the field of cultural analysis.

Seen through considerations of individuals, the relation between feminism and modernism took several dynamic forms. First, the cultural figure of the feminist often functioned as a symbolic substitute for a more general modernism. The dynamic of symbolism and substitution meant that the feminist also—paradoxically—could represent the repressed other of modernism, or that which modernism had purged or rejected. As agents of representation, feminists also acted to subvert, undermine, and generally poke holes in modernist beliefs, not only about women, but also about art and cultural representation generally. Feminism was enmeshed in a process of cultural mediation and appropriation: figures of feminism functioned as both avant-garde figures because they represented a change in the meaning of "woman," so important in modernist discourse, and as popular, feminized consumers that emptied modernism of its revolutionary potential. Finally, the politics of cultural representation forced some feminist modernists into positions of abjection, unable to write or to act. But this very position of extreme marginality led them to critical and representational dissent.

In addition to my engagement with the history of feminism and women's literature, my view of feminism has emerged from a new approach to the cultural history of modernism. In the introduction to a special issue on modernism in *American Quarterly*, cultural historian Daniel Joseph Singal claims that a kind of paradigm shift had taken place in modernist studies. Rather than looking at formal practices and texts of an elite group of intellectuals and artists as "modernism," Singal sees that modernism was more properly a new "historical culture," one that replaced Victorianism starting in the late nineteenth century.[21]

This approach has opened up the field of modernist studies considerably, revealing modernism's generic diversity and interrelationships and making it possible to study and write about modernism from an interdisciplinary vantage point. Further, it engages the polarities of culture—the divisions between high and low, popular and avant-garde—relationally rather than exclusive of each other, showing the indebtedness of middle-class hegemony to movements in avant-garde art and ideas as well as in popular culture. The dynamics of the cultural transformation of American life from Victorianism to modernism, however, have not been fully clarified.

The very wealth of cultural phenomena that is designated "modernist" creates the need for large explanations that can pull these tendencies together. For example, Singal sees in modernism a progressive, even redemptive power that healed the philosophical dualisms, social rifts, and ideological rigidity that he sees as characterizing much of nineteenth-century culture and politics. And, indeed, this belief echoes modernist declarations of what was new and modern about the twentieth century. Singal calls this a belief in "wholeness" that brought intellectual movements into harmony with broad-based changes that we associate with modern culture. But to emphasize "wholeness" as the overarching tendency in American modernism risks ignoring the dialectical qualities of modern culture. Wholeness—whether a belief or a critical strategy— tended to suppress the dynamic of marginality and dominance, dissent, contestation, and competing tendencies in modern culture. The very capaciousness of the definition of *modernism* as a historical culture tends to empty it of the process of formation in relation to mass culture. In light of these concerns, wholeness remains an important guiding idea in modernism, but it is also a desire whose expression foreclosed its other side, which was the impossibility of any stable resolution of either identity or cultural formation.

To tell the story of modern feminism, one must thus also tell the story of the intertwined connection between modernism and mass culture. The terms *modern culture, mass culture,* and *modernism* are not always used in the same way in the field of modernist studies, and different terms altogether are often used in U.S. cultural history. The polarity between mass culture and modernism is in many ways designed to illuminate the critical position that modernism holds toward commodity capitalism, the media, and the sensibility of audiences and consumers shaped by these institutions, all encapsulated in an already pejorative term, *mass culture.* Cultural history in the United States has complicated such a polarity, preferring such terms as *popular culture* and *consumer culture* to highlight the diversity of "the masses" and sites of resistance in "mass culture." While *modernism* should not be narrowly defined as a group of movements confined to the visual arts and literature, neither should the term be generalized to such an extent that it stands for the entire culture of the early twentieth century, since that risks eliminating the contestation and conflict so key to the period. *Modernism* is a term that is strategically useful to illuminate dissent, imaginative engagement with and intellectual wonder at the transformations of American life. Further, the modernist opposition to mass culture should itself be seen as one indication of the dynamics of cultural formation, in which critique is always, inevitably enmeshed with identification, mutual influence, and appropriation. Together, modernism and mass culture formed what can be called *modern culture* from about 1890 to 1940 in the United States.[22]

The most important movement in modernist studies since the paradigm shift discussed by Singal has been to reveal the artistic, critical, and political dynamics of dominance and marginality in modern culture. This scholarship has not only rediscovered but also created new interpretive models for work that the canon of high modernism excluded, especially the cultural production of socially and politically marginalized groups and peoples. Literary historian Cary Nelson described this approach as "repression and recovery."[23] This movement in scholarship has retrieved writers and artists that had been lost to us and argues for the very centrality of displaced and forgotten movements, texts, and people for the creative power of modernist culture.[24] Efforts to change the representation and lived conditions of gender were embedded in these power dynamics in modernism and its history, what is remembered, forgotten, and recovered about it. Feminist modernism was both marginalized in history and complicit with the dynamic itself.

In engaging key moments in feminist modernism, *The Secret Treachery of Words* seeks to show not only the high tides of feminism but also its low ebbs, arguing that both constituted the representational possibilities for women in modern culture. Feminism and modernism emerged in American intellectual and cultural life in the years just preceding World War I. In 1913 feminism became a key word to describe theories and practices of women's emancipation; the year was also marked by one of the most spectacular demonstrations of modernism—the opening of the Armory Show of independent art, which, like feminism, provoked extensive commentary. In the 1920s the expressions of both feminists and modernists were marked by alienation and self-doubt. By the end of the thirties, the possibilities of a feminist modernism had contracted, largely as a result of the cultural politics of the Depression and the war mobilization. The representation of women and their productive power suffered under New Deal and Left populism, because both called for the subordination of experimentalist formal practices to realism and resurrected traditional gender ideologies. Significantly, though, articulations of feminist modernism did not vanish without a trace in the Depression but instead became a kind of dissenting countercurrent under the dominant representational tide of the period.[25] Looking at feminist modernism provides a way of seeing across debates over art and politics over the course of the early twentieth century, rather than sticking to distinctions between the "Roaring Twenties" and the "Socially Conscious Thirties."[26]

Within the broader time frame between 1910 and 1940, I trace feminist dynamics in four American modernist contexts: the Left intellectual and artistic circles of the teens known as cultural radicalism; the literary avant-garde established by little magazines; the social criticism that developed in the bohemian enclave of Greenwich Village; and the beliefs and politics of the thirties Left. In these contexts, I interpret four cultural figures, well known in specific fields but not necessarily in a general context for feminist modernism: the dancer Isadora Duncan, editor Margaret Anderson, writer Floyd Dell, and writer Josephine Herbst. Through these portraits, I expose how certain tendencies in the lives and thought of these figures symbolized and produced the dynamics of feminist modernism in both vanguard and dominant culture.

To live feminism and modernism together was difficult and sometimes impossible for these figures, given the fissures as well as the intersections of these two movements. Not surprisingly, the themes I focus on also reveal the limitations of how feminism and modernism have been understood or ignored long after the influence of these figures waned. I read lived experience as part of the discursive production of modernism (thus intervening in the textual orientation of high modernist studies) and I read modernist discourse as central to and empowering for feminism (thus intervening in women's history, which has tended to segregate feminism and modernism).

Chapter 1 investigates the cultural theories and performances of the modern dancer Isadora Duncan, and their reception by cultural radicals who were profoundly affected by her from the height of her popularity in the United States around 1908 to her death in 1927. Duncan was one of the most important figures to establish modernism in dance and was known as a trailblazer for women's emancipation. Her life has become the stuff of legend, and she is remembered as a heroine, especially by the sexual revolutionaries of the 1960s. Aspects of her life, especially her outspoken critique of marriage and her many, open love affairs, all testified to in her wonderful autobiography, have been appropriated in popular culture, in films and novels, as archetypal for the "liberated woman."[27] As many dance historians have pointed out, this understanding of Duncan has obscured her aesthetic views and tends to marginalize her as a significant dancer, choreographer, and theorist.[28] Yet retrieving Duncan is no simple matter.

The cultural anxieties of modernism, which Duncan herself often expressed, also have obscured her significance for and the implications of her feminism. I depart from the domain of dance criticism to show how feminism and modernism interacted in Duncan's life, thought, and impact on others, producing both the liberationist mythology and what was seen then as revolutionary in her performances. I focus particularly on Duncan's elaboration of a theory of wholeness, the ethos of indissoluble connection between art, politics, and life that Singal identified as so important to modernist culture. Duncan used the rhetoric of early feminism and created a visual code to enact what she believed would be the liberation of women from the divisive constraints of Victorian culture. At the height of her career, modernists saw Duncan's body in performance and theory as an enactment of their beliefs in wholeness. Yet, Duncan's later career, which declined as African American–influenced popular culture rose, is as important to account for; Duncan's waning cultural power and her attempts to shore it up rested on an implicitly white appeal to civilization. Duncan's decline in relation to a wider popular culture in America helps to explain the presumptions and contradictions in both modernist and feminist desires for wholeness. Despite the utopian promises of wholeness, the desire for it produced racialized and nationalistic ideas and reified the visual conventions and literary metaphors through which the female body was understood.

In order to assess the significance of a figure like Duncan, it has been necessary to widen the definition of what counts as an important cultural text. Duncan's performances as a dancer were ephemeral because they were largely undocumented except for the impressions and descriptions of those who saw them. Though much scholarship in modernism has focused on texts—paintings, poems, novels—a figure like Duncan presents an interpretive problem that demands the reevaluation of the relationship between text and context. As the work of Jerrold Seigel on bohemian Paris has shown, the primary texts of modernism rest on and cannot be understood fully apart from their context in the beliefs and activities of people who supported, indeed created the conditions for such achievements.[29]

The cultural work of such support is the starting point of my second chapter, which investigates avant-garde editor Margaret Anderson, who as a member of Chicago's artistic circles in 1914 created one of the most important little magazines for modernist writing in the United States, the *Little Review.* Anderson sought out and published the work of such high modernist figures as James Joyce, T. S. Eliot, and Ernest Hemingway, and indeed could be seen as an authentic figure for a heroic modernism, as opposed to Bromley's inauthenticity. After all, Anderson published Joyce's *Ulysses* in the United States, suffered the ire of the *Little Review*'s readership, who didn't like it, and then was accused of publishing obscene materials by the Society for the Suppression of Vice for printing the novel in the first place. Despite these deeds, Anderson's critical reputation has suffered under a masculine bias that emphasizes text over context. Her editorial practice has been characterized as that of an undiscriminating dilettante, whose magazine only became artistically worthy when it gained the contacts and critical acumen of Ezra Pound, who became foreign editor in 1917. Anderson, then, has been seen as a consumer rather than a producer of modernism, a position that became degrading especially because it was feminized.

Recent feminist studies of Anderson, particularly the work of Shari Benstock, have shown the importance of Anderson's battles with both dominant American culture and with the very modernists she collaborated with, including Pound.[30] Mathilde Hills's research also has recovered Anderson as a radical lesbian ahead of her time—a woman who celebrated her relationships with other women at a time when lesbian literary themes emphasized the maudlin and the abject.[31] Anderson also is known as a key figure among American expatriates in Europe in the twenties and thirties.

My study of Anderson proceeds from the perils and possibilities of self-expression, a core idea of the modernist rebellion. Significantly, Anderson did not see herself merely as a mediator and facilitator of other people's work; rather, she saw an opportunity to create herself in the pages of the magazine. Although the *Little Review* published a lot of subsequently famous work, Anderson believed the magazine first and foremost to be an expression of herself. Though this idea seems prosaic, to Anderson self-expression represented all that she had been denied in her bourgeois upbringing and everything that she sought in a transformed culture. Self-expression was a central principle of modernist self-formation, informing the poses of bohemians, dandies, and feminists alike in their adoption of particular styles, vocabularies, and fashions.[32] Through focusing on self-expression, the chapter dramatizes women's attempts to transcend older models for women's cultural work, to create new relations to art, and to challenge the representation of sexuality. Just as important, the chapter reveals the extent to which the strategy of self-expression was enmeshed with other, more denigrating perceptions of women's roles and activism in modernism.

Certainly one of the most troubling perceptions that informed the gender politics of modernism was the symbolic association of women with mass cultural figures who threatened modernist innovation. However, the status of the feminist has been a significant absence in interpretations of this configuration of gender in modernism. Because it challenged the social and political effects of gender difference, feminism muddied the equivalence established between masculinity and modernism, femininity and mass culture. Not simply a variable in an abstract logic, feminism was a key topic of discussion in modern culture, especially its progressive—and dangerous—qualities.

One of the most important developments in early-twentieth-century America was "the revolution in manners and mores," a sexual revolution that was celebrated for replacing Victorian repression with modern expressiveness. The institutions of consumer capitalism such as advertising and the new popular media of movies and radio flourished by appealing to a new heterosexual partnership between men and women in which dissatisfaction and hostility between the sexes were banished and fulfillment and happiness were the order of the day. Recent studies in women's history and the history of sexuality have traced the making of this middle-class ideology and its roots in both bohemian and working-class culture, emphasizing the role of young women as the newly sexualized archetypes of modern culture.[33]

While this new culture of heterosexuality celebrated pleasure, it also viewed with suspicion those who resisted it or did not fit. Homosexuality, especially, became a threat to be contained and suppressed, its behavior punished and its symbolic expressions condemned. Many viewed modernism and feminism as suspect precisely because of their perceived gender exclusivity, even though the critique of Victorianism in modernist thought and the emphasis on sexual freedom by feminists had been appropriated and popularized in the middle-class sexual revolution. While modernism was often construed as a masculinist enterprise, feminism also was criticized for excluding men.

Chapter 3 takes up these questions by looking at the thought and persona of Floyd Dell. Dell was one of the most famous bohemians in Chicago and New York in the 1910s and 1920s; he edited the *Friday Literary Review* and later the important magazine of cultural radicalism, *The Masses,* and he wrote novels, poetry, plays, and social criticism, which met with varying degrees of success. Like Anderson, Dell found his most important subject in himself. In his case, however, his writing often concerned his repeated attempts to establish exciting, fulfilling, yet stable and supportive relationships with women. Dell's subject matter, then, was the sexual revolution, and he believed that feminism was one of the most important innovations in this process. Though his search for a meaningful, romantic partnership was carried out rather conventionally, in two marriages and several love affairs, Dell explored the possibilities intellectually and culturally as well. He studied and wrote about the theme in philosophy and the history of modern literature, and he undertook psychoanalysis. He saw feminist possibilities everywhere, not only in his bohemian haunts, but in his excursions to working-class cultural arenas such as dance halls and burlesque clubs. These explorations found their way into much of his writing, and while his topics were typically bohemian and eclectic Dell's commitment to creating a new heterosexuality was a serious, deep-running theme.

In the early 1930s Dell published a social-scientific treatise on modern sexuality that advocated much more traditional views of masculinity and femininity and seemingly recanted his earlier radicalism. Discussions of Dell have focused on his contributions as an editor and a novelist and his lifestyle as a cultural radical, or his later role as a spokesman for the gender conservatism of sexual thought in the twenties and thirties.[34] This chapter charts how Dell's explorations of new relations between women and men evoked an important narrative about the interrelations of feminism and modernism. While Dell arrived at entrenched formulations about family, gender roles, and social responsibility, what makes him important for this study was his championing of and then later rejection of feminist modernism for remaking heterosexuality. Dell's changing ideas revealed feminism's importance in modernist and mass culture, and the relations between them.

While each chapter charts a dynamic of liberatory possibility and treacherous reconsolidation as central to the cultural politics of modernism and feminism, the last chapter considers this dynamic through the relation of modernism to historical representation itself. In the thirties, the decades-long modernist experiment was thrown into sharp relief by the economic and political crises of the period. In response, the Depression era produced a remarkable level of social engagement by artists and writers, staging a rapprochement between the popular and the avant-garde in their belief that art and activism should be intertwined. Populist styles, realism, and the Soviet-influenced propaganda art known as *proletcult* all sought to represent the lives of ordinary Americans and to persuade and incite them to confront and change the conditions that had produced the Depression.

In the process, the combative, experimental tendencies in modernist feminism were labeled socially and politically irresponsible, even counter-revolutionary, and fell by the wayside.[35] In their place, traditional symbols of gender were used allegorically to represent the people, the nation, and the potential for progressive change out of the state of devastation and dispossession that so many had experienced. Gender conservatism became an intrinsic part of cultural representation, a legitimation of political and economic change, not an aspect of the social critique leveled at American institutions. Symbolically and politically displaced, women writers and artists shaped by the movements of the teens and the twenties nevertheless carved out a place on the margins of the new cultural moment and produced a significant body of work that deeply expressed the sexual, economic, and political anxieties and desires of the period.

In this context, the status of history—of what could possibly explain the crisis and why the recent experiments had failed—became a recurrent theme. Chapter 4 turns to the historical imagination in the 1930s and its gender politics by examining the work of writer and activist Josephine Herbst. Widely known in the Depression decade as a novelist producing a new American history in the trilogy of historical novels she wrote between 1933 and 1939, Herbst participated in the Left movement to discover the dialectical quality of the American past. Herbst also cast a critical eye on contemporary developments as a Left journalist, reporting on labor strikes in the United States as well as on her travels in Russia, Germany, Cuba, and Spain during its civil war. This chapter looks at the interplay between Herbst's view of the past in her historical novels, her extensive reporting on both domestic and international politics in her own time, and the very shifts in feminism and modernism that *The Secret Treachery of Words* engages. This interpretation foregrounds Herbst's historical insight: how, as if she were a modern Cassandra, she both resisted and fell victim to the conservative gender politics of the era. The chapter also emphasizes the importance of representation; while Herbst deeply believed in the idea of a usable, and therefore accessible, past, she employed an experimental form that reproduced feminist modernism as a position of critical dissent.

There is much to be gained by looking at how people saw themselves as cultural historical agents, and how their views about gender and modern culture changed as representational politics changed. Though I focus on individual lives, my approach is less biography and more intellectual portraiture. I don't focus on the ebbs and flows of individual success and failure, nor do I discern the teleology that explains an individual's life.

This book tends to chart histories of failure, not success. It seeks not to celebrate these individuals as having found the "right" or "progressive" or "good" way to live feminist modernist lives; rather, it seeks to understand how these individuals struggled with a set of often contradictory, always protean expectations. As feminists they often confronted a representational politics that put women in subordinate positions or that led them to dead ends such as nationalism, racism, conservative heterosexuality, and disaffected marginality.

This book emphasizes less the outcomes of history than the process of historical engagement itself. The difficulties that each figure faced in challenging and recreating the cultural representation of gender are revelatory of modernist culture. The critical reputations of each of these figures speak to the qualities I am trying to tease out: each is well known and yet figured as an artistic failure. My aim is not to turn the critical tables, but to show how their very positions reveal the larger dynamic of interpreting gender politics in modernism.

Both women and men discussed feminism in their modernist desire to build a new American civilization, in their rebellious embrace of self-expression to defy the hold of ideology upon them, in their confrontations with mass culture, and in their efforts to create a revolutionary politics. These efforts were significant, but I am not celebrating the results; I focus rather on the contradictions feminism introduced and revealed in modernism. Through these examinations I hope we will begin to see feminism as centrally a part of, not separate from, American intellectual engagements with culture.

CHAPTER 1

From Event to Monument

Isadora Duncan and the

Desire for Wholeness

In 1915 Mabel Dodge Luhan, a philanthropist who was helping to spark an artistic and political renaissance in New York, organized a party at Isadora Duncan's studio. The party was intended to persuade the city's political elite to support the modern dancer's current project. Duncan wanted to convert the city's armory building into a school and theater, a place where Duncan could develop and spread her ideas. Among the guests were the mayor, John Mitchel, and Walter Lippmann, the progressive political theorist. At this gathering, Duncan and her students, the Isadorables, gracefully reclined on couches or floated in their draperies among the guests in the dimly lit, moody room. Luhan was fascinated by the scene they created at the same time that she "felt . . . shorter and more square than I had ever been in my life before, and my gloves suddenly ceased to fit my hands." As there was no furniture in the room except low couches, pillows, and a grand piano, Lippmann sat stiffly on a pillow, and "his clothes creased in the wrong places, looking ungainly and uncomfortable, losing in authority." Meanwhile, Luhan was thinking about Duncan. "There was something frightening about her actual presence in a place; the vibrations became loosened up, broader, more incalculable. She made one nervous. Anything might happen."[1]

And something did happen. Though Duncan was supposed to present her case for the Armory along with a brief performance by her students, she digressed from this plan, instead hotly discussing the case of a mother

1

accused of murdering her children, a story then current in the news-papers. While she was preoccupied with this discussion, Duncan's "dress slipped from her shoulder and showed her breast."[2] According to Luhan, Duncan's speech and disarranged clothing deeply embarrassed the guests. Lippmann was so horrified by this incident that he withdrew from the project and retreated from the renaissance that Duncan sought to create. He wrote later to Luhan,

> I'm utterly disgusted.... I went into this because like a damn fool I deluded myself into thinking that we could have one spot of freedom and beauty. I should have known better. Those spots exist only in the imagination we weave about performers like Miss Duncan. I should have known better than to be dazzled into a short cut to perfection—there are none, and Isadora is not the person to show the way.[3]

With this incident, Lippmann's hopes for a modernity that privileged "freedom and beauty" were dashed. And while we should not make too much of this incident for shaping Lippmann's approach to American po-litical reform, his comment revealed both how attached he had been to the dazzling ideals Duncan seemed to express, and how disillusioned he was when she disappointed those ideals. Lippmann's letter suggested a larger dynamic shaping the alliance between feminism and modernism.

In the early twentieth century, Duncan sought nothing less than to change the world by emancipating both the female body from its socio-cultural limits and contemporary dance from its aesthetic limits. This philosophy had a profound influence on American modernism: experi-enced as enactments of unfettered freedom, Duncan's performances were celebrated as major events, and her philosophy of the liberated body cir-culated widely among intellectuals and artists seeking to redefine the meaning of art, politics, and sex. Duncan symbolized "our own twentieth-century consciousness," according to the visionary urban planner Lewis Mumford.[4] She was often mentioned as a symbol of both freedom and beauty in essays, memoirs, and poetry by feminists and women writers as diverse as Charlotte Perkins Gilman and Jean Garrigue.[5] Devoting a chapter of her autobiography to her encounters with Duncan, Luhan found her own desire for liberation reflected back to her in the dancer's poses: "I recognized what she did in the dance.... Power rose in her from her Center and flowed vividly along her limbs before our eyes in living beauty and delight. We saw a miracle happen before us when Isadora stood there, passive, and Pure Being incarnated itself in her."[6]

When outdoor dancers appeared on the cover of *Vanity Fair* in 1918 and tunic-clad college students were seen reveling in May Day celebra-tions in the early 1920s, it was evident that Duncan had influenced American culture more widely.[7] The image of women dancing lyrically in transparent, fluttering tunics gave visual evidence of the impact of femi-nism. Despite Duncan's personal difficulties, she became a symbol of lib-eration that bridged artistic and political ideals with progress for women. While there is a rich scholarship on Duncan's contributions to modern dance, she is more well known now as a heroine of "sexual liberation." Her autobiography, *My Life,* contributed to this mythology, as have sev-eral novels and films about her.[8] Two feminist classics also took Duncan's lifelong effort to bring together her work and her love life as a case study of the difficulties faced by women artists. The importance of understand-ing Duncan as both a feminist and a modernist was suggested soon after her death by the journalist and editor Max Eastman, who wrote in his memorial tribute to her in 1927: "Few people realized how far beyond the realm of art—how far out and how deep into the moral and social life of our times the influence of Isadora Duncan's dancing extended."[9]

The reverence that Duncan inspired as well as the disillusionment she provoked stamps this history. While there were many individual respons-es to the eccentric, capricious, glamorous dancer, the shift from reverence to disillusionment was pronounced after World War I. While her earlier performances were greeted with an almost ecstatic enthusiasm, many be-lieved that Duncan was stuck in a kind of cultural impasse by the early 1920s. This change could be seen as part of the pessimism and alienation that many intellectuals and artists experienced as a result of World War I. However, such an interpretation obscures a crucial point. No longer a firebrand, as Duncan grew older she was seen more as a relic of a lost artistic and political radicalism, and the signs of her body's aging became signifiers of her decline as an artist and of the ideas she embodied. As the later commentary of her contemporaries clearly indicated, this perceived decline in her art and philosophy was understood primarily through her body; instead of signifying utopia, her body signified the dreaded physi-cality of the aging woman.

Duncan herself articulated a deep sense of estrangement from domi-nant American culture in the 1920s. Returning to the United States from a year-long visit to Bolshevik Russia, she angrily confronted a hostile press and conservative audiences. But Duncan's disaffection was more than a political confrontation between her revolutionary sympathies and an anticommunist American public. It was also a result of the wide gap that emerged between Duncan's philosophy of dance as a means to create a new civilization and the development of racially diverse and sexually expressive trends in popular music and dancing. As a result of this cultural divide, the link that Duncan had forged between feminism and modernism was seen as irrelevant and residual. For many of her contemporaries, Duncan became symbolic of a hopeful but incomplete transition from Victorianism to modernism. Duncan's performance of a liberated female body must be read both as the vibrant emancipating force behind her centrality for early American modernism and, ironically, as the grounds on which she was rendered insignificant by those same modernists—and those who have written their history.

The Event of Isadora Duncan

Duncan's lightly clad body dancing in simple, seemingly spontaneous movement on a spare stage inspired fascination and, sometimes, catharsis. For art critic Elie Faure it was as if the burdens of an oppressive past had been lifted.

> Yes, we wept when we saw her. It was no longer to our eyes, nor to our ears; it was no longer to our nerves that she spoke. From deep within us, when she danced, there arose a flood that swept away from the corners of our soul all the filth which had been piled up there by those who for twenty centuries had bequeathed to us their critique, their ethics, and their judgments.[10]

With emotions like these aroused, it is not surprising that Duncan's performances during her tours of the United States in 1908–10, 1914–15, and 1922–23 were much anticipated, often drew large audiences, and were discussed frequently in both the mainstream and radical press. Her concerts excited the imagination of a wide range of American modernists, including writers, artists, and editors of the magazine of cultural radicalism, *The Masses,* members of Alfred Stieglitz's artistic circle, and progressive intellectuals of all stripes. Many who saw Isadora Duncan dance came away believing they had experienced liberation, and because this promise was so central to the hopes and dreams many had for the twentieth century, Duncan's performances were singular events. Eastman wrote, "She was an event not only in art, but in the history of life."[11] Duncan's dances were *events* through which the past was swept away and dreams for modernity were somehow realizable and attainable.

Wholeness

The event of "Isadora Duncan" included her performance style, persona, and philosophy, as well as the response to her by her contemporaries, revealing several important connections between feminism and modernism. Duncan's expression, body, and ideas appeared to enact a philosophy that profoundly moved modernists—that art and life should be inseparable. While many cultural critics and intellectuals worried that twentieth-century culture under capitalism fragmented identity, divided labor from life, and substituted materialist consumption for real social transformation, Duncan suggested the possibility of wholeness.[12] Far from being an artist living only for art, Duncan seemed to bridge fundamental dualisms between body and mind, self and world, the individual and social collectivity. Envisioning a modernity in which the arts would merge into one aesthetic whole, and seeing in art the possibility of political and social change, Duncan's beliefs resonated with other attempts to blend artistic practices with new relationships between women and men, and progressive and socialist political beliefs. These beliefs implicitly expressed a historical outlook: wholeness was often contrasted to Victorian culture.

Duncan herself and the commentary about her linked the desire for wholeness to women's emancipation. Duncan's particular contribution to the formation of American feminism lay in the meaning of and visual perception of the female body. Duncan was both a modernist and a feminist because she represented a whole female body, restored from the divided sensibility and physical constraints associated with a Victorian past that moderns were struggling to escape. For writer Floyd Dell, Duncan showed how important the body was to changing woman's condition: she "made us see . . . the goodness of the whole body. This is as much part of the woman's movement as the demand for a vote."[13]

Duncan's innovations in costume, stage design, and movement were crucial components of both her aesthetic and her cultural critique. These elements of her performances gave visual imagination and spatial dimension to the search for wholeness and its integral connection to women's emancipation. Duncan's costume, especially, became an emblem of change from the Victorian to the modern. Duncan danced in a sheer, short tunic secured at the breast and hips. While there is evidence that the tunic was lined with a leotard, her body appeared to many to be nude under this light costume.[14] Duncan herself played upon the illusion of nudity. She believed that her tunic's revelation of her unbound body and bare feet replaced constraint with unity and fusion as the basis for beauty. "It has never dawned on me to swathe myself in hampering garments or to bind my limbs and drape my throat, for am I not striving to fuse soul and body in one unified image of beauty?" she asked in the early

1900s.[15] In its signification of transparency, the tunic let the female body be perceived as a unified whole.

A female body without a corset, with no petticoats, no drapes of heavy fabric, for many, was a body that had been liberated. "She ripped off all the corsets and let herself go," as one admirer said, describing his sense that Duncan had freed the female body from its nineteenth-century constraints.[16] Playing on the metaphor of loosening the bonds of clothing to express her critique of dominant aesthetics in dance, especially the use of stocking, corsets, and slippers by female dancers, Duncan wrote, "Everything must be undone."[17] Duncan's critique was powerful, and shocking for many, because it was literal and physical: she stripped away the tight and heavy layers of Victorian culture by taking off shoes, stockings, and corset, which for Duncan were signifiers of constraints on the female body and its expressive potential.

Though Duncan believed that her costumes were timeless and universal, they were symbols of Duncan's rebellion from late-nineteenth-century fashions. Deceptively simple—a length of sheer cloth and a cord—Duncan's costumes were also an element of her intervention into the history of women's public performance. Like many turn-of-the-century intellectuals, Duncan found simplicity and harmony in Hellenic images and forms, which were compelling because they seemed to be the opposite of the elaborate, heavy decorations of Gilded Age style. While her light tunics were modeled on how women were dressed in the bas-reliefs, sculpture, and pottery of Greek antiquity, Duncan also imitated Renaissance and Romantic conceptions of Hellenism. Her costumes in the early 1900s were designed to make her look like the Botticelli Venus figure come to life, and she later settled on an even simpler version of the tunic, as she continued to go back to the ancient Greeks for inspiration. Seeing an essential female body in Greek and Roman images of women, Duncan thought that she could establish a true, natural form for women. She wrote in one of her many essays on dance, "The Venus of Milo stands on her pedestal in the Louvre for an ideal; women pass before her, hurt and deformed by the dress of ridiculous fashions; she remains forever the same, for she is beauty, life, truth."[18] Promoting what she thought of as an image that was beyond history, Duncan sought to transcend the contemporary ideal of the tightly cinched hourglass figure.

Duncan's costume also should be seen *against* those of other dancing women in the early twentieth century, in both the popular culture of vaudeville revues and the high culture of the ballet.[19] Duncan condemned those costumes because they made women's bodies "illicit" by playing upon the erotic appeal of stockings, corsets, and décolletage as signifiers of undress. Duncan believed that she could remove culture's distortions of the female body by stripping away the elements of conventional costumes, but she did not emerge nude; rather her costumes were meant to suggest what she called "a new nakedness" in which legs, feet, breasts, and torso were seen as a unified whole, not as fragmented, fetishized objects to arouse the audience.[20] Duncan's hostility to both high culture and popular culture was a common point of view among modernists. More important, her emphasis on how women's costumes had distorted femininity and exploited sexuality revealed the centrality of feminism to this cultural critique.

To be sure, some comments on Duncan's costume had little to do with such high-flown ideas. One review, for example, associated Duncan's tunic with a negligee.

> Spectators in the front rows gasped when they saw the famous barefoot dancer leaping forward from the shelter of the dark curtains hung at the back of the stage clad only in the lightest, scantiest, and most translucent silk. One glance sufficed to show that beneath this airy raiment . . . nature was unadorned. . . . Anthony Comstock himself would have been surprised.[21]

Despite Duncan's efforts to reveal the body as a source of wholeness, such comments showed how difficult it was to pry apart the representation of women's bodies from a discourse of eroticism and obscenity.

Nevertheless, Duncan's beliefs about costumes extended to everyday life and fashion, and this continuity strengthened the perception that she was creating a holistic philosophy of life. Duncan looked completely different from other women as they appeared in public in the early 1900s, wearing narrow tailored jackets and long skirts, with elaborate, large hats and buttoned boots. In her simply draped linen or wool tunic and sandals, often with no hat, Duncan's uncorseted form and bare or sandaled feet became a symbol of the reform of the image of women before the war. Though it may seem that Duncan was subverting dominant cultural expectations for women's fashion and respectability (and, indeed, her style later influenced the avant-garde Parisian fashion designer Paul Poiret), her practices were expressions of her belief that the core of culture itself had to be changed. Her clothing style was against fashion, because it was against the contemporary construction of womanhood through which image changed but which kept women's essential inequality intact. Her dress and costume were in themselves a radical performance of her search for a universal principle of women's freedom.

Isadora Duncan in everyday costume. Postcard, about 1908.

Duncan's stage design and dance movements expanded the symbolic possibilities suggested by her costume and everyday dress. In her appeal to wholeness as a principle for both culture and women's emancipation, Duncan sought to blur the static structures of female inequality into a dynamic, moving performance of liberation from those structures. Claiming that she had eliminated artifice to allow for the play of invention and imagination through spontaneous movement, Duncan actually used the techniques of lighting, music, and Greek motifs to establish a context for dance in which unity and connection were not only suggested to the audience, but experienced by them.

The stage design was simple, so simple that it suggested that there was no design at all. A backdrop of long, blue-gray curtains, a carpet, and diffuse lighting in rosy colors made it seem that illusion and artifice had been done away with. The music came up, but no set or dramatic moment occurred to announce the artist's entrance. When Duncan appeared unassumingly from the shadowy corners of the stage, audiences saw a form of dancing quite different from the rigid commonplaces of the ballerina's steps and the displays of soubrettes at popular revues. At those, the shapeliness of the female form was the entertainment, and Duncan did not want her performance to be experienced as a form of entertainment. She did not offer acrobatics, tricks, or songs, nor did she use choreography and the *mise en scène* of the ballet repertoire to tell tragic or charming stories. Duncan claimed that she was dissociating her art from the bourgeois taste for the trivial, superfluous, and merely entertaining.

In contrast to the static lines of the ballerina's poses and the mechanical steps of a set choreography, Duncan's movements magnified those of everyday life—walking, running, leaping, and skipping—through which she expressed an unmechanical relation to the world. Duncan believed that everyday movements were holistic rather than mechanical. Often called "natural" and "expressive," Duncan's movements emphasized nature over industry, simplicity over technique. She bounded and leapt across the stage, but also fell and lay down, acknowledging the weight of her body. She posed, then rhythmically dissolved that stance and slowly formed another pose; she mimed childhood games; she lay down on the stage for long moments or left the stage altogether as the music continued playing. Her movements were repetitive, mimetic, and rhythmic, and they seemed to express the emotional quality of music.

Duncan's appeal to wholeness encompassed an attempt to integrate dance and music into an aesthetic unity. Duncan did not perform to conventional dance music but to orchestral music she considered in itself transformative—Gluck and Wagner operas, Tchaikovsky and Beethoven symphonies, and Chopin concertos. Though her success with this approach was debated, Duncan did not believe music merely accompanied her performances; rather, her movements stemmed from the music, creating a spatial, visual bond with the experience of listening. In creating a three-dimensional space for the music, Duncan represented the seemingly oppositional elements of harmony and ecstasy, building an arc between the ancient Greek polarities of the serene, contemplative Apollonian and the dissonant, abandoned Dionysian. While Duncan's plastic poses and playful mimes emphasized harmony, she also suggested dissonance, with frenzied, wild skipping, head flung back and hands in claws, suggesting the maenads and Furies of the Greek chorus.[22]

Duncan's costume and movement vocabulary were part of the modernist attempt to dismantle aesthetic categories and to bring art into the practice of everyday life. Duncan often made pronouncements about her innovations in costume, set design, and movement that suggested that she was going beyond the limits of dance itself. She vehemently dissociated herself from the cultural connotations of being a dancer, stating, "I hate dancing. I am an expressioniste of beauty. I use my body as my medium, just as the writer uses his words. Do not call me a dancer." She also liked to say that she had dismantled the performance conventions of dance, which was a way of resisting the tendency of critics to place her within an outmoded history of dance and theater. "I never danced a step in my life. I hate all dancing. . . . I am not a dancer. What I am interested in doing is finding and expressing a new form of life."[23] Not a codified, repeatable set of movements, Duncan's dance was the expression of philosophy that rebelled against a culture she considered conventional, complacent, and destructive.

Aesthetics and Woman's Condition

Duncan's ideas about performance were framed by her beliefs about the social, economic, and political situation of women. In her autobiography, for example, Duncan linked her childhood discovery of the imaginative power of dance to her realization that marriage often meant miserable dependency for women. *My Life* paints a vivid picture of what women's legal and economic disfranchisement meant to her and her family, especially their desperate circumstances after her parents' marriage fell apart and her father abandoned her mother and the four Duncan children. Duncan's stories of her family's poverty sounded the sentimental themes of Victorian novels that often expressed covert critiques of women's condition. Yet they set the stage for Duncan's explicitly feminist declarations.

> I was deeply impressed by the injustice of this state of things for women, and putting it together with the story of my father and mother, I decided, then and there, that I would live to fight against marriage and for the emancipation of women and for the right for every woman to have a child or children as it pleased her, and to uphold her right and her virtue.[24]

Duncan proposed abolishing marriage (even though she did eventually marry, disastrously, a Russian poet); she encouraged women to experience passion in sex and to seek it outside of marriage; and she also believed in free motherhood and thought the state should provide services like daycare and health care for all mothers and children. She wrote in 1927, "At the present time I believe my ideas are more or less those of every free-spirited woman, but twenty years ago my refusal to marry and my example in my own person of the right of the woman to bear children without marriage created a considerable misunderstanding."[25] Such statements indicated the emergence of feminism as a key part of the transformation of American culture.

Duncan's social critique merged with her aesthetic theories in her claim that women's control over their bodies was the foundation for their freedom. Duncan's feminism was rooted in her rather heroic approach to liberating women from weakness, dependence, and deformity by training the body itself. Duncan also conveyed strength and autonomy for women in her dances by imitating the powerful stances of classical statues. By modeling her body in this way, Duncan shifted the emphasis from the female body parts eroticized in her own time to a less sexualized image. A French critic responded, "Imagine for yourself a woman with a body that suggests the perfection of Greek sculpture, without the slightest resemblance to the modern French figure." Duncan, rather, was "straight, slender as a sapling, robust hips, with legs at once feminine and virile, bust fragile."[26] She did not resemble the "modern French figure" because the gaze of the viewer shifted from her bust to her powerful legs.

By calling upon images of women in antiquity, Duncan was also reinforcing beliefs that progress for women in the twentieth century went hand in hand with a new view of civilization. Women's emancipation would be the basis for a new civilization, not, as in an older view dominant in the nineteenth century, a civilizing influence. This sometimes raised tensions between Duncan and women reformers, who tended to emphasize women's weakness in order to protect them from physical and economic exploitation. When one such woman uneasily criticized Duncan's continuing to perform when she was visibly pregnant, Duncan insisted that her concern rested on an old-fashioned notion of modesty. Duncan, rather, believed her pregnant body suggested a natural process of life creation: "Oh, but my dear Mrs. X, that's just what I mean my dancing to express—Love—Woman—Formation—Springtime. . . . Everything rustling, promising new Life."[27]

Duncan's social and artistic views advocated women's right to be an erotic subject, not an erotic object. But this belief led to a distinct contrast between the conduct of Duncan's public performances and her personal life. Duncan not only recounted her passionate affairs in her autobiography, a tactic that surely did not hurt sales of the book, but often proclaimed the healthfulness of sexual pleasure.

> Now that I had discovered that Love might be a pastime as well as a tragedy, I gave myself to it with pagan innocence. . . . Some people may be scandalised, but I don't understand why, if you have a body in which you are born to a certain amount of pain . . . why should you not, when the occasion presents, draw from this same body the maximum of pleasure?[28]

Yet she attacked eroticism and sexual display as a mode of expression in dance. "I don't like to look at stage dancing. . . . All I see in what people call dancing is merely a useless agitation of the arms and legs. . . . This is the sort of dancing based on sexual desire. . . . We see all the outward movement. But what of the inward movement, the movement of the mind?"[29] Wholeness, for Duncan, could only be experienced when audiences stopped eroticizing the female performer. She wrote in 1908, imagining the female dancer of the future: "She will dance not in the form of nymph, nor fairy, nor coquette, but in the form of woman in her greatest and purest expression."[30] For Duncan, women would become artists and not entertainers when they performed themselves rather than merely following assigned roles in the trite and eroticized dance repertoire.

Duncan often went out of her way to demand that audiences stop equating the nude female body with obscenity, to jolt them out of their misperception. For example, she stopped a performance in Boston in 1922 when the audience began jeering after her breast slipped out of her costume. Victor Seroff, Duncan's companion and biographer, wrote that she told the audience,

> "To expose one's body is art; concealment is vulgar. When I dance, my object is to inspire reverence; not to suggest anything vulgar. Nudity is truth,

it is beauty, it is art. Therefore, it can never be vulgar; it can never be immoral . . ."

And then she tore her tunic down to bare one of her breasts and cried out, "This—this is beauty!"[31]

By baring her breast in public, Duncan shifted the meaning of the breast as signifier of women's sexuality to something that was probably more shocking to a bourgeois audience, namely the possibility that women could be agents of representation rather than objects of it.[32] In contrast to erotic paintings that tell viewers they are seeing bodies that are sexually arousing, Duncan wanted the revelation of her body to disrupt the association of codified women's bodies with sexual temptation and submission.[33] Duncan thus used the discourse of female purity, a woman's body divorced from its own passions, to change the perception of the female body and remove cultural associations of what women ought to look like. Such displays were not always successful, as the response of the scandalized audience in Boston tells us. But in representing the female body as a source of wholeness rather than a site of weakness and immorality, Duncan allied women's emancipation to central ideas of modernism.[34]

A Symbol of Cultural Liberation

Duncan was an "event" because of the innovations that she introduced and her self-fashioning as an artist, and because there was so much commentary about her. As Duncan situated her ideas about dance within a larger cultural project, modernists claimed her as an apostle; her performances often were the site around which intellectuals placed and dated their own visions and dreams. The hyperbole of her contemporaries commented little on what Duncan actually did but rather noted the inspiration she aroused in them. In the bohemian rhetoric of the 1910s in America, Duncan was perceived as a "pagan" who was fighting the "Philistines."[35] Duncan's claim, "I could not do anything without seeming extravagantly different from other people, and therefore shocking," became a familiar bohemian stance in the 1910s: to be different and shocking was a goal that most shared.[36] In Duncan cultural radicals saw a way to unload their intellectual and familial baggage and to see the praxis of art and life they valued.[37]

The event of Duncan encouraged physical, sensory images of change and transformation. Cultural radical Floyd Dell, for example, found in Duncan's performance a way to represent his own claim to a new ethos and its difference from a decrepit social order. He wrote in 1916,

A strange and dark century, the nineteenth! . . . When I think that if I had lived and died in the darkness of that century I should never have seen with these eyes the beauty and terror of the human body, I am glad of the daylight of my own time. It is not enough to throw God from his pedestal and dream of superman and the co-operative commonwealth: one must have seen Isadora Duncan to die happy.[38]

In Dell's rhetoric of light and vision, Duncan dispelled the "darkness" of the nineteenth century. Yet she is not one of the philosophers of the metaphysical breakdown that shaped modern consciousness; she embodies those ideas. Through the shock of "seeing" Duncan's body, Dell recognized himself as modern, albeit with a utopian's sunny view of the twentieth century. For Dell, Duncan literally and physically enacted the change from Victorianism to modernism.

In addition to such literary assessments, Duncan's emphasis on the body made her a subject of representation in a range of visual mediums—drawings, prints, paintings, and photographs—by artists associated with modernism. The artist Abraham Walkowitz, who was part of Alfred Stieglitz's circle, made over 5,000 sketches from memory of Duncan's poses. He explained his thrall in 1920 by saying, "She didn't dance according to rules. She created. Her body was music. It was a body electric, like Walt Whitman."[39] While Walkowitz's description was a common assertion of the artist as rebel, his perception of Duncan's "latitude" led to a kinetic, cinematic representation of her body; grouped as a series on a single page, his drawings suggest an endless series of movements not reducible to a single repertoire.

Artist John Sloan's 1911 painting of Duncan represented the dancer as a symbol of freedom. As a member of the Ash Can School, Sloan was one of a group of American artists breaking away from the techniques and subjects of academic, genteel art and moving toward representing life as they found it—on the streets and from the rooftops of immigrant neighborhoods—with a style to depict both the beauty in everyday life and the injustice they saw around them. Duncan was a special subject for Sloan because she helped him to see in aesthetic terms a new iconography of the body different from both mannered portraits of society women and academic conceptions of the nude. Sloan's depiction of Duncan performing on a darkened stage attempted to capture the event of Duncan in paint, and his broad strokes arrest Duncan in a lyrical moment. Her body is figured with head back and arm flung wide, with the fluttering tunic draped lightly and transparently over her body.

The event of Isadora Duncan. *Isadora Duncan,* by John Sloan, 1911. Oil on canvas, 32¼ x 26¼ inches. Milwaukee Art Museum; Gift of Mr. and Mrs. Donald B. Abert. Printed by permission of the Milwaukee Art Museum.

Duncan's associations with intellectuals and artists of all types re-inforced the perception that she was an innovator dedicated to an inte-grated rebirth of all the arts. The link between innovation and rebirth was expressed through a familiar gendered rhetoric that attributed re-productive power to Duncan's performances. One passionate, youthful devotee of Duncan wrote in 1920, "To love you with understanding is to conceive a new religion—to give birth to a god; and what throes and pangs and ecstasies attend such a delivery!"[40] Such metaphors of birth associated Duncan's art with abilities specific to women and located the desire for transformation within the female body. Unlike most understandings of the artistic process, to enter into Duncan's vision of modernity was not an escape from the body of the mother but a physical act of rebirth centered in the female body.

Duncan's belief that the emancipated body would allow women to overcome weakness and dependency implicitly used eugenic ideas.

> It is not only a question of true art, it is a question of race, of the development of the female sex to beauty and health, of the return to the original strength and to natural movements of woman's body. It is a question of the development of perfect mothers and birth of healthy and beautiful children.[41]

Sloan also fell into the discourse of eugenics when describing why Duncan's body was powerful to him.

> Isadora as she appears on that big simple stage seems like all womanhood—she looms big as the mother of the race. A heavy solid figure, large columnar legs, a solid high belly, breasts not too full and her head seems to be no more important than it should to give the body the chief place.[42]

Such rhetoric connected Duncan to the figure of the mother so important in both Victorian discourse and modern racialist social science. In this set of concerns, Duncan's body is suggestively described as the origin of a new approach to the body.

Sloan's interest in Duncan, moreover, was not erotic, and most modernists did not talk about the inspiration that they took from Duncan's performances in terms of an expressive sexuality—even though liberating sex from the repression associated with Victorianism was a widely shared goal. Rather, Duncan's contemporaries emphasized that her performances were freed from a relation to sex, a freedom they characterized as abstract, pure, and natural. The critic Carl Van Vechten wrote after seeing her perform in New York, "[I]t was pure and sexless . . . always abstract emotion has guided her interpretations."[43] To prove the artistic stature of Duncan's work and to undermine the association of her performances with her famed lifestyle of "free love," her conductor, Martin Shaw, wrote, "There was no sex appeal in Isadora's dancing."[44] Watching Duncan enabled viewers to see health and natural beauty in the female body. In 1917 critic André Levinson connected nature imagery to the absence of a decadent femininity, writing that Duncan was an "artist-andragyne": "There is something bucolic about her. There is no tragedy. No eroticism. There is no real femininity in her essence. In her there is a simple grace, strength, the joy of youth."[45] The absence of sexuality in Duncan's dance was itself a form of freedom for these observers, and it freed them to see her contributions to modernist concerns with abstraction and simplicity.

From Civilization to Modernism

Duncan's ideas about the liberated female body referenced a larger problem, that of the impact of modernity on those who lived in the rapidly changing metropoli of the early twentieth century. Modernity was both a promise and a threat: the rapidly expanding cities, the waves of immigration, the spectacular array of material goods and activities produced by capitalism were in themselves enormous changes, and they made even more change possible. One of the key problems of modernist thought was how to grapple with the dualistic nature of modernity—its great wealth and pervasive poverty, its acceleration of work and expansion of leisure, its tendency to both wound and gratify the soul. Many modernists met the divided nature of life in the twentieth century with ambivalence. On one hand, they argued that the development of capitalism would eventually usher in a society free from class, race, and sexual division. On the other, they worried about how the technology and pace of modernity affected the body and the mind. In their own lives, they sought to loosen the bonds of routinized labor and to pursue dreams of self-fulfillment.[46] They embraced change, but they found themselves shaking the bars of the iron cage of modern life. In this sense modernists were simultaneously the critics and utopian dreamers of modern life.

Duncan's own ambivalence toward modernity produced a compelling, dissident view of the dizzying pace of change and the tumultuous conditions of life in the early twentieth century. She believed that dance could lighten the pressures of modern life; she emphasized depth and harmony in order to counteract the disorienting effects of an increasingly accelerated and alienated twentieth-century world, a world she called "strident, clamorous dissonance."[47] She sought to connect body and soul when industrialization tore them apart, and she emphasized simplicity when fashion and mass production combined to make embellishment and the accumulation of things a never-ending process.[48] Duncan's aim was to slow things down, to calm what she called the paroxysms of modern life.[49] Her personal presence indicated this: Those who met Duncan consistently pointed out that she was calm, that she always moved slowly and gracefully, and that her voice was melodious and soothing.[50]

Modernist perspectives on urban, capitalist life also encompassed a critique of "civilization," the idea that those who reaped the economic rewards of capital also stood at the moral and cultural apex of its society. In Duncan's theory of the body's centrality for change and freedom, the morality of Victorianism had damaged the body by attempting to civilize it. In her 1909 essay, "Movement Is Life," Duncan wrote, "With the first conception of a conscience, man became self-conscious, lost the natural movements of the body; today in the light of intelligence gained through years of civilization, it is essential that he consciously seek what he has unconsciously lost."[51]

While civilization had repressed the consciousness of the body, through dance the expressive body could be rediscovered. The individual would rediscover an embodied relation to the world through sense—nerves, muscles, and perception—and Duncan theorized that if one was trained to make the most of this encounter with the world, then one also had the means to resist the moral and social prohibitions that dominate the body. The purpose of dance was thus to disarm the power of civilization to dominate and control the body, and through dancing the body would be the agent of progressive change.

While Duncan sought to strip away the civilized conventions guiding the perception of women like so much nineteenth-century clothing, her emphasis on ancient forms prevented her from coming to grips with the changes wrought by modernity in the early twentieth century.[52] Duncan believed that the bonds tying the individual to machines, to consumption and to repression, could be loosened and indeed should be escaped altogether. This misunderstanding prevented her from seeing the extent to which she was part of a process of historical change, of what modernity exacted from women as well as the progressive changes it introduced. Her belief in the essential integrity of the body did not acknowledge the body's mediation by the machines of capitalism, either the assembly lines of industry or the telephones, automobiles, and cameras of consumer culture.[53] Indeed, Duncan believed that she could preserve an unmediated aura as a performer when that aura was increasingly disappearing from the autonomous work of art. Significantly, while Duncan was photographed by such well-known artists as Arnold Genthe and Edward Steichen, she refused to be filmed by a motion-picture camera, believing that the technology distorted her practice as a dancer and distanced her from the audience.[54]

Timelessness and Collectivity

While in this account Duncan seemed to be fully immersed in her historical moment, her primary desire was to break free from that moment and move into the realm of timelessness. The ambivalence with which Duncan confronted the features of modernity stemmed from her appeal to the past as "primitive" and thus purer than the supposed signs of progress in the early twentieth century. Duncan's evocation of a "pure" past was an attempt to get outside of the structures of history, just as she appealed to a seemingly timeless Hellenic costume to disrupt the history of women in performance. To dance was to be, to exist in a continuous present outside of time.

This desire for timelessness was shared by many modernists. Gordon Craig, theater designer and father of Duncan's first child, wrote to Duncan in 1919, "'The past'—'the present' . . . 'future' . . . all these are words which have some meaning when used in speaking of most people—they have nothing whatever to do with you."[55] After watching Duncan in Paris, Gertrude Stein used Duncan's suspension of time in dance to emphasize space and motion as a model for the continuous present and a prose without narrative in her essay, "Orta, or One Dancing":

> [C]omplete connection being existing in her being one dancing between dancing being existing and her being one not being one completing being one, she was one dancing and being that one she was that one and being that one she was that one the one dancing and being the one dancing being that one she was the one going on being that one the one dancing. She was dancing. She had been dancing. She would be dancing.[56]

Stein's essay replicates a sense of timelessness in the reader, where boundaries dissolve and "one" could move in "all" directions, freed from the structure of a linear narrative. Tenses shift; dancing is everywhere but has no place in time. Yet Stein's use of the continuous present to dissolve the structures of the self in place and time points to a larger problem for women artists like Duncan.

Duncan both wanted to reveal the unique and exceptional quality of her artistry, yet erase the distinct contours of her individuality in order to produce the sensation of abstraction, timelessness, and simplicity. Duncan tells us in her autobiography that early in her career she stood for hours in front of a mirror and finally discovered the origin of movement within her body, at the solar plexus, rather than from an exterior source. "I was seeking and finally discovered the central spring of all movement, the crater of motor power, the unity from which all diversities of movements are born, the mirror of vision for the creation of the dance."[57]

While Duncan clung to the centrality of a coherent inner self, she also thought of her body as only a medium for the music and the audience's sensation of freedom. Duncan often said her motto was *"sans limites."* The desire to be both unified and without limits—both coherent in self and encompassing the world—was a contradictory way of explaining the situation of the self in history. Duncan described herself as a "magnetic center," a point of emotional consciousness. "Often I thought to myself, what a mistake to call me a dancer—I am the magnetic centre to convey the emotional expression of the Orchestra."[58] That she dissolved boundaries between performer, music, and audience thus pointed away from the centrality of the self, and individuality, as the locus for change and transformation. This dynamic of dependence on a self that then is dissolved presaged her erasure within modernism.

Duncan appeared to bridge the tension between individualism and collectivity in her performances by displacing the notion of dance as a solo performance. This was appealing to modernists focused on their individual, psychic development at the same time that they were involved in social movements that included class struggle, the vote for women, and other collective demands for rights. Claiming "I have never once danced a solo," Duncan believed that her performances molded individual expression into a collective social presence.[59] Duncan's essays insisted that she meant both to play upon the individual's access to harmony and to make the audience aware of itself as a collective presence reflected in the movements on stage. One of her phrases about her method is evocative: "call and response, bound endlessly in one cadence."[60] Her performances sought to break down the barriers introduced by spectacles and to bind the audience and the performer together into a collective event; like Whitman, whose *Leaves of Grass* she carried with her everywhere, Duncan wanted her body to "contain multitudes." She expressed collectivity by evoking the impression of a moving chorus rather than the solitary dancer on a spare stage. To proclaim the unity of self and collectivity was not so much a contradiction but a utopian claim.

Interpretations of Duncan's movements often made them into allegories of cultural and political movements. In claiming that she danced the part of the chorus, not the soloist, Duncan pointed to a political, social arena for artistic expression. Her dances often seemed to tell allegories of revolution, and their progressions were likened to socialism and utopian views of history. Marxist editor Michael Gold wrote in 1929, "She prophesied the future, when in a free society there will be neither money nor classes, and men will seem like gods, when the body and mind will form a radiant unity. Her own mind and body approached that unity."[61]

In evoking collectivity and a socialist body politic, Duncan equated her own persona with what she believed were universal feelings and drives. Luhan suggested in her memoirs, "[T]his life she let loose up through her body was not good or bad but merely undifferentiated and voluminous."[62] Duncan called this "multiple oneness," and theorized movement as not merely evoking but enacting collective social action.

> In order to realise these dreams, a single gesture of appeal will be able to evoke a thousand extended arms, a single head tossed back will represent a bacchantic tumult. . . . It seems to me that in this music is concentrated the . . . whole cry of desire in the world. . . . I repeat, I do not fulfill it, I only indicate it.[63]

Duncan's power to represent wholeness and unity in this dialectic of individuality and group identity relies upon her belief that freeing the female body would unlock all the other doors of freedom as well. Through dance, she evoked wholeness and unity as a woman at one with her body, which was effective because women were most closely associated with the fragmentation wrought by modernity. Intervening in the discourse that structured the perception of women as hopelessly split between body and mind, intelligence and animality, Duncan reached for harmony: "She will dance the body emerging again from centuries of civilized forgetfulness, emerging not in the nudity of primitive man, but in a new nakedness, no longer at war with spirituality and intelligence, but joining with them in a glorious harmony."[64] To express wholeness, then, was to "dance the freedom of woman."[65]

Duncan's contribution to a feminist modernism was in her effort to resolve the opposition between mind and body for women in their collective, everyday lives and also in the idea of "woman" in the discourse of civilization. But we can see how radical and how problematic this effort was when we look at the representation of Duncan as both a feminist and a modernist figure in history. In many ways, Duncan was understood as a feminist body that would create an artistic and social revolution. Max Eastman and Floyd Dell, for example, wrote about Duncan as a symbol of women's emancipation that connected feminism to the new art.

Duncan was understood as making a social and symbolic leap from the Victorian to modernism. But she also demonstrated how difficult that leap was to make. Floyd Dell saw women's emancipation in Duncan's dancing body; he included an essay on Duncan in his collection of feminist portraits, *Women as World Builders,* because he believed, "[I]t is to the body that one looks for the Magna Charta of feminism." The world-builder Duncan was writing one of the founding texts of feminism with her body. But crucially, for Dell, Duncan represented the leap from the political and social agitation of feminists and suffragists to the realm of "truth" and "beauty," thus disconnecting art from politics and removing the taint of social change from what we consider to be art. "It is only when the woman's movement is seen broadly . . . that there comes the re-alization that here is a cause . . . from which sincere lovers of truth and beauty have nothing really to fear." In doing so, he reestablished her as someone who posed no threat to those who have a "proper regard for literature and art" and preserved the boundaries of what constituted that literature and art.[66]

Duncan was also understood as a feminist pioneer in new historical territory for women. Eastman, for example, characterized Duncan as "the most advanced outpost of the movement for woman's emancipation." But Eastman's rhetoric of trailblazing and pioneering tied her to history in a parody of the early women's rights activists; her tendency to make speeches, he said, was "didactic," and her intellectual pretensions made her a "bluestocking." Feminism, in the person of Duncan, was thus susceptible to the modernist attack on Victorianism, symbolized here as the woman who forsakes her desirability for intellectual pursuits. "To put it in another way, she was a spiritual child of Susan B. Anthony as well as Walt Whitman, and the strain of the iron reformer was strong in her."[67] The coupling of Susan B. Anthony, fighter for women's rights, and Walt Whitman, poet of the body, had produced a child with all of their sins as well as their strengths.

The Monument of Isadora Duncan

Duncan's support for U.S. involvement in World War I marked a change in her reception among cultural radicals. The "iron reformer" was much on display in John Sloan's 1915 drawing of Duncan for *The Masses.* Like Lippmann, Sloan was going through his own disillusionment with the Duncan mystique. Titled "Isadora Duncan in the 'Marche Militaire,'" the drawing mocked Duncan's style and body in order to criticize those who supported the war mobilization. Duncan's hair is messy and lank, her face appears haggard, and her eyes are smeared. The signature tunic is misshapen, and Duncan appears flatfooted, heavy, and almost clumsy, if not for the determined, forceful overstatement of the march step. With her arm thrust forward, her hands fiercely clutching a taut scarf, Duncan's pose was a parody of the lyricism, reverence, and utopian longing with which Sloan had greeted her performances four years previously. This drawing, rather, provokes a feeling of revulsion; in contrast to Duncan's abstract gestures to a utopian modernism, here her gesture is meant to be seen as a repellent patriotism. The betrayal that Sloan may have felt at Duncan's sentiment toward the war was more than avenged by his appropriation of her body to signify the war and those who supported it as ugly objects of contempt. Just as Duncan's body could be represented as a lyrical, timeless gesture to wholeness, it also could be appropriated in an antiwar parody.

While the modernist response to World War I was not the only turning point in the reception of Duncan, the Sloan drawing was suggestive of an impending transformation. The visual apprehension of Duncan's performing body as the unity of a new definition of womanhood and utopian aspirations for the twentieth century fragmented as Duncan herself confronted difference and change in modern culture. She had always had an uneasy relationship to dominant culture as it was unfolding in the America of the Progressive Era. Janet Flanner, essayist for the *New Yorker*, wrote, "Exalted at the concert hall by her display of Greek beauty, limbs, and drapes which though they were two thousand years old she seemed to make excitingly modern, her followers, dazzled, . . . went home to Fords, big hats, and the theory of Bull Moose, the more real items of their progressive age."[68] While the main line of progressivism had supported the war effort, those who dissented from U.S. entry into the war faced suppression, and the Red Scare that followed the war made cultural expression of dissent even more difficult. By the end of the war, radical trends in American modernism had fragmented, weakening the situation in which Duncan had flourished as a feminist modernist.

In this context, the interpretation of Duncan's performing body changed. While many critics and observers at the time laid this change at the door of Duncan's advancing years, aging body, and her experiences of great personal tragedy, including the deaths of her two children, a more abstract rhetorical and visual transformation was also taking place. She began to be recognized not as a dynamic event, but as a monument—an immobile allusion to a lost moment of freedom, part of a nostalgia on the part of cultural radicals for their prewar heyday. The perception of Duncan's body froze into a tribute to liberation, not a process of liberation.

Duncan the "iron reformer" in Sloan's antiwar parody. "Isadora Duncan in the March Militaire," by John Sloan, from *The Masses* (May 1915). The Tamiment Institute Library, New York University; used by permission.

Just as a monument stands for a symbol of and myth about the past, the discourse of monumentality neutralized Duncan's avant-garde gestures and cloaked her negative reaction to popular culture. Duncan's body continued to represent modernist sensibilities. But now the mood of Duncan's contemporaries was marked by a sense of failure, pessimism, and a romanticized desire to persist in a cultural project made marginal by the repressive politics of the Red Scare and the rise of consumer culture. The shift in rhetoric from the transformative event of Duncan to the monumental Duncan thus is central to the interpretation of Duncan's ideas about the expressive body, her role as an artist, and the historical assessment of feminism in modernism.

Despite the alienation from American culture expressed by many modernists, developments in mass culture after the war were not all conservative. In a broader sense, the impact of the war distilled a process of cultural change: the ideal of wholeness dimmed amid the growth of a popular culture less focused on the cause of unified, collective change and more intent on diverse experience. Trends in urban culture, especially the popularization of jazz as well as African American and working-class dance styles, were more racially diverse, sexually expressive, and appealing to young people. The new music and dancing were expressions, indeed, of the loosened sexual mores and cultural revelry of the twenties. In the context of an ever-expanding consumer culture and a new morality, Duncan was caught between the ideal potentialities she had seemed to embody and the actualities of a changing culture. Her alliance between women's emancipation and the modernist ideal of wholeness was mired in a generation gap.

Race and Sexuality in Popular Culture

Duncan was aware of the widening split between her theory of wholeness and elements of popular culture. Fearing that she would not be able to draw an audience when dance crazes were sweeping the country and capturing the imagination of young Americans, her rejection of the conventions of dance took a new rhetorical turn. While she continued to dance, her strategy of self-promotion became less focused on movement and philosophical persuasion and more on polemical attacks. She believed that her conception of dance was being contaminated by popular expression.

> If, twenty years ago, when I first pleaded with America to adopt my school and my theories of dancing in all the public schools, they had acceded to my request, this deplorable modern dancing, which has its roots in the ceremonies of African primitives, could never have become dominant.[69]

Duncan's later speeches and autobiography opposed her goal of a unified national culture to the music of jazz and popular trends in couple dancing, and in doing so she used an explicitly racist language. Imagining a national music to match her vision of dance, she wrote,

This music would have a rhythm as great as the exhilaration, the swing or curves of the Rocky Mountains. It would have nothing to do with the sensual lilt of the jazz rhythm: it would be like the vibration of the American soul striving upward, through labour to harmonious life. Nor had this dance that I visioned any vestige of the Fox Trot or the Charleston—rather was it the living leap of the child springing toward the heights, towards its future accomplishment, towards a new great vision of life that would express America.[70]

Duncan's use of this rhetoric was not uncommon in the twenties, when, for example, heightened racist and nativist reactions to cultural pluralism led to the revitalization of the Ku Klux Klan.

Harlem Renaissance poet Claude McKay made it clear that this polemic was Duncan's limited representation of a larger culture influenced by African American popular forms. In describing an argument he had with Duncan in her studio in Nice, France, he wrote: "Isadora was . . . severe on Negro dancing and its imitations and derivations. She had no real appreciation of primitive folk dancing, either from an [a]esthetic or an ethnic point of view."[71] Duncan not only could not appreciate African American folk culture, as McKay said, but her utopian belief in the integration of art and life was in tension with what she saw as the "primitive" allure of popular culture.

Racial language also affected Duncan's ideas about dance and gender; it increasingly became a part of the discourse that Duncan and those who wrote about her used to talk about womanhood. The dance critic Levinson, for example, wove racial metaphors into his argument that Duncan's dance was dissociated from connotations of sexuality. Through these metaphors, Duncan's performance became comprehensible not only as that of a new woman, but as a white woman's.

> The cult of athleticism, of the strong, lithe, healthy body, gave rise to talk . . . of the "racial" quality evidenced in Duncan's art. The aesthetic character of her dance carries this typically anglo-saxon impression. . . . She was the product of a race that had no past. . . . Her bare soles trod virgin ground from the outset. . . . It was not only the reasoned discipline of classical ballet that was trampled by her white feet. It was the general effect of the social and intellectual conventions upon which civilized society lives.[72]

By describing Duncan's "racial quality" and white feet as being Anglo-Saxon and without a past, Levinson suggests that Duncan created art not only through the female body but through whiteness as well.

Duncan's own use of Hellenic images and myths became more force-fully racialist in her manifestos written in the twenties. She had written in the early 1900s, "It is not only a question of true art, it is a question of race, of the development of the female sex to beauty and health, of the re-turn to the original strength and to natural movements of woman's body."[73] In contrast to this concern with race as a form of human evolu-tion or development, Duncan later understood race in terms of cultural difference and morality: "It is of the utmost importance to a nation to train its children to the understanding and execution of movements of great heroic and spiritual beauty; . . . [to place] prohibitions on the frivo-lous caricatures and symbols of sex which are found in such dances as the fox trot and Black Bottom."[74]

Duncan mobilized the implicit association between new womanhood and whiteness that had characterized her early thought to make an explicit distinction between white Anglo-European culture and black African culture in contemporary American life. Jazz and popular dancing became specific racial signifiers that replaced the universal image of "woman" in Duncan's rhetoric.

While Duncan's attack on the civilized constraints of Victorianism had been effective for showing how important the body was for women's emancipation, her ability to see the progressive possibilities for women in the popular culture of the twenties was much less so. She argued that women's consumption of black culture threatened their moral uprightness and bodily purity. While she had despised the civilizing reformers who had chastised her in her own youth, Duncan, now in her forties, began to use a rhetoric of morality and purity to talk about young women's behavior. She wrote in 1927: "It is extraordinary that mothers who would be intensely shocked if their daughters should indulge in a real orgy . . . will look on with smiling complacency at their daughters indulging in licentious con-tortions upon a dance floor, before their very eyes."[75]

In claiming that popular dancing was overly sexual, she fell back upon a Victorian discourse of a mother's duty to protect her daughter's morali-ty. In making this connection, Duncan was contributing to a racist his-tory that saw blackness as a threat to white womanhood.[76] Moreover, Duncan's emphasis on the licentiousness of popular culture undermined the coherence of her theory of women's sexual agency; young women performed the dances popular in the 1920s at their peril.

A seemingly modest young girl would not think of addressing a young man in lines or spoken phrases which were indecent and yet the same girl will arise and dance these phrases with him in such dances as the Charleston and Black Bottom, while a negro orchestra is playing Shake that thing![77]

Duncan rightfully saw that sexual expressiveness, not women's explicit control of their own bodies, had become central to modern culture in the twenties. But her emphasis on suspending the association of sexual pleasure with the female body had become moralistic. Duncan's belief that harmonious, natural movement would produce a new woman who was strong, healthy, and independent had been a dynamic and radical feminist strategy when it was articulated in the context of an abstract wholeness. But the more this abstract emphasis was displaced in her later rhetoric, the more static her idea of womanhood became.

The spontaneous, temporary, fragmented nature of popular dancing subverted Duncan's emphasis on dance as a productive, generative philosophy of life. Nevertheless, wholeness and unity could only be posited when the invisibility of African Americans made it possible to do so. Duncan's utopian narrative had been based on negating difference all along. But that negation was not visible, and certainly not so shrill or overtly negative until African American styles and traditions became more influential in dominant culture.

Nationalism

Duncan's move to revolutionary Russia in 1921 was fueled in equal parts by her cultural despair and her attraction to the possibilities of building a new world. "With all the energy of my being, disappointed in the attempts to realise any of my art visions in Europe, I was ready to enter the ideal domain of Communism."[78] She described her sojourn there as if it were an escape from Western civilization and an entrance into a wide open space where the distinctions between high and popular culture had been eradicated. Duncan initially turned to the revolution to give her inspiration and the raw material for her own blueprint for the future, but she was soon influenced by the tales of revolution and struggle she encountered. Some of her dances told these stories, her body's movements literally expressing the political narrative from oppression to freedom. Rather than the aesthetic and emotional transformation of self-consciousness, her dances became propaganda: an upward movement of the arm matched a music crescendo that together expressed the will of the people.

What was rejuvenating about Russia for Duncan seemed very different to her contemporaries in America. When she returned to the United States to tour in 1922, she was met with hostility by the government, the press, and the larger public, who taunted her with such anticommunist epithets as "scarlet woman" and "red whore." This reception exacerbated Duncan's sense of estrangement, expressed in her belief that dominant American culture was hostile to art and artists and that popular culture was contributing to the demise of culture itself. Faced with being labeled a Bolshevist, moreover, Duncan began to emphasize that her idea of America was not about freedom, but about nationality.

Even though Duncan spent most of her life in Europe, she had always claimed that her emancipatory ideas were intrinsically American. A more distinct nationalism expressed her opposition to the direction of popular culture. She wrote in her 1927 autobiography,

> It seems to me monstrous that any one should believe that the Jazz rhythm expresses America. Jazz rhythm expresses the primitive savage. America's music would be something different. . . . America will be expressed in some Titanic music that will shape its chaos to harmony, and long-legged, shining boys and girls will dance to this music, not the tottering, ape-like convulsions of the Charleston.[79]

While such remarks displayed Duncan's racism, the most important result of such rhetorical intensity was that her persona became that of a demagogue, and her posturing both in performance and in her speeches became more rigid.

Duncan's fluid notion of self also hardened into a concrete, stable narrative. Believing herself a heroic American at the same time that she felt doomed to exile by its dominant culture, Duncan produced a story that gave her a stable identity in a sea of cultural contention. Duncan's story emphasized her origins as an American against an oppositional culture that nearly characterized her as a traitor. She was, she wrote, the product of both immigrants and pioneer settlers, the heroic nation builders of the American mythology. She was the grandchild of Irish pioneers making their way across the country in a covered wagon, with her grandfather fighting off Indians while her grandmother gave birth to her first child. The young Isadora, in turn, inherited the spirit of her grandmother's Irish jigs, absorbing

> some of the gestures of the Redskins themselves and, again, a bit of Yankee Doodle. . . . I learnt it from her, putting into it my own aspiration of Young America, and, finally, my great spiritual realisation of life from the

lines of Walt Whitman. And that is the origin of the . . . Dance with which I have flooded the world.[80]

This story represents Duncan as a pioneering ethnic American, against the cultural influence of jazz and its hybrid link between the African and the American. Often repeated in Duncan's late speeches and essays, this story of Duncan's multiethnic roots attempted to establish a stable, usable past for her in an increasingly unsure present and an elusive future.

Memory and History

As if to corroborate Duncan's movement from an abstract collectivity to a rigid Americanism, many writers and artists claimed that Duncan was symbolic of America, and that American ideals would be exhibited by American bodies. Perhaps in his own effort to defend the tradition of American radicalism, Max Eastman celebrated the emergence of a national as well as a feminist female body produced by Duncan's influence. "All the bare-legged girls, and the poised and natural girls with strong muscles, and strong free steps wherever they go—the girls that redeem America and make it worth while to have founded a new world, no matter how badly it was done—they all owe more to Isadora Duncan than to any other person."[81] Such assessments were rhetorical monuments to Duncan that gestured toward a utopian lost moment but that were not grounded in the conditions of Duncan's career in the changing culture.

In this context, the division between being a subject—Duncan's control over the process of being both an artist and a woman—and an object of representation—how others described, photographed, and drew Duncan—asserted itself powerfully in the twenties. This division was channeled metaphorically into the perception that Duncan had aged, a convenient discourse but one that had everything to do with a generation's anxiety over the failure of a cultural idea.[82] Her contemporary intellectuals were dismayed by the changes in her dances and in her aging body. As Duncan entered middle age, her body no longer signified an artistic, philosophical, cultural unity; instead, her body got in the way of the visual apprehension of her ideas. Levinson wrote in 1929,

> The art of Isadora Duncan had aged with her. Those who had not seen her when she was twenty had not seen her. It was at the Trocadero, in May of 1923, that these inexorable ravages were apparent to me for the last time. . . . How I remember from the upright and noble carriage of her small head, to the torso of a robust amazon. . . . Yesterday, tortured, I sought those traits in her heavy face, the nape of her neck, and her mas-

sive thighs, revealed by an overly short tunic. . . . The arms, the wrists had lost their suppleness. . . . [A] single memory stays with me. I see the dancer, again with arms crucified as on an imaginary cross, the body weighed down, knees bent, legs broadly, brutally split apart. Then the head rolls back, the chest follows and the short head of hair sweeps the floor.[83]

The stream of metaphors that Duncan's performances had generated earlier in the century stopped abruptly in the 1920s. Her tunic no longer signified transparency and sexlessness, and her body referred to nothing but itself. Rather than being described as symbolic of abstract concepts such as freedom, unity, nobility, or images drawn from "nature," Duncan was described as a body in parts: legs, breast, and head. Modernists could not watch her without remembering what they had seen years before in her performances, and they could not brook the comparison. To many, Duncan had become monstrous.

But in their desire to hold onto the possibility of cultural transformation, even though it no longer could be produced through the event of Duncan, her intellectual companions used militaristic and majestic imagery in their writing about her. By this time, when Duncan was in her forties, her performing costumes remained simple, but her daily garb became more theatrical and elaborate. In contrast to the straight and streamlined fashion of the times, she wore, for example, red boots, green velvet capes, lace stockings, gold sandals and belts, beaded turbans, and orange smocks on her trip to the United States in 1922–23. Victor Seroff, Duncan's companion at the end of her life and one of her biographers, wrote, "She astonished me by her unnaturally theatrical appearance. . . . This was not a woman, this was some kind of theatrical king."[84] By becoming more theatrical and majestic in her daily costumes, Duncan had introduced a split between her performances and her daily life; they were no longer one and the same, unified, coherent presentation of a transformed womanhood.

Using his memory of Duncan to explain his own crusade against the sexual politics of "Puritanism," Eastman cast Duncan in the mold of a militant hero in battle armor, in contrast to the fluidity of the transparent, silky tunics that had marked earlier descriptions. He wrote:

America fighting the battle against Americanism—that was Isadora. From that battle incomparable things are to come—things that will startle and teach the world. And Isadora led the way into the fight all alone, with her naked and strong body and her bold character, beautiful as an Amazon. If

America triumphs over itself—over its cheap greed and prudery, its intellectual and moral cowardice, it prurient puerile senility—if America triumphs over that, Isadora Duncan will be sculptured in bronze at the gate of the Temple of Man in the new day that will dawn.[85]

Even as Eastman built a monument to Duncan's struggle against social constraint, the complexities of her ideas and her performances, not just her polemical posturing, were lost. The image of Duncan as a statue occurred frequently in tributes to her, for example, by a gushing admirer in 1920: "No man who lives is great enough to build a permanent monument to you."[86] Though monumentalizing her is understood to be impossible by this devotée, his desire to do so remained.

Duncan grew impatient with those who wanted to memorialize her while she was engaged in an ongoing struggle. She said in 1921, "I know you will put up a monument to me fifty years after my death, but what good will that be? I will then be far away from the agony and struggle and unable to give you a great school and a great idea that you cannot understand or appreciate."[87] Her autobiography, which she finished two months before she died in 1927, recorded Duncan's inability to reconcile her sense of her body and the process of monumentality to which it was subjected. For her this was a problem of representation. The first few pages of her autobiography are a caution to her readers: "How can we write the truth about ourselves? Do we even know it?" This caution does not affect our ability to believe her memoir, written as it is in a straightforward, first-person, chronological narrative. But occasionally, the narrative does break from its story and we read passages that suggest Duncan has thrown up her hands in despair, and she addresses the reader directly: "here I am, trying to write the truth of all that happened to me and I greatly fear that it will turn out an awful mess."[88]

This ambivalence extended to the way Duncan believed history would place her, which she did not resolve by preserving her work.[89] The photographs, drawings, and sculptures of Duncan suggested movement, but they did not reproduce it. Duncan refused to be filmed, believing that the technological distortions of early cinema would not fully represent her project. Indeed, she wanted to avoid completely the process of mechanical reproduction and instead preserve an unmediated aura, what she believed was an essential bond between audience and performer. Needless to say, this desire to retain the purity of performative connection distanced her from the development of modern culture. But Duncan saw that the visual and literary images of her body that alluded to the stature

The monument and Isadora Duncan. *Isadora Duncan at the Portal of the Parthenon,* by Edward Steichen, 1921. Reprinted with permission of Joanna T. Steichen.

of her ideas and her fight for women's freedom would not solve the problem of history and representation.

Duncan thus wrote her autobiography in part to define for herself a place in history. Duncan wanted to preserve her project for history, but her language, her vehicle of representation, was dance and not words, as she said often.

Memory, Memory—what is Memory? A cracked tankard from which the wine has all leaked out, leaving it dry and to quench no thirst. When I try to remember events that were so marvelous, so vibrant—like an apple orchard bursting with ripe apples—and when I put this in these words, a medium I don't understand, they seem like dead leaves, dry, parched, no juice or interest left—but that is because I am not a writer. When I dance it is different.[90]

These gaps between memory, words, and dance were not bridged in Duncan's autobiography; instead, they were articulated over and over again in terms of her sense of her body. The gap between words and the social world produced a rhetoric of dualism for her, played out on the landscape of the body as she tried to grapple with her persona as a mythical figure. As in most myths, Duncan's tale was drenched in tragedy and pathos. The pathos masked but did not completely hide Duncan's deep sense of pessimism about modernity.

[T]rying to recollect my life, I am filled only with a great disgust and a feeling of utter emptiness. The past seems but a series of catastrophes and the future a certain calamity. . . . What is the truth of a human life, and who can find it? . . . In the midst of all this anguish and delight; this filth and luminous purity; this fleshly body filled with hell fire, and this same body alight with heroism and beauty—where is the truth?[91]

Duncan's extreme use of metaphors of purity and contamination reflected her later sensibilities. In a larger sense, they expressed the difficulty of the shift from Victorianism to modernism. Despite her despair, her autobiography contributed to and did not negate the process of monumentality.

Duncan's resigned question, "I know you will put up a monument to me, but what good will that do?" was answered in ways that fulfilled her fear of history. Making Duncan into a monument was an ideological move that was easily codified: she was substituted for that other ideological emblem of freedom, the Statue of Liberty. Seroff claimed, "The time will come when freedom-loving Americans will throw the Statue of Liberty, that symbol of so-called freedom, into the sea, and raise in its place a statue of Isadora Duncan, who was the personification of true freedom and who called for the brotherhood of nations."[92] Eastman made the association even more boldly: "She looked like a statue of real liberty."[93] The appeal to a national symbol further shifted Duncan from an abstract dialectical notion of self to a stable, mythological one as an "American."

Conclusion: The Scarf

The figuring of Duncan as a monument helps to explain the criticism and distance expressed by a younger generation of modernists who found little to value in her experiment for their own struggles for self-expression. Some emphasized that Duncan had become anachronistic: "She . . . was being bypassed in the onrush of the modern."[94] Margaret Anderson, editor of the *Little Review,* castigated Duncan's performance because she saw in it both a frightening nationalism and a sentimental portrayal of the body. Anderson turned her experience of seeing her perform into an opportunity to express how her idea of art differed from Duncan's. She used the metaphor of monument-building to establish her critique of sentimentality:

> You must not insist to us that Isadora Duncan is an artist. This generation can't be fed on any such stuff. We are tired of that kind of loose valuation. . . . Isadora Duncan, as you will know after seeing her once, is a . . . monument of undirected adolescent vision, an ingrained sentimentalist.[95]

Others, however, remembered the significance of Duncan's transformation of gender and the conventions of representation, her stance as both an artist and a liberator. For example, Janet Flanner, who wrote cultural criticism for the *New Yorker* and paid particular attention to the participation of women in modernist culture, liked Duncan's performances during her later career. Flanner saw the tension between aging and Duncan's aesthetic project, but believed that modernists such as Levinson saw failure and monstrosity as a result of their own anxiety over the fate of an artist's career. In Flanner's view, the cultural memory of Duncan neutralized her explosive, uncomfortable presence that had opened a trail for women's artistic expression. Yet even Flanner's reverent rhetoric cannot escape the emphasis on Duncan as a monument: "Only Isadora, animator of all these forces, had become obscure. Only she, with her heroic sculptural movements, had dropped by the wayside, where she lay inert like one of those beautiful battered pagan tombs."[96] Though Flanner and Anderson perceived Duncan in radically different ways, both women's perceptions were mediated by the logic of the monument.

The reification of Duncan from an event significant to the history of women in modernism into a sentimental monument to a lost moment for cultural radicals can be seen clearly in assessments of Duncan's death. In 1942 Eastman wrote about his ambivalence about Duncan as a hero of emancipation. "As an aging woman, she needed a truer and more austere wisdom than she had," he wrote. "She could not live on gestures any longer. . . . If the scarf had really been given life by her dance, it could not have acted more loyally."[97] The scarf that Eastman refers to is the one that broke Duncan's neck when it wrapped around the wheel of a Bugatti sports car in southern France in 1927. While the viciousness of Eastman's statement denied Duncan's humanity and his feeling of friendship for her, his statement also referred to Duncan as an image and a character, a symbol of "Isadora Duncan" in a web of ideas about the meaning of cultural intervention in American life in the 1910s and 1920s. The scarf acted loyally by creating Duncan as, finally, a monument, rather than an ongoing event: the scarf fluttered gaily in the wind, dropped into the spinning wheel, was pulled tight, straightening the dialectical disorder and fluidity in a moment of abandon into a line of separation marking a dualistic framework. The ideas that Duncan depicted through her body were worthy of expression for most moderns—oppression and freedom, the desire for wholeness—but casting the body into a statue reified her ideas and has immobilized our perception of Isadora Duncan by making her an inert legend, dropped by the wayside of history.

Like many other people of her time, Duncan sought to understand what it meant to be a woman at a moment when Victorian notions about culture, gender, and art were under serious attack. Significantly, her popularity coincided with the moment when feminism first entered our mainstream vocabulary. At the height of Duncan's career, feminism provided a way for her to inhabit a modernist stance, and the broad support she received from other modernists and feminists at the time indicates that they, too, saw her as negotiating this intersection. However, as her career continued into the 1920s, for most Duncan ceased to embody a feminist modernism. Instead, she became a symbol of the impossibility of thinking through feminism and modernism at once. Duncan's project and the way it was taken up sheds light on early feminism's significance to modernism but also on the blind spots and attenuations of both movements.

The tendency to cast Duncan's body into a statue has tended to immobilize our perception of her accomplishments both as a dancer and as a feminist modernist who initiated new ways to conceive of women as subjects of representation. Crucially, it has also obscured the extent to which Duncan herself was not simply an iconoclastic firebrand but was susceptible to and productive of some of the most corrosive American tendencies toward racism and nationalism. Her theory of wholeness and its implications for representing the female body led to both dynamics.

While many discursive histories see claims to liberation as merely new forms of control and regulation, this history attempts to understand what was both enabling and limiting in Duncan's claims to freedom. Such an approach seeks to make Duncan more available to history and, by doing so, restore feminism as a central tendency in American modernism. Feminism was both celebrated in modernism and mobilized in relation to nationalism and in opposition to other discourses of difference, including race. These intersections help to show both how gender rebellion became part of a cultural movement and how women's cultural agency came to symbolize that which must be eradicated and suppressed.

CHAPTER 2

A Battle with "Reality"

Margaret Anderson

and the Cultural Politics

of Self-Expression

In 1921 Margaret Anderson and her coeditor, Jane Heap, were charged with publishing obscene materials in their magazine, the *Little Review*. They had been running installments of James Joyce's *Ulysses,* the first appearance in the United States of what would become the most important novel of the twentieth century. Under scrutiny by the Society for the Suppression of Vice were supposedly harmful passages from the novel, and the newspaper headlines were sensational rather than protective: "Greenwich Girl Editors in Court," announced the *Chicago Examiner*.[1] The editors were supported by friends and colleagues during the trial, but, not surprisingly, they were found guilty and fined.

Though at the request of her lawyer she had been quiet, even demure, during the two weeks of the trial, Anderson created a commotion at the police station when officers attempted to fingerprint her. "I examined the thick fluid into which I was supposed to dip my well-kept fingers and insisted upon elaborate advance preparations to guarantee its removal. . . . [I]t became their responsibility to convince me that there would be no permanent disfigurement."[2] While we could joke that Anderson resisted the mark of cultural suppression at the station, she had not always been so fastidious about her manicure; she had certainly soiled her hands marking up the page proofs of the *Little Review*'s provocative installments of *Ulysses.* Anderson's worry over her manicure was a parody of proper femininity, a feminist act within a larger politics of self-expression.

Anderson's arrest was one of many among feminists who confronted the law in pursuit of rights and opportunities, including Margaret Sanger for opening a birth-control clinic and Alice Paul during the militant demonstrations for women's suffrage. Anderson's fingerprinting also was a significant moment in the long battle to create a forum for avant-garde, dissenting ideas in American culture.

The Politics of Self-Expression

Anderson edited the *Little Review,* widely considered one of the most important of the modernist magazines in America. She was also a flamboyant personality, and she used her beauty, her sense of style, and her disregard of all things conventional to create a buzz—the impression that the *Little Review* was on the cutting edge of the cultural renaissance in Chicago and, later, New York. Anderson fashioned her self and her activities into symbols of avant-garde aspirations and pretensions, an early version of what we would now call "celebrity."

Margaret Anderson's contributions to American modernism have been interpreted within two distinct frames of reference. In the literary history of canonical modernism, Anderson is primarily understood as a dilettante who happened to be in the right place at the right time, surrounded by the right people, especially Ezra Pound, to publish groundbreaking modernist writing, including the work of Sherwood Anderson, Ernest Hemingway, Djuna Barnes, Wyndham Lewis, and James Joyce. Feminist literary history has highlighted Anderson's participation in the expatriate lesbian community of Paris in the 1920s as well as her discerning efforts as an editor and publisher. Anderson's unconventional womanhood has been the basis for her dismissal as a serious modernist figure and a source of celebration. Both assessments, indeed, structure the history of feminism in modernism.

The role of self-expression as a basis for both gender rebellion and cultural innovation was in question when Anderson published her autobiography in 1930, which, reflecting her intention to fashion herself as a cultural rebel, she titled *My Thirty Years' War.* Matthew Josephson, a young writer who wrote one of the many reviews of Anderson's book, pinpointed the importance of self-expression for women involved in the production of modernism.

> The revolutions of poetry and art in the United States during the twentieth century were conducted largely by inspired women. These female crusaders and zealots—Amy Lowell, Isadora Duncan, Harriet Monroe,

Margaret Anderson, and numerous others—toured and stumped the country in behalf of free verse and realism, free dancing, or free love. Many of the younger writers of today may recall how in their youth, somewhere between 1914 and 1924, they were sheltered and nurtured by the forensic prowess of these amazons. . . . Militant women were making literary history and artistic history in those days; and often in so doing they showed strong points of resemblance to their grandmothers or great-aunts of Abolition and Temperance-Ball days, save in one important respect: that they were largely for "self-expression" rather than for measures of repression.[3]

This passage from Josephson's review suggested a change in women's subjectivity and sensibility that characterized their participation in modernism, from "measures of repression" to "self-expression." Significantly, Josephson praised women's groundbreaking efforts and their cultural leadership in the new forms of expression that became known as modernist, in the arts, literature, and the world of manners and mores. Many women involved in modernism were creative artists and writers, while others played key roles as editors, publishers, and patrons.[4]

Josephson acknowledged the various roles that women played in a wide-ranging modernist revolution. His perspective, indeed, helps to retrieve the significance of modernist women who are not as well recognized today because the practices that supported the formation of the historical culture of modernism were suppressed in order to elevate the autonomous work of art. Modernist style took shape in the pages of the *Little Review* between 1914 and 1929. Anderson's acts of self-expression in editing the magazine and her eventual retreat from those acts highlight the gender politics in the formation of modernism as "high art."

Self-expression was both an artistic creed and a tenet of feminism in the 1910s, encompassing beliefs about the imaginative, creative potential of the self and ideologies of cultural independence. Because it was associated with new roles for women as well as art, the ideology of self-expression shows connections between feminism and modernism. Women were activists for a cultural revolution that would allow them to express ideas that were distinctly counter to the nineteenth-century ideal of proper womanhood, an ideal of self-sacrifice and nurturing dedication to others.[5] To believe in your own self-expression was to declare independence from this dominant idea about what proper women should be.

Affiliation with self-expression helped women to break with codes of gender identity and behavior, and in this sense modernist feminists sometimes expressed ideas that went against the grain of those of their reformist and suffragist sisters. For example, Elizabeth Stuyvesant, one of the contributors to a series on modern feminism published in *The Nation* in the mid-1920s, wrote about her coming of age in a Midwestern city:

> My thinking was profoundly affected by a group of choice souls out of that smug, crass, over-uplifted, over-settlement-housed city—a printer . . . ; a bookseller . . . ; a few foreign-born workers . . . ; a dancing teacher, fresh from the influence of Isadora Duncan, making a daring struggle for beauty and self-expression.[6]

Stuyvesant was responding to the well-established belief that women elevated, educated, and redeemed a corrupt public sphere. This belief had legitimated women's presence in public life and thus their expanded role in the social world. In the early twentieth century, for Stuyvesant and others like her, the usefulness of these practices had gotten in the way of a more creative, imaginative womanhood. Because self-expression was that which enabled the possibility of an as-yet-unimagined womanhood, it was often seen as a form of gender rebellion.

Self-expression also was one of the underlying ideas informing the avant-garde rebellion from genteel, bourgeois culture in America. Modernists often declared that they were less interested in reforming others—Josephson's "measures of repression"—than in discovering themselves. Self-expression became a code for a new way of living as well as the new writing. According to Malcolm Cowley, author of one of the key accounts of his modernist generation, *Exile's Return,* self-expression was a principle of the bohemian lifestyle: "Each man's, each woman's, purpose in life is to express himself, to realize his full individuality through creative work and beautiful living in beautiful surroundings."[7] Self-expression was a form of generational rebellion from bourgeois style, a code of living in beauty rather than in the drab, enervating surroundings of conventional homes and offices. It was a stance to be encouraged and defended among others, a badge of bohemian outlawry. As both the subjectivity of many feminists and the creed of the cultural rebels, self-expression was an exemplary instance of the connection between feminism and modernism.

Anderson sought to create a magazine that would be both "ardently feminist," in her words, and one that would contain the writing of what the writer Sherwood Anderson simply called "the New Note." What brought both these efforts together was the magazine's promotion of self-expression and its opposition to sentimentality. Thus, in an important sense, we must see the discontinuity of feminist cultural practices with nineteenth-century women's writing and social activism and their affiliation with modernist aims. Anderson used self-expression in both modernist and feminist ways. In order to understand the significance of her rebellion, we need to go back to the beginning of the battle, when Anderson's declaration of personal independence from her well-to-do family led to the *Little Review*'s declaration of independence from American culture.

"Submerged in the Ghastly Sentimentalities"

In 1911 Anderson told her parents that she wanted to leave her suburban Midwestern home and get a job in Chicago. While this story calls to mind other tales by New Women who escaped from the conventional expectations for daughters of the upper class—Jane Addams's discovery of her social usefulness or Elsie Clews Parsons's dedication to her intellectual ambitions—Anderson's struggle to leave her suburban Indiana home was an aesthetic one. "I really couldn't see this as my life, which was to be beautiful as no life had ever been," she later wrote in her autobiography. In persuading her parents to let her make an independent life for herself, she simply, yet defiantly used the trope of self-expression, rather than more high-minded ideas of moral duty or social usefulness. "I said it was being able to think, say and do what you believed in."[8]

Anderson's declaration of familial independence was also a rebellion from a common language of sentimentality used about womanhood found in popular novels, magazine stories, and diaries, as well as the tracts of social reformers. Anderson attacked sentimentality for encouraging women to accept the limits placed on their lives and tethering them to ideals of domesticity, self-sacrifice, and dependency. In one of her essays in the *Little Review,* for example, Anderson evoked how difficult it was to become independent by describing a young woman drowning in sentimentality, appropriately enough, as if she were a character in a novel:

> She is submerged in the ghastly sentimentalities of a tradition-soaked atmosphere—and heaven knows that sentimentalities of that type are difficult to break away from. It takes not only brains, but what William James called the fundamental human virtue—bravery—to do it. And so the girl gives up the fight and moans that circumstances were too much for her. The next stage of her development shows her passing around gentle advice to all her friends on the noble theme of not being "hard" and living

only for oneself; how one must sacrifice to the general good—never having had the courage or the insight to find out what the general good might
really be. Thus are our incapacities extended.[9]

Here and elsewhere, Anderson saw self-expression as a rejection of the
idea that women must deny their interests, desires, and the possibility of
participating in public life. In rejecting the system of self-denial that
Anderson sees as structuring the middle-class woman's life, Anderson
both comments on the struggle for her own self-expression and theorizes
a historical break for women in general; by drawing upon James's idea of
bravery, she says, women will get out of the ideological cul-de-sac of the
nineteenth-century emphasis on domesticity and self-sacrifice.

Such a struggle was not only discursive and literary; it also entailed a
generational break. It was no easy matter to break the codes of gentility
and respectability that so clearly defined and circumscribed middle-class
women's lives in the early twentieth century. In 1911 Anderson gained a
measure of independence in exchange for the propriety of living at the
YWCA and having an older woman look out for her, two concessions she
characterized as "how a perfectly nice but revolting girl could leave
home."[10] Her chaperone was the social reformer and editor Clara Laughlin,
who assured Anderson's parents that she would guide the gamine
Margaret. Under Laughlin's patronage, Anderson took a job as a book reviewer at a religious weekly, the *Continent,* later becoming the book-page
editor for the magazine.

While Anderson's early lifestyle in Chicago was respectable, she resisted the terms of self-sacrifice and social mission that had allowed many
New Women to leave home and that Laughlin had promised Anderson's
parents she would instill in her. Anderson was not interested in social reform as such, and by emphasizing self-expression in her autobiography
she tells us that she refused an older model of legitimate, middle-class
feminine activity in the city. Laughlin told her: "Go stand on the bridges
and watch life. . . . Feel the story in every poor vagabond you may meet
there, in every poor waif of a girl who may be wanting to throw herself
into the river." Like many progressives, Laughlin believed in clear-eyed,
rational approaches to the problems of urban poverty, but she aroused
sympathy through her representation of the poor. Anderson was not
moved by the sight of human misery; in fact, she could not even see it.
Anderson responded, "She loved human interest. So did I; but in great
poetry not in those sentimental human stories she was always writing. I
knew I would never know any story but my own. . . . But I went and stood

on the bridge one day. . . . By the time I came to the bridge I saw no people at all. I saw only boats and foreign ports."[11] Celebrating "great poetry" instead of "sentimental human stories," Anderson displaced the focus on humanity and social conditions that characterized progressive reform, putting her self at the center of her cultural script.

Looking back on such scenes in her autobiography, Anderson constructed a narrative that put her in a deliberately contrary position—here, her refusal to be moved by human interest—to shock and disrupt the association between the middle-class woman reformer and her encounter with the city. While Jane Addams, the founder of Hull House, had appealed to young people to discover in themselves what she called "The Subjective Necessity of Social Settlement," Anderson was discovering other subjective necessities that connected feminism to Chicago's cultural renaissance. Anderson found much to embrace in the wider world beyond "the life of golf and bridge" she had left behind, but she also found generational conflict and competing models for female behavior in the city. Even after leaving home, Anderson remained a "revolting girl," and Laughlin became another mother figure against which she revolted. In criticizing the language of sentimentality, Anderson broke the ties that connected women across generations and across class through sympathy and reform.

Anderson's story of her rebellion and her embrace of self-expression was not only a narrative of a New Woman; it was also reminiscent of those of many modernists who revolted against small-town or suburban life and moved to the city to start their creative lives. Anderson's rejection of sentimentality and intense self-interest—"I knew I would never know any story but my own"—was related to her aesthetic experiences and involvement in cultural radicalism. Anderson's code of self-expression was part of a wider movement to forge bonds between art and life, and she fashioned herself within Chicago's arts and commerce and its bohemian subculture. Curious, wandering, observant, but with no discernible purpose or destination except the pleasure of seeing and consuming, Anderson walked the streets of Chicago, gloried in views of Lake Michigan, wandered through galleries and museums, sat writing letters in hotel lobbies, shopped in department stores, lunched in cafeterias, and attended concerts.

Anderson's enthusiasm for the city blended the struggles of New Women in the 1910s with an older, masculine model of modernist consciousness rooted in Europe. Anderson's descriptions of her immersion in Chicago cultural life in 1911 recall the figure of the flâneur so important to Charles Baudelaire's vision of modern life in the mid-nineteenth century in Paris.[12] The flâneur was a tourist, an observer who walked through the crowded streets but was not of those streets. Most important, the flâneur crossed the borders between the bourgeois surface of the city and its bohemian subcultural spaces. Anderson's wanderings attempted to blur the lines between her middle-class background, her love of art, and the independence that working-class young women had already carved out for themselves in the city. She wrote, "I was always pretending that I was a poor-working-girl, always forgetting that I was really poor—also a working girl."[13] While the early flâneur had been a male figure partaking of pleasures in public space that proper woman could not occupy, Anderson's presence on the streets of Chicago presented a new way for middle-class women to enter public space in the 1910s, one in which class distinctions did not disappear.[14] Anderson's were not a politics of solidarity with the working class; she grasped that her identity was rooted in her subversion of what it meant to be middle class.

Anderson came to Chicago at a time when the city's cultural life was undergoing a renaissance that included vibrant movements in literature, theater, and architecture.[15] In this fertile context, Anderson made flânerie into a vocational pursuit as a book reviewer and later a bookshop clerk. Book reviewing intellectually enacted the position of the consuming, observing tourist, making self-expression into both a persona and a paying job. Anderson followed the advice of Floyd Dell, then editor of the *Friday Literary Review,* who told the many young women who reviewed fiction, including Anderson, "In heaven's name, don't tell the story of the book! Bring to bear upon the book, in aesthetic terms, your attitude toward life."[16] Such advice encouraged Anderson's own definition of "self-expression" as doing and saying what she believed in. Moreover, her sense of subjectivity—her exceptional qualities and her intense preoccupation with her own taste, desires, and difference—gave her a resistant perspective on dominant culture. By taking Dell's advice, Anderson shifted the narrative of any book under consideration to her own interests and concerns. Under these permissive guidelines emphasizing self-expression, she was very successful and prolific as a book reviewer.

Yet Anderson's easy, lighthearted tourism of Chicago's urban cultural spaces was more difficult to accomplish in print. Her critique of the effect of sentimentality upon young women did not mean that she herself escaped its discursive hold. In one of her book reviews for the religious, family-oriented *Continent,* for example, she said she thought Theodore Dreiser's *Sister Carrie* was a good book. While Anderson could not have failed to note that both Dreiser's heroine in the novel and she were "perfectly nice but revolting girls" who tried to make it in Chicago, she realized too late that her own self-expression was not strong enough counterpoint to challenge the imperative of morality for a book page in a family magazine.[17] Refusing to condemn the novel's story of seduction and celebrating Dreiser's naturalist style, Anderson transgressed the code of book reviewers as moral arbiters and unwittingly identified herself with a tale of moral degradation. "I made the discovery that what they wanted of me was moral rather than literary judgments," she later wrote.

> Since this hadn't occurred to me, letters began to pour in protesting. . . . The editor of the *Continent* urged me not to give up my book page but state facts as they were, which simple process would keep me out of trouble. This sent me from paroxysms into paralysis.
>
> What facts? And what do you mean—as they are?
>
> Very simple, said the simple man. When a book is immoral, say so.
>
> How will I know?
>
> That's one thing that everyone knows, he said kindly.[18]

Anderson wriggled out of the problem by claiming not to know "facts as they are," the ideology that says that good novels reward young heroines for being good and punish them for being bad. Of course, Anderson knew this "fact," but the claim allowed her to say that she was not a part of this reality, either as literature or as a code of moral life. Anderson's experience with *Sister Carrie* served as a founding moment that radicalized her, in part, because the reaction to her review posed a threat to her own self-expression. The act of telling one's own life story through reviewing a book became an act of transgression. By allying herself with Dreiser's novel, Anderson affiliated a feminist perspective on self-expression—that which resisted the codes of gentility, sentimentality, self-sacrifice, and dependency—with a modernist text.

Self-Expression and the *Little Review*

In a larger sense, the cultural context of Chicago's renaissance made political acts of "expressing oneself" possible. Anderson's stand at the *Continent* was supported by the artists and intellectuals she met at Browne's Bookstore in the Fine Arts Building and at salons held by Margery Currey and Floyd Dell, who lived in quarters originally built for the 1893 World's Columbian Exposition.[19] When Anderson came up with the idea of the *Little Review* in 1914 at the age of twenty-five, she was buoyed by this community and inspired by the need for an ongoing cultural conversation that would enable more experimental voices to be heard. Her inspiration was by no means original—the *Little Review* was one among many experimental magazines created across the country during this period—but its inclusiveness and directness made it a vivid documentary of the spirit of the times.[20] Art and ideas intermixed; its reviews, criticism, forums, and reports were all intrinsically associated with the production of new art.

The masthead for the new monthly magazine read "Art Literature Poetry Drama," but the predominance of criticism and reviews and cultural reports made it clear that the *Little Review* was about a vibrant subculture as much as art in itself. The magazine presented writers associated with the Chicago Renaissance, including Maxwell Bodenheim, Ben Hecht, and Sherwood Anderson, along with energetic articles on the philosophical trends that engaged cultural radicals in Chicago in the 1910s. Early issues also revealed the importance of European thought on American modernists; various articles celebrated Henri Bergson and Friedrich Nietzsche and showcased Imagist poetry and Futurist plays. Overall, the magazine was an expression of the American bohemian belief in the 1910s that artists and political radicals shared much common ground and were united in opposition to complacency and sentimentality in American culture. Anderson's desire that the *Little Review* would be "something absolutely alien to the American tradition" connected the magazine's eclecticism to its oppositional character.[21]

The alienation from "American tradition" announced by Anderson was rooted in a profound sense of cultural transition; many believed that the nineteenth-century foundation for American civilization was crumbling. The war in Europe also created deep unease and political dissent among artists and intellectuals in the United States. Many pieces published in the first three years of the magazine proclaimed a belief that an older order had broken down, that the world had fallen apart. Sherwood Anderson's essay, "The New Note," in the first issue was representative of the rhetoric of a literary and political generation shaped by World War I: "Something has happened in the world of men. Old standards and old ideas tumble about our heads. In the dust and confusion of the falling of the timbers of the temple many voices are raised."[22] While many spoke out in opposition to the perceived causes of the war, such as imperialism, greed, patriotism, and private property, the *Little Review* was less a forum for these voices than a space apart from the cultural order that reflected those causes. "Nineteenth-century civilization has overwhelmingly and dramatically failed," an anonymous essayist wrote for the magazine. "What shall we build now?"[23] The devastation wrought by the war thus became a metaphor for the demise of an older culture.

Violent imagery was also used to symbolize cultural militancy. In talking about the impact of the *Little Review* on his life as a writer, for example, Maxwell Bodenheim used the imagery of bomb-throwing rebels to evoke the magazine's role in American culture.

> From the pages of the *Little Review*, . . . a great laugh, shout of anger, and whisper of imagination combined and rose against the forces of a country and utilized them without their understanding or permission. New Figures made their appearance in this Andersonian factory of gunpowder and delicate tissue.[24]

In juxtaposing these contrasting images of loud explosions and quiet delicacy, Bodenheim evoked how deeply felt and yet how militant stands for self-expression were. The cultural work of the *Little Review*, indeed, was to make the laughs, shouts, and whispers of self-expression heard and to make visible the alternatives to dominant American culture that were being created in its midst. The production of the *Little Review* thus was a subcultural practice that both provided the context for and supported not only the texts of modernism, but also the ideas and people who made them.[25]

As an outlet for a modernist subculture, the *Little Review* promoted self-expression as both an artistic creed and a critique of "reality," Anderson's word for how dominant culture made its organization seem natural, the ways things just were. "It really all comes to one end," Anderson wrote in the *Little Review*, "Life for Art's sake." Evoking Nietzsche, she went on, "We believe in that because it is the only way to get more Life— a finer quality, a higher vibration . . . a step beyond the old Greek ideal of proportion and moderation. It pushes forward to the superabundance that dares abandonment."[26] While making one's life a form of art may seem hopelessly decadent and insulated from real social and political conditions, with this outlook one could take "a step beyond" seemingly natural divisions between work and leisure, production and consumption, public and private, which had characterized nineteenth-century Victorian culture. In her autobiography Anderson characterized the process of creating the magazine every month as a form of productive play, which tended to confuse the tight corollaries of work and production, play and consumption. She claimed, "Anything I want will happen if I play at it hard enough. I can't say work at it because anything I work at never seems to come out right."[27] As Anderson's life became more and more identified with the *Little Review,* a literal enactment of "life for art's sake," the distinctions habitually drawn between private and public eroded.

The passionate rhetoric of abandoned play and abundance ran counter to the neurasthenic lethargy that had plagued American intellectuals and artists since the late nineteenth century. For Anderson and her theorization of the *Little Review* as an outlet for the self-expression of her generation, a key word, indeed, was "intensity." Often described by others as possessing great energy and enthusiasm herself, Anderson exalted intensity over aesthetic purity or moral goodness. "Certainly I want for the *Little Review,* as I want from life, not merely beauty, not merely happiness, but a quality which proceeds from the intensity with which both beauty and ugliness, pleasure and pain, are present." Intensity, whether it be painful or pleasurable, was what distinguished the artistic life from a life defined as complacent, conventional, sentimental, restrictive, and hypocritical. Intensity marked the space in which there was no distinction between art and life, and it distinguished this space from alienated, ordinary, humdrum everyday life.

> I grant you that it also becomes silly to talk eternally of "feeling" without qualifying or defining. It is like taking refuge behind that vaguest phrase in the language—"life itself." But by "feeling" I mean simply that flight of wings which makes walking unnecessary; that dazzling tight-rope performance which takes you safely over the chasm of Experience but leaves you as bruised as though you had fallen to its depths.[28]

Anderson's attempt to describe the intensity of self-expression mixed a lot of metaphors, but it revealed the extent to which she tried to take the *Little Review* a "step beyond."

Margaret Anderson's Suit

Anderson's belief that the magazine's development was like the development of an artist foreshadowed the dynamic through which her own contribution would be understood. She became an emblem of the *Little Review* and a symbol of its cultural outlawry. Like her avid tourism of Chicago's cultural scene, crossing the lines of high culture, commerce, and bohemian subculture, Anderson's sense of personal style seemed to blend a bohemian avant-gardism with dominant ideals of fashion and beauty, especially in a moment of great change in women's fashions and appearance. Women's fashion was in its own revolt against Victorianism, and the new styles of shorter skirt lengths, less fabric, and simplified, straighter lines began to be called "modern." Changes in hair and make-up went along with the new fashion: lipstick and rouge became respectable, and by the twenties bobbed hair had become mainstream. Photographs of Anderson show her as the embodiment of this new style: she was often pictured in a tailored suit, a silky blouse, and a closely fitting hat over short hair, dark lipstick, along with gloves and high heels. Reflecting on her fashionable appearance, Anderson wrote, "I was extravagantly pretty in those days, extravagantly and disgustingly pretty. I looked like a composite of all the most offensive magazine covers." One reviewer even called her a "Model American Girl."[29] While Anderson parodied this perception, she did not contradict it. Indeed, she identified herself with modern fashion rather than the loose dresses and sandals worn by other bohemians and dress reformers.[30] She fostered an image of being up to date, and she buttressed that image with her opinion of what fashion should mean for modern women, writing in the *Little Review*, "[W]omen have such a splendid chance to look straight, unhampered, direct, lithe. I don't know just why, but I want to use the word 'true' about the new clothes. They're so much less dishonest than the old padded ways—the strange, perverted, muffled methods."[31]

This image of Anderson as both modern and fashionable, however, must be seen through the contradictory juxtapositions in which she wore her suit. Anderson not only looked like the magazine covers of dominant culture; the suit also became an emblem of bohemia. Anderson appeared to link modern style to ideas about freedom and unconventional lifestyles. She also had an enviable ability to look great in difficult situations, as one famous anecdote made clear. Having run out of money, Anderson, her sister, and some friends decided to live in tents on a Lake Michigan beach rather than pay rent for an apartment. Newspapers ran several stories on the bohemian encampment, portraying Anderson bathing in the lake in a scandalously tight bathing suit, yet emerging from her tent every morning looking fresh and perfectly dressed.[32] Anderson's ability to position herself as both the model of modern women's fashion and as the editor of a magazine of the cultural revolt made her iconic in representations of Chicago's renaissance.

In some descriptions, bohemia figured itself as Margaret Anderson. Ostensibly writing about innovative movements in Chicago's art scene, poet Eunice Tietjens wrote, "The adventure was Margaret Anderson."

> In her severe black suit and little black hat, under which her blond hair swept like a shining bird's wing, she stood pouring out such a flood of high-hearted enthusiasm that we were all swept after her into some dream

Margaret Anderson and "the suit." *Margaret Anderson*, by Man Ray, 1930. Copyright 2001 Man Ray Trust/Artist Rights Society (ARS), NY/ADAGP, Paris. Reprinted by permission.

of a magazine where Art with a capital A and Beauty with a still bigger B were to reign supreme, where "Life Itself" was to blossom into some fantastic shape of incredible warmth and vitality.[33]

Ben Hecht, who started out as an avant-garde writer in Chicago and became a Hollywood screenwriter, associated the suit Anderson wore with the cultural role she played. "During the years I knew her she wore the same suit, a tailored affair in robin's-egg blue. Despite this unvarying costume she was as chic as any of the girls who model today for the fashion magazines."[34] In contrast, the *Little Review*'s "wrenlike tan covers" demurely dressed a magazine that was, for Hecht, "nakedly and innocently, Art." While Hecht wanted to woo Anderson, he found himself devoted to the cause of the *Little Review* instead. Playing upon the common understanding of fashion as an indicator of taste or a tool of seduction, Hecht described Anderson's suit as a vehicle of artistic inspiration.

> Miss Anderson's genius consisted of making young writers want to please her rather than a larger, more lucrative public. It was a genius that demanded Art of its admirers as some pretty girls demand jewels and love nests of them. It was a genius, also, for filling others with a vision which it was unable, itself, to express. . . . In Miss Anderson's case the demand and applause were more impersonal. It was Art before which she sat uttering her flushed bravos. I was young, without direction or aesthetics, and it may be I saw no Art. But it is certain I saw Miss Anderson. Thus the Art I served in the *Little Review* may have been only Miss Anderson in her robin's egg blue suit.[35]

Anderson played the siren, but rather than her own pleasure she sought devotion to the higher, almost religious, calling of art. Tietjens said Anderson's stark black suit represented art, and Hecht associated the robin's-egg blue suit with the act of publishing his work; while colors differ, the perceptions of the cultural work the suit performed were similar. More so than the "innocently naked" ideas advocated in the *Little Review,* Anderson's suit lured artists to the life of self-expression.

The emphasis on the image of the modern woman as advocate for art and an inspiration for bohemia, however, was precarious as a mode for feminist modernist self-expression. Anderson's subversive self-fashioning could easily be stripped of its challenge, turned merely into a figure for the literary imagination or an emblem of artistic consumption, an object to be consumed. Abstracted from the irony of Anderson's subversive use of fashion, her stylish beauty merely fit the more conventional narrative of an artist's muse or the Pygmalion story. Writer Sherwood Anderson wrote about Anderson, "You were a character in a play. You were a novel or a painting come to life."[36] With the dismissiveness that lurks around most such compliments, Sherwood's meditation on the alternative space Margaret represented—"You had but to walk through the street. . . . You were not like the rest of us, . . . going constantly, falteringly, in and out of our unreal world"—made her, simply, part of its imagination, but not its reality.

The objectification of Anderson's self-fashioning made her more of an advertisement for modern art than its advocate or arbiter. In Anderson's efforts to fund the *Little Review,* for example, Anderson canvassed stores and businesses for advertisements, even going from door to door in office buildings for subscriptions, confident that her personal appeal represented the modernist appeal of the magazine. The financier Otto Kahn, who considered being a patron of the magazine in the early twenties, articulated most clearly the position Anderson found herself in as an advertisement for the *Little Review.* Kahn suggested that his money could pay not only for printing the magazine, but for some "pretty dresses" for the editor. Anderson, whose only suit was getting shabby, said, "Wonderful! Then we can go everywhere. And we can talk everywhere. We really can make the most interesting talk." Kahn replied, "Oh no one wants to hear any talk. . . . Just go about. Let people see the color of your eyes and your hair and the way you wear your clothes. No one cares about anything else nowadays."[37] As Kahn's comments implied, Anderson's self-fashioning did not enhance her control over the *Little Review.* In a wider sense, women's participation in modernism is filled with such devaluations, and a similar dynamic characterized the reputations of such figures as Nancy Cunard, Zelda Fitzgerald, and Djuna Barnes.[38] While the roles of "advocate" and "advertisement" have often overlapped, the stakes for a feminist presence in modernist culture were high; the image of Margaret Anderson as modernism threatened to strip the power of speech and active determination from her.

Feminism, Sexuality, and Women's Cultural Independence

Despite the gender dynamics that undermined the power of her cultural role, Anderson conceived the *Little Review* as a feminist magazine. As she exclaimed in the first issue, "Feminism? A clear-thinking magazine can have only one attitude; the degree of ours is ardent!" The *Little Review* was itself understood in connection with the women's rights movement; it "came when the biggest battles were waged by militant suffragists, when women's rights in government and marriage were still violently debated." Anderson's role as the *Little Review*'s editor was also associated with feminism: "A feminist before her time, Margaret Anderson was the spark who turned Chicago into the hottest literary town in the world." Through a figure like Anderson and her editorial practices, the militancy of feminism and the vibrancy of the cultural renaissance in Chicago were linked.[39]

In the first few years of the *Little Review,* considerations of art mingled with reports on birth control, free motherhood, and the new theories of sexuality. Feminists Margery Currey, Cornelia Anderson, and Susan Glaspell contributed articles on women writers and thinkers. And while most calls for greater sexual freedom were made assuming a heterosexual norm, references to homosexuality occasionally surfaced. Anderson chided Edith Lees Ellis, the wife of sexologist Havelock Ellis, for talking only about perversion and not about inversion when she gave a talk in Chicago in 1914. "Mrs. Havelock Ellis was criticized for her failure in a recently given Chicago lecture to include explicit approval of 'free love, free divorce, social motherhood, birth control, and the sex morality of the future.'" "She knows," declared Anderson, "of boys and girls, men and women, tortured and crucified every day for their love, but was silent concerning them."[40] The eclectic nature of the *Little Review* enabled the consideration of art, reform, and sexuality.

Though the *Little Review* only rarely addressed the plight of sexual outlaws, Anderson's lesbianism was covertly identified with the subcultural status of the magazine, and it underlay the magazine's militant stands for self-expression. Anderson's epigraph to her autobiography reads: "My greatest enemy is reality. I have fought it successfully for thirty years." Claiming "I have always held myself quite definitely aloof from natural laws," Anderson used the idea of reality both as an aesthetic declaration and an avoidance of conventional gender expectations, especially those of heterosexual romance. Because Anderson so extravagantly personified other feminine gender ideals, such as her sense of style and her beauty, her inaccessibility to men and their romantic designs on her only increased her symbolic aura as a kind of fairy princess of the new art and cultural rebellion.

Her resistant sexual status helped others to see themselves as cultural outlaws. In this sense, lesbianism was figured as the "beyond" that modernists sought to go; it was intertwined with the modernist critique of "reality," especially as that reality came to mean dominant cultural expectations.[41] "Let's admit that," Sherwood Anderson wrote, "we are an outlaw people."

Those of us who write words, tramp the boards of the stage, spread paint on canvas . . . trying to reach into unreality through the real, do not belong. . . . The outside world, the world of reality in which we are compelled, it seems, to live . . . drags us down constantly out of the unreal into the real.[42]

The *Little Review* was special for him not simply because the magazine published his early work, but because Margaret Anderson offered an alternative space to "outlaw people." "I saw men of my own real-unreal world all drawn together," he wrote. Margaret Anderson, to him, existed wholly in this other space he called "unreal." Sherwood Anderson's commentary contributed to the myth of a magical bohemia—the idea that it was possible to escape from the dominant culture.

Anderson was "unreal" in part because she did not fit the usual narratives in modernist literature and social criticism that relied on heterosexual romance to express liberation and personal freedom, the struggles by women and men to forge new relationships based on mutual love and companionship.[43] Anecdotes by and about Anderson emphasized her contempt for bohemian sexual politics. For example, when Sinclair Lewis rebuked Anderson for ignoring the attentions of a man who cared for her, he only succeeded in provoking her bored impatience.[44]

Anderson's imperviousness to conventional romance made her perhaps even more powerful as a symbol of modernist beliefs; it was also central to her own self-definition. Anderson sidestepped heterosexual categories, saying, "I don't know just what kind of thing I am." Neither a young heroine trapped by "ghastly sentimentalities," nor a partner in a bohemian love story, Anderson believed she existed outside of "natural laws." She wrote in her autobiography:

I have never felt much like a human being. It's a splendid feeling. I have no place in the world—no fixed position. I don't know just what kind of thing I am. Nobody else seems to know either. I appear to be a fairly attractive woman in her thirties. But such a human being falls inevitably into one or more of the human categories—is someone's daughter, sister, niece, aunt, wife, mistress or mother. . . . I am no man's wife, no man's delightful mistress, and I will never, never, never be a mother.[45]

Anderson's syntax suggested that being a woman intrinsically meant being possessed and located by "a man." Instead of being a man's woman, Anderson represents herself as having "no fixed position." This passage alluded to the doubleness of women's roles in modernist culture; women were often both artists and wives, artists and mistresses, artists and mothers. Because of this double identity, women were often taken less seriously than men, who were supposed to be able to assume a singular cultural position. Not only did Anderson avoid possession by a man, her autobiographical self-definition negated the heterosexual construction defining women's relation to modernism.

Stances like Anderson's were seen as threatening in a broader context of thought about the "independence" of feminists in their quest for self-expression. The problem, according to many contemporary intellectuals, was not that women sought to become writers, professionals, or artists, but that they did not need men for their self-realization. Ellen Key, the Swedish feminist whose books on voluntary motherhood were much admired in the United States during this period, worried that young women sacrificed the pleasure of romantic love by focusing so intently on self-expression.

> [F]or many of these modern, aesthetically refined, nervously sensitive young girls the aesthetic point of view is decisive. And since the modern woman knows that, in the sphere of spiritual values, nothing can be attained without sacrifice, she prefers to keep free agency and to sacrifice love.[46]

Anderson certainly did prefer to keep free agency, except that she did not sacrifice "love" so much as point out that its construction did not apply to her. Alfred Kreymborg, poet and editor of the little magazine *Others,* also wondered about the new independence women associated with being modern: "A modern note comes to light: here is a girl, a woman, who does not kneel to her lover."[47] Women, to Kreymborg and many other male cultural radicals, were not playing by the rules of either chivalry or submission that the structure of romance demanded; they identified themselves as artists instead of potential lovers or wives. In a larger sense, the independence of feminists was worrisome because it eliminated the love plot from the cultural script.

In this heterosexual discourse about art, the "threat" of the independent woman who valued her own self-expression above love implied the absence of a partner. Anderson, however, met artist Jane Heap in 1916, and the two formed a partnership as companions, lovers, and coeditors of the *Little Review* that lasted over ten years. While Heap was well known as Anderson's coeditor, references to the full nature of their relationship were rare but provocative. William Carlos Williams, for example, wrote, "I used to visit the apartment of Margaret Anderson and Jane Heap, the editors of the *Little Review*. There was a huge swinging bed suspended from the ceiling. We poor males would look timidly at it and marvel."[48]

While Williams's comment is suggestive, tinged with the straight man's erotic curiosity about lesbianism, Anderson neither suppressed nor eroticized her relationship with Heap. Rather, she emphasized how important her partnership with Heap was through the trope of self-expression. Avoiding the maudlin abjection that characterized the most famous novel of lesbian life in the early twentieth century, Radclyffe Hall's *The Well of Loneliness*, Anderson gave meaning to her relationship with Heap through language: words, conversation, dialogue. She wrote in her autobiography about their first meeting, "Jane and I began talking. We talked for days, months, years."[49]

More than a code for love or sex, language was important to Anderson's characterization of her life with Heap because it gave her a way to express who she was, and because it was a quality she valued in Heap. For Anderson, who had dedicated her life to creating a cultural conversation, Heap was the "world's best talker." "[H]ere was my obsession—the special human being, the special point of view. I never let anyone escape her psychological clairvoyance." In joining forces with Heap, Anderson moved from self-expression as a discourse about her own personality to a more dialogic relation, which raised questions about the primacy of individual expression for both of them. Anderson described her relationship with Heap through the metaphor of conversation, but she also despaired that she could not fully transcribe the quality of hers and Jane's conversations. "It isn't a question of words, facility, style. It isn't a question of erudition. It isn't even a question of truth. . . . It is entirely a question of ideas," Anderson wrote. Anderson wanted Heap to "express herself" as well but Heap, she says, resisted being Anderson's partner in the crusade. "It's an awkward role for me. You're the buzz and I'm the sting," Heap said. "She didn't at all share my obsession about enlightening the world," Anderson explained.[50]

Despite Heap's hostility to the role of "enlightening the world," she nevertheless played that role in Anderson's autobiography. There, the metaphor of conversation and dialogue, of language itself, became a way to represent what had been unrepresentable, a loving, productive, long-term partnership between two women. In this sense, the thematic of language and representation—of feminist modernist self-expression—provided a usable discourse for lesbian sexuality in the early twentieth century.

"Rebels for Their Own Liberation"

The idea of self-expression was entwined with declarations of cultural outlawry and modernist fears of women's independence. It was also a theme in debates over the relation between artistic creativity and political goals. Anderson took the struggle of the *Little Review* into more overtly political territory when she "converted" to anarchism in 1914. She wrote with characteristic flippancy, "May. . . and the third number of the *Little Review* was going to press. I heard Emma Goldman lecture and had just time to turn anarchist before the presses closed."[51]

Anderson's engagement with anarchism took place amid a much broader movement to join the innovative power of the new art to political goals. The socialist magazine, *The Masses,* for example, featured drawings and cartoons by artists John Sloan and Robert Henri that expressed both deep anger and biting sarcasm. Other attempts included the spectacular Paterson Pageant in 1913, which was staged in New York's Madison Square Garden and dramatized the plight of textile mill workers in Paterson, New Jersey, in a bitter strike. Though the agit-prop pageant did not successfully arouse the sympathy and support of general audiences, it represented a utopian attempt to create a community of artists, writers, and the Paterson strikers themselves. Such events reveal the interrelations of modernism and radicalism.[52] In this context, there were many debates about the nature of what was truly revolutionary, as labor struggles became metaphors for the artistic process, and artists struggled to find an elusive common ground between formal innovation and political usefulness.

The *Little Review*'s interest in self-expression was certainly compatible with anarchist political theory, a critique of any authority that hampered the free activity of individuals. Anderson's conversion, however, was inspired by listening to Emma Goldman, the famous anarchist and a gifted, riveting orator. Goldman's ideas appealed to Anderson in her desire to break with conventional standards and with the institutions of American culture and politics. Moreover, Goldman linked the critique of "institutions" specifically to feminism. Deeply critical of the reformist politics of the suffrage movement, Goldman argued that the more important issues for women were birth control and sexual expression. Goldman's economic and cultural critique of marriage and suffrage and her support for homosexual rights coincided with Anderson's own position, and the two were friends and colleagues until Goldman's death in 1940.

Each portrayed their friendship in their autobiographies, and the intertextual encounter revealed the significance of self-expression in the larger debate over the relationship between art and politics. Like Anderson's earlier confrontation with Clara Laughlin and the *Continent,* the significance of self-expression for feminist modernism was inflected by a sharp generational divide. Goldman was, of course, on the far left of the Progressive Era political spectrum, and Anderson was compelled by her reputation: "Her name was enough . . . to produce a shudder. She was considered a monster, an exponent of free love and bombs." Persuaded less by Goldman's political ideology and more by her aura of revolt, Anderson wrote in the *Little Review:*

> I have heard her twice—once before the audience of well-dressed women who flock to her drama lectures and don't know quite what to think of her, and once at the International Labor Hall before a crowd of anarchists and syndicalists and socialists, most of whom were collarless but who knew very emphatically what they thought of her and of her ideas. I came away with a series of impressions, every one of which resolved somehow into a single conviction: that here was a great woman.[53]

Just as Anderson found herself roused and inspired by Goldman's lectures, the *Little Review* impressed Emma Goldman. The magazine was something she had been looking for, something rebellious, alive, and "free from the mawkish sentimentality of most American publications." Goldman continued, "Its main appeal to me lay in its strong and fearless critique of conventional standards, something I had been looking for in the United States for twenty-five years."[54] Anderson's declaration that Goldman was a "great woman" and Goldman's praise of the *Little Review*'s "strong and fearless critique" coalesced in a moment of feminist appreciation.

The first meeting of the two women, however, was fraught with the tension of misrecognition. After making a date, Anderson arrived at the appointed time, but Goldman turned away from her. She explained, "I was surprised to see a chic society girl. . . . Her butterfly appearance was disappointing, so radically different from my mental picture of the *Little Review* editor." Anderson concurred in her autobiography: "I probably looked so frivolous she was scorning me."[55] While Goldman thought Anderson's high style belied her critique of "conventional standards," Anderson was disappointed that Goldman was made "all of one piece." Not at all the monstrous exponent of bombs and free love construed in the popular legends about her, Goldman was in Anderson's estimation a motherly, sentimental woman who simply could not stand to see people hurt. They were drawn to each other through their reputations as rebellious women, but when describing each other they fell into a gap between feminist generations—Goldman was sentimental and thus tied to the old culture despite her reputation, while the modern Anderson was frivolous, only interested in style and appearance.

As this generational conflict developed between them, it revealed the importance of self-expression for modernist feminist views of politics and its break with an older view. Sitting in Anderson's empty apartment with views of the lake filling the windows, Goldman listened while Anderson played the piano. She wrote,

> Margaret's playing exerted a peculiar effect, like the sight of the sea, which always made me uneasy and restless. I had never learned to swim and I feared deep water, yet on the beach I would be filled with a desire to reach out towards the waves and become submerged in their embrace. When . . . I heard Margaret play, I was overcome by the same sensation and an uneasy craving.[56]

When Anderson finished, Goldman said, "You are a great artist." Goldman's pronouncement pleased Anderson enormously. She wrote, "It was the first time in my magazine-cover existence that I had been taken at another valuation. I was filled with gratitude."[57]

Just as Goldman had given Anderson "another valuation" as an artist, Anderson also considered Goldman an artist whose medium was revolutionary struggle. She editorialized,

> And Revolution? Revolution is Art. You want free people just as you want the Venus that was modelled by the sea. . . . All my inadequate stammerings about Emma Goldman have been to show her as the artist she is: a great artist, working in her own material as a Michael Angelo worked in his.[58]

While Anderson attempted to theorize Goldman's politics as themselves a form of art, Goldman could not believe that Anderson's feminist modernist beliefs in self-expression were a legitimate politics. Indeed, Goldman accused Anderson and Heap of being "rebels for their own liberation." "[T]hey had broken the shackles of their middle-class homes to find release from family bondage and bourgeois tradition." Goldman was simply not able to recognize the legitimacy of Anderson's more complicated use of self-expression, in which the escape from the middle-class family was part of an attack on a discourse of normality and respectability. While Goldman was heartened to find a young woman "seriously interested in modern ideas," she bemoaned the lack of social consciousness in the editor of the *Little Review*.[59] Anderson, on the other hand, thought Goldman should have been just as inflammatory and rousing in her lectures on modern drama as she was about labor struggle and women's rights to control their own bodies.

Anderson's embrace of anarchism and her enthusiastic articles on Goldman caused the magazine to lose financial backing and provoked a police inquiry. Despite this evidence of the magazine's political militancy, Anderson appropriated the anarchist principle of direct action for the realm of art and ideas. Her revolution, as she saw it, was in art: as Bodenheim wrote, Anderson made the bombs to blow up genteel culture. Goldman's famous aphorism, "[W]oman is confronted with the necessity of emancipating herself from emancipation, if she really desires to be free," found a parallel in Anderson's situation as emblem of both rebellion and creator of a "free space" for writers.[60] It was as an editor that Anderson took the "direct action" so prized by anarchist agitators.

The Blank Issue

In the 1910s and 1920s the *Little Review* was one among many small magazines and publishers. In publishing, advertising, and distributing new writing and art, these presses collectively created modernist literary culture. Recent scholarship has explored the important role that women played in the alternative literary publishing movement in the United States, Britain, and Europe—Nancy Cunard's Hours Press and Sylvia Beach's bookstore, Shakespeare and Company, were two prominent examples.[61] Assessing the contribution of women editors has required some qualification, however: women's efforts have been characterized as valuable but secondary to the analysis of real art; they enabled the work of others, but were not creative in themselves. In the cultural politics of self-expression, Anderson defied this logic; the editorial role was valuable because it was not "real art."

Since her days as a book reviewer Anderson had "expressed herself" through her consumption of the work of others. In the *Little Review* a very different dynamic appears. Unlike her book-reviewer persona, who facilitated the self-expression of others, as an editor Anderson foregrounded the editorial practices of the magazine, in which her own self-expression took center stage. What was peripheral in most magazines was central to the form and structure of the *Little Review*—the editorials, announcements, and letters, and its reflections on its own status, problems, and triumphs. The magazine was a monthly manifesto advertising the *Little Review*'s battles for modern art in the face of the forces that attempted to suppress it. The magazine's contemporary aura grew from these textualized battles, leading William Carlos Williams to say, "Much of what the *Little Review* prints is bad, but the *Little Review* is good."[62] Williams believed that Anderson's role in making the *Little Review* was not a secondary consideration; its editing was a central cultural practice. Valuably, such a reading grounds the production of literature and the production of modernism in a historical context: we can't read the *Little Review* merely as a collection of modernist literary texts; rather, we must read it as a cultural practice. This insistence on the priority of cultural production is where Anderson made her mark.

In contrast to editors who believed their primary identities were as novelists or poets, Anderson never considered herself anything except an editor. This realization was valuable to her because it enabled her to take up many positions in relation to art. "I'm not a writer. In fact I have never thought of myself as a writer at all. I am not a creator; I'm an appreciator, a discusser, a moralizer, a propagandist, an illiterate, and a dilettante."[63] By refusing the status of the modernist writer, Anderson placed at the center those positions that had been relegated to the margins of artistic practice, because they were perceived as noncreative. Editing was a form of self-expression because she had no other primary medium.

> I was having a marvelous time being an editor. I was born to be an editor. I always edit everything. . . . I edit people's clothes. . . . I edit people's tones of voice, their laughter, their words. . . . It is this incessant, unavoidable observation, this need to distinguish and impose, that has made me an editor. I can't make things. I can only revise what has been made.[64]

Similar to Isadora Duncan's pronouncement that she was not a dancer, which disrupted the codified meanings of dance to connect her project to a more general renaissance of the arts, Anderson's refusal to call herself anything but an editor was central to her wider notion of artistic production. Anderson's comments shifted the perception of her capabilities from limitations into avenues of self-expression.

The *Little Review*'s publication of the famous "blank issue" in 1916 clearly showed the value of editing as a cultural practice. Here, Anderson did not simply proclaim that she was free from the constraining aspects of editing the already produced and received; her stance became an act, finding a "significant form." The editors issued an ultimatum in 1916: unless they received "art," the magazine would be published with no art at all.

I loathe compromise, and yet I have been compromising in every issue by putting in things that were "almost good": and "interesting enough" or "important." There will be no more of it. If there is only one really beautiful thing for the September number it shall go in and the other pages will be left blank. Come on, all of you![65]

But no one managed to respond to the editors' call to art, and as a result Anderson and Heap did indeed leave blank the pages reserved for art in the September 1916 issue.

The blank issue functioned both as a rejection letter to the *Little Review*'s community of readers and contributors and as an invitation to produce something else; they disrupted the conventional, already given reception of "art" and foregrounded the editorial act of publishing the issue. The blank issue of the *Little Review* has been interpreted mainly as either an avant-garde prank—a publicity stunt for the editors—or an act of feminine creativity. Literary historian Susan Gubar, for example, argued that the blank pages were a distinctively feminine form of imagination; the blankness was a "brilliant illustration" of the substitution of the womb for the penis.[66] This analysis, however, depends upon the absolute blankness of the magazine, and Gubar claimed the issue consisted entirely of sixty-four blank pages, a misunderstanding that Anderson started in her autobiography. The issue was not entirely blank; only thirteen of twenty-eight pages were, and even these were printed with running heads and page numbers, along with the sentence, "And the other pages will be left blank." The remaining fifteen pages included the editorials, letters, and political analysis of recent events that were part of the usual format of the magazine. These, however, assumed an unusual importance because there was nothing else to read. What was essentially blank and, by implication, empty was the place reserved for "art" in the *Little Review*; there was no fiction or poetry. In an editorial, Heap and Anderson called that space a "Want Ad."

The blank pages themselves invited response and demanded creativity from those who bought the issue. Since the pages were blank, one could write or draw anything one liked. One reader sent a letter to the editors written on the blank pages, which was published in the next issue: "These pages are a record bearing on life and art and you," Roy George of San Francisco wrote. "And this is not youth saying I will do as I damn please, but judgment saying I will avoid doing what I please not; not a baby demanding the moon at all—merely a proper young entity refusing a rotten piece of cheese."[67] This reader got the joke of the blank issue and rendered it into an act of revolt, yet it is difficult to know whether the pages to which George referred were the letter he sent or the issue he received. In any case, both were pages bearing on the life of Margaret Anderson.

The visual composition of the issue promoted this ambiguity. A two-page cartoon was prominently featured in the middle of the issue, dividing the blank pages from the regular departments. Titled "Light Occupations of an Editor While There Is Nothing to Edit," the cartoons of Anderson were drawn by Heap, and they parodied the photo layouts of debutantes on the society pages in newspapers and magazines.

They depict Anderson in a gamut of unconventional activities made somehow ordinary by their lightness and irony, eating fudge for breakfast, wearing a skimpy bathing suit, attending lectures by Emma Goldman, and haranguing a sheriff about free verse and anarchism. The cartoons mark the border between art and the secondary practices that support art, its connection to and grounding in the world, and they moor the *Little Review* to the life of the editor, rather than merely to the "art" the magazine sought to present. Moreover, their representation of Anderson's life stood out even more since the surrounding pages were blank.

Self-expression at the center of the *Little Review*'s blank issue. "Light Occupations of the Editor While There Is Nothing to Edit," by Jane Heap, 1916. John Hay Library, Brown University.

The blank issue was an avant-garde editorial act because it could not be appropriated and there was nothing to consume. It represented a moment when self-expression, not tied to art per se, was foregrounded. Yet it also marked a transition; over the next few years, the magazine's "Want Ad" for art was clearly answered, and the *Little Review* published work that has certainly become some of the most important of the century, especially Joyce's *Ulysses*. Yet the larger project of the *Little Review* as an "advertisement" for self-expression was derailed, appropriated by the very forces of "art" it claimed to support. While feminist forms of self-expression, such as the blank issue, disrupted the conventions of art, this political aesthetic was squeezed out by the refinement and reification of literary art that rose to take the place of the older culture the *Little Review* had helped demolish.

The Rise of Literary Modernism

Ezra Pound wrote from London that he was impressed with the gutsy blank issue and suggested that he might be able to fill those blank pages, which he did with his customary gusto. Heap and Anderson were looking for real "art" and Pound promised to provide it. In return, he and his circle were promised a place where they could appear regularly in an American publication. As foreign editor Pound solicited and gathered together material for an issue and sent it to Anderson and Heap in New York. Anderson and Heap continued to solicit material for about one-third of the magazine. They were responsible for editing, proofreading, and distributing each issue. Pound received money directly from benefactor and lawyer John Quinn to pay authors while the *Little Review* itself was mired in money troubles.[68]

Pound's resulting control over the magazine has been well documented. The *Little Review* continued to be significant not in the larger arena of the avant-garde or of cultural radicalism, but through the more narrow definition of literary modernism that Pound and his group promoted and then later came to represent. Ruthven Todd's 1939 remarks were typical: "Immediately upon Pound's assuming the foreign editorship the *Little Review* became a paper that people bought and kept. The next three years were its great years; from 1917 to 1919 the monthly publication of the *Little Review* was an important event in literary history."[69] As writers such as Pound, T. S. Eliot, Wyndham Lewis, and Ford Maddox Ford became privileged by American literary scholars trained in the New Criticism, the period in which Pound was foreign editor of the *Little*

Review became regarded as the best, and certainly the most famous, phase of the magazine's history.

This assessment of the *Little Review* during the "Pound era" ignored the negative reaction by readers to the changes in the magazine. Readers were flabbergasted by the material brought in by Pound, and they protested vigorously in a barrage of letters. The editors published the most representative of these protesting letters in the "Reader-Critic" section of the magazine, and many attacked the "foreign element" that Pound represented. Mrs. O.D.J. wrote in 1917, "I have great faith in the artistic life of America, and I don't think Ezra Pound's notions of it are very healthy. I sincerely hope the trend of it will not emulate the 'smart' or dissipated literature which . . . can hardly come under the head of 'good letters.'" H.L.C in Chicago wrote, "I wish you didn't have such a craze for foreigners and self-exiled Americans." Another reader complained, "The Ezras know too much. Their minds are black, scarcely smouldering logs. . . . After all . . . you are still persisting at the impossible and the miraculous."[70] The readers wanted more of Anderson and Heap, and less of the "great art" the editors claimed to have found and through which they sought to change the shape of artistic life in America.

Anderson responded to these attacks on the magazine's changes with defiance rather than conciliation. The dialogue in the magazine through responses to the letters and critical forums became more combative and contentious. In the end, she renounced the role of the audience, the public, the reception of "art" altogether. She did not endeavor to cultivate a small but defiant bohemian community for the magazine. The editors firmly rejected the idea that there was an audience at all for the magazine and insisted that this lack was in fact the basis for its cultural necessity. The banner that had announced new issues of the *Little Review* changed in 1918 from the encompassing "Literature Art Drama Music" to the combative "Making No Compromise with the Public Taste."

The United States' entry into World War I and the increased use of censorship only increased the editors' sense of marginalization. The *Little Review* was denied the mails in 1918 when it published a wartime short story by Wyndham Lewis about a British soldier who seduced and abandoned a young French woman. The story evoked the degrading effects of the war through the sexual imagery in the story of seduction, but the story's tale of immorality led readers to believe that the magazine was taking a decadent and libertine stance in the face of the seriousness of the war. One reader said, "These are times for men to be attending to more serious things than aesthetic oddities." Anderson responded, "The layman says that we are now given over to the bizarre and the 'aesthetic' (that adjective which in America means something vaguely inconsequential, if not something shameless and immoral)."[71] While one reader was relieved that the editors managed to escape explicitly discussing the war, Anderson and Heap were more concerned to battle the effects of wartime notions of propriety, morality, and the suppression of cultural experimentation. Overall, the desire by readers for more from Anderson and less from Pound suggested that the "self" that the *Little Review* was expressing during these years was more Ezra Pound's than Margaret Anderson's. As literary modernism began to champion its male heroes, the limits of feminist modernist self-expression became clear.

The *Ulysses* Trial

Anderson's involvement with *Ulysses* solidified the gender politics of self-expression. In 1918 the *Little Review* started running installments of the novel, which was already being heralded in the Pound circle as James Joyce's masterpiece. Yet most readers at the time found the novel's experimental prose impossible to understand and the erotic musings of its central character, Leopold Bloom, vaguely smutty, even immoral. It was not surprising that these issues came to the attention of John Sumner and the Society for the Suppression of Vice, an organization that saw itself as a guardian of public decency and targeted many modernist and politically radical magazines. The *Little Review* editors were charged with printing obscene material in 1920, and the trial took place in early 1921. The lawyer for the editors, John Quinn, focused on defending the novel's status as literature rather than on the rights of the editors; in a larger sense, the trial represented modernist heroism in the face of cultural suppression. Interpreting the meaning of this episode for Anderson, and not for Joyce and his novel, allows us to see, finally, the limits Anderson faced in her championing of self-expression as both an artistic and political stance.

Anderson's role as editor of the magazine that printed Joyce's novel implicated her in the reception of Joyce's novel as "unintelligible" and "immoral." When Anderson claimed that *Ulysses* was "the most beautiful thing we will ever have," she knew that most readers at the time considered the novel thoroughly ugly and corrupt and that the magazine risked censorship. Janet Flanner, a journalist who wrote insightful essays about cultural politics for the *New Yorker* during this period, suggested that *Ulysses* indelibly marked Anderson. Flanner wrote,

She was first tinged by fame when it became known that it was she herself, with her exceptionally handsome hands, who had labored over the endless bundles of sullying proofs, including the libidinous sections—how was this possible for so pretty and feminine a creature as she looked to be?[72]

Flanner put Anderson's femininity in relation to the production of modern art: like the fingerprint ink at her arrest, the messy proofs both sullied Anderson and tinged her with fame. Anderson did not inspire Joyce to write *Ulysses*, but her role was key to its publication in the United States, and the idea of the "model American girl" literally touching and handling the obscene passages affected its reception.

The serialization of *Ulysses* got the editors into trouble long before it caught the attention of the Society for the Suppression of Vice. Some readers were not only affronted by the unintelligibility of *Ulysses* and the immorality of some of its passages, but thought these qualities tainted Anderson. Letters to the *Little Review* criticized her decision to publish installments of the novel, with readers explaining that the immorality of Leopold Bloom contaminated their perception of Margaret Anderson. "With all the force of my being I reject thinking of you as part of this hellish business," one reader wrote. "I loathe the possibility of your continuing to associate yourself with such degradation."[73] Anderson was compelled to answer the letter and used the exchange as an example, her response turning the rhetoric of contamination back on the letter writer.

> You received a copy of the *Little Review* at your own request. That was a tacit agreement to deal with it courteously. You have heard me speak of James Joyce with reverence. And yet you did not hesitate to speak of him to me with grossness. . . . On what then is your temerity toward me based?[74]

In contrast to her earlier writing, Anderson here used the gender conventions of chivalry and politeness to deal with this critic, when it was exactly those things that the reader was trying to uphold and that Anderson was trying to get rid of.[75] Anderson refused to explain why subscribers to the *Little Review* should overcome their distaste and read the novel; they were supposed, merely, to accept Anderson's judgment that she revered Joyce and that *Ulysses* was beautiful. She was in a unique position as a cultural mediator, a "model American girl" and a champion of the avant-garde, to explain the power and possibilities of Joyce's critique of modern life as well as why publishing the novel represented so strongly her own embrace of self-expression. But instead she retreated behind the language of convention.

The trial of the *Little Review* followed the pattern of retreat from the cultural contestation that had characterized self-expression. While it became the most famous episode for the magazine, it also illustrated the perils for Anderson and Heap in defending their rights to self-expression. Quinn's case depended upon arguing that *Ulysses* was literature and therefore incapable of harming readers by contributing to immorality.[76] Women constituted the frail readership in question, and so, Quinn reasoned, the fact that the editors were women undermined his case. In order to create the appearance of propriety, Quinn insisted that Anderson and Heap be silent during the court proceedings and that they surround themselves with schoolgirls in the courtroom audience. Anderson and Heap appeared at the trial not as advocates for an art that circulated outside conventional and normative images of gender and sexuality, but as figures of proper, and seemingly innocent, womanhood.

In the end not only were the editors literally silenced by Quinn, but the judge thought they were incapable of knowing what they were doing, although the two had eagerly sought the opportunity to publish the novel, had read it thoroughly, and had edited the proofs. Anderson, especially, came to represent the object that legitimated the discourse of obscenity during the trial—young womanhood corrupted by immoral literature. She wrote,

> One of the [judges], regarding me with a protective paternity, refused to allow the obscenity to be read in my hearing. But she is the publisher, said John Quinn, smiling. I am sure she didn't know the significance of what she was publishing, responded the judge, continuing to regard me with tenderness and suffering.[77]

The authority of the editors was denied in favor of a court display in which Anderson and Heap become ignorant creatures in need of protection, not the knowing, hardy editors of the *Little Review.* Anderson was trapped by the ideology of morality that she had so long sought to escape. In a larger sense, the role she had played was diminished by the modernist movement she helped to create.

Nevertheless, the irony of the case was not lost on her. Quinn had defended Joyce's right to self-expression in exchange for the women editors' silence and acquiescence to the idea that they did not know what they were doing. This strategy placed the editors in a weak position to defend their own right to self-expression—their own right not only to publish

Joyce and therefore to facilitate his self-expression but to support what they believed was an honest, if bleak, portrait of the human condition and the role of sexuality in it.

In this sense, the trial was a reprise of the review Anderson had written of *Sister Carrie* in 1911; she again came up against "facts as they were" in 1921. After the trial ended and the editors were fined $100, Quinn exhorted Anderson, "And now for God's sake . . . don't publish any more obscene literature." "How am I to know when it's obscene?" Anderson fired back. "I'm sure I don't know."[78] But unlike the *Sister Carrie* scenario, in which her literary judgment facilitated her own self-expression, the *Ulysses* trial did not lead to a new articulation of the relation between self-expression, feminism, and modernism. Here, self-expression had hardened into a modernist truism. For Anderson, silence, not self-expression, became a form of protest: "I will protect my sensibilities and my brain cells by being unhearing and untalkative." Heap told her, "Don't try to talk; don't put yourself into their hands."[79]

While self-expression had been a form of assertion, Anderson used her own silence as a form of refusal that Anderson called "self-preservation." The shift from self-expression to self-preservation was linked to Anderson's perception that the work of the magazine—both the work to put it out and the work presented in its pages—was becoming a part of the "reality" of social expectation and responsibility, rather than an act of resistance to it.[80] "I am definitely giving up the *Little Review*," Anderson told Heap. "You can't give it up. You started it. . . . You have no sense of responsibility," Heap replied. "Self-preservation is the first responsibility," Anderson concluded.[81] Withdrawing from confrontation and contestation, Anderson found that the *Little Review* no longer was a vehicle for her self-expression. Having concluded that, Anderson left the magazine in Heap's hands and joined the exodus of American writers, artists, and intellectuals to Europe.[82]

"Our Function Is Finished"

Though Anderson had less input into the magazine's final years, she and Heap together compiled a final issue of the magazine in 1929. They advertised this issue with much fanfare, promising again, like the blank issue of 1916, an issue containing "no literature and no art." Unlike the blank issue, however, the editors had come to the conclusion that there was no more "art" to be found, and they solicited the "confessions" of artists, writers, and others whose work the *Little Review* had published during its fifteen-year run. Sending around a questionnaire, which was a tool surrealist and dadaist groups had also used to challenge their contemporaries, the editors goaded their authors, "Here is a chance to tell the truth about yourself as no interviewer, critic, or historian could do."[83]

The flyer advertising the final issue seemed to promise this truth, listing "the great personalities" who had contributed the magazine from its early days in Chicago to its later years as a forum for the Parisian avant-garde, from Sherwood Anderson, to H.D. and Ernest Hemingway, to Man Ray. The flyer conveyed the sense of having fought a battle and, in a sense, having won it:

> to our public: after a turbulent, gay, and pioneering life of more than a decade we are bringing the *Little Review* to an end. we have discovered, promoted, and slain. we have fought, starved and faced jail. we have kept a record of all the most energetic manifestations of contemporary art. the files of the *Little Review* present a wide-world cinema of the art of this time. contemporary art has come into its own. today there is only emulation . . . there will be repetition for a hundred years. our function is finished.[84]

While the 1916 blank issue had left empty space as a signifier for art not-yet-produced, the final issue was a self-conscious act of closure, a culmination of Heap and Anderson's efforts on behalf of contemporary art.

While this announcement conveyed a sense of discovery, battle, and public contestation, the questions put to contributors were resolutely individualist and seemed to be designed to prompt responses that would not connect the artist to the cultural struggle the editors had waged. One question asked, "Why wouldn't you change places with any other human being?" Another asked, "What is your world view? (Are you a reasonable being in a reasonable scheme?)" Reading the responses, one can see on one hand a tribute to the idea of self-expression as a motor for modernism. On the other hand, the confessions were scripted, prescribed, and limited by the questionnaire.

The questions baffled respondents; many avoided addressing the questions directly or wrote eulogies to the magazine instead. For Ezra Pound, the idea of "no literature and no art" was infuriating. "Print what you've got on hand," he told the editors, angry that work he had sent earlier had been "suppressed." Emma Goldman, then living in exile in the south of France, refused to engage with the terms of the questions themselves, writing to Anderson, "I find the questions really terribly uninteresting and do not know what one is to answer to them. Do you really think the *Little Review* would gain by such material? I mean, since the questions are so ordinary the replies can be naught else."[85] As Goldman correctly foresaw, the reader learns little from those who methodically addressed each question, because their responses often resulted in laundry lists of likes and dislikes, reinforcing the impression that the artist's relation to the social world was solely a question of individual taste. By equating self-expression with individuality, the editors unwittingly helped to erase the consideration of cultural production that they had emphasized for years.

Perhaps as a result, Anderson and Heap were disappointed by the responses in the final issue. For Anderson, the final issue represented an opportunity to return to the original premise of the *Little Review,* a forum for artists to carry on a cultural conversation. But in going back to that premise, Anderson realized that the moment for the conversation she sought was lost. "As this number will show, even the artist doesn't know what he is talking about. And I can no longer go on publishing a magazine in which no one really knows what he is talking about."[86] Within the framework of self-expression that had legitimated the work of the magazine, in an essay titled, "Lost: A Renaissance," Heap wrote, "Self-expression is not enough; experiment is not enough; the recording of special moments or cases is not enough. All of the arts have broken faith or lost connection with their origin and function, . . . a pronounced symptom of an ailing and aimless society."[87] Both Anderson and Heap ended their editorials on a note of pessimism and failure, but, like the blank issue, they used the editorial role to express their sense of "historical truth."

Conclusion: A Dilettante's Revenge

In contrast to the final issue, Anderson's autobiography retrieved the significance of self-expression and its importance for feminist modernism. Self-expression was not simply what she fought for as an editor; it was what Anderson had to explain about her own life.

The reception of Anderson's autobiography, however, revealed how little room there was for such a perspective. In 1930, in the context of hardening opposition between aesthetics and politics, there wasn't much sympathy for Anderson's dedication to art and beauty, no matter how subversive it might be. For Marxist critic V. F. Calverton, the editor of *Modern Monthly* and a sophisticated proponent of literary radicalism, Anderson's battle with what she subversively termed "reality" was actually a decadent's posturing. For Calverton, a more responsible cultural politics would actually try to change real, material conditions.[88]

The reception of Anderson's autobiography by the literary modernists was less severe, but was in the end more damaging. This group of critics, interested in cataloguing the achievements of modernist writers in the teens and twenties, consigned Anderson to the marginal and anecdotal role of the woman who encouraged and published modernist writers. At the same time they attacked her autobiography for not being a "good history": flippant, breathless, episodic, it was not a seamless narrative of the period. Matthew Josephson (whose own autobiography, *Life Among the Surrealists,* appeared soon after Anderson's) complained,

> All of Miss Anderson's twentieth-century Odyssey through the cultured purlieus of Chicago, New York, and Paris offers valuable documents for the future biographies of many potential immortals. But is it good history? Why do so many presumably fascinating and original characters among whom she passed shrink to small stature in her narrative?[89]

Revealing more than a hint of masculine anxiety, Josephson thought Anderson focused too much attention on herself rather than on the "immortals" she had published. Alfred Kazin, writing forty years later upon the reissue of Anderson's autobiography, agreed: the problem with the book was that Anderson stopped being an enabler for others and used her experience editing the *Little Review* to tell her life story.

> Margaret Anderson's life, as told by Margaret Anderson, is the all-too-authentic example of that now unbelievable belief in "life as a work of art" that was once believed in by connoisseurs, dilettantes, epicures at the great feast of art provided by other people.[90]

In a modernist focus on texts as the signifier of significance and importance, Anderson herself wasn't "real."

The history of self-expression shows the extent to which modernists erased their own cultural formation in order to elevate and standardize art and literary style. This process was gendered in ways that were profoundly negative for the legacy of such figures as Margaret Anderson. Maxwell Bodenheim wrote that her autobiography "indicates the futility of self-biography when it is written by an ultra-radical outcast retiring to private life and temporarily exhausted by the secret incoherence and treachery of words."[91] Through the construction of her as a silly dilettante we can see the process of the formation of the gendered narrative of modernism, from something that men and women created together as the practice of forming new living arrangements and a cultural style to represent such beliefs to the professionalized establishment of a canon that excluded much of the effort women had expended on behalf of creating the possibilities for that art.

Yet Anderson's use of self-expression made her a compelling figure for many writers and artists in American modernism, not only because she published their work, but also because she embodied the avant-garde claim to rebellion and creativity. While Anderson's attempt to escape the "reality" of the bourgeois woman's life through her engagement with both bohemia and modernist writing was not successful as a permanent act of rebellion—the *Ulysses* trial effectively reconstructed her as subject to sentimental appeals to pure womanhood—the attempt nevertheless revealed some of the stakes in women's attempts to define their roles in an artistic revolution as well as political struggle.

To recognize the importance of self-expression, it is necessary to highlight modernism's process of formation, not simply the texts that rose out of that historical culture. Though she did not consider herself a "writer" or an "artist," Anderson was a feminist and modernist because she facilitated and became an emblem of a radically new culture and cultural style. Focusing on self-expression reveals possibilities in modernism that were suppressed in the creation of modernism as a form of high art. The cultural practices of modernism were ways in which women forged possibilities for themselves, but the increasing focus on texts occluded the importance of that history and enabled a narrative that posited that modernist men were rebelling from an older, residual culture associated with women. That is why it is important to reread stories like Margaret Anderson's, the vibrant rebels for self-expression, with all of their problems and contradictions. Her embrace of self-expression as a feminist and modernist stance led her to reject the discursive construction of "reality," as defining categories of womanhood. Her self-description in her autobiography never departed from her belief that conventional language—the language that constructed her as a woman and that made cultural laws seem natural—could not represent who she was or what she did. Through this reading, we can understand Anderson's autobiography as a feminist disruption of canonical modernism.

CHAPTER 3

Home from Bohemia

Floyd Dell and the

Crisis of Feminism

in Modern Culture

In 1926 the writer and editor Floyd Dell issued a challenge to his generation of writers and artists, men and women who had been shaped by
the modernist and feminist rebellion but were exhausted and disenchanted by the postwar world. Using the familiar rhetoric of breaking
from the Victorian past, Dell asked what their next step would be: "When
old ideals are broken, we must make ourselves new ideals. . . . But—it is
hard to drive the sore and wounded human spirit to the task of making
workable new ideals! It is easier to nurse our wounds in a corner."[1] For
Dell, the task of making new ideals was necessary not only for the art that
his generation would create but also for the lives that they would lead and
the influence they would exert.

> It may not be impossible for . . . a younger generation to begin to formu-
> late and erect into socially acceptable *conventions,* and where possible into
> laws, some healthy modern ideals of courtship, marriage, divorce, and the
> relations of the sexes in general. It may not be so difficult for them to find
> the political terms upon which they can accept and serve and use a ma-
> chine civilization. It may be quite natural for them to think of the arts as
> means of communication rather than merely opportunities for irrespon-
> sible self-expression. And their chosen literature is, in that event, likely to
> be a literature which, among other things, will help them to love gener-
> ously, to work honestly, to think clearly, to fight bravely, to live nobly.[2]

Dell's guiding ideas in his manifesto for the social responsibility of artists and writers, *Intellectual Vagabondage,* suggested a turn away from subversion and experimentation in an adversarial subculture and toward the creation of a new voice in dominant culture. In so doing, Dell rejected the rebellious tenets of self-expression that had guided the beliefs of such figures as Margaret Anderson. Dell abandoned self-expression in favor of communication, implicitly saying that revolutions in style and language had not produced a strong enough foundation for the civilization his generation must build. While the modernist impulse to entwine art and social life remained, here Dell introduced newly solidified ideals of a family-centered sexuality. His explicit focus on conventions and laws governing the lives of young men and women seemed to harden the meaning of the sexual revolution.

Dell's call for social responsibility was noteworthy in part because he was a modernist intellectual deeply engaged with feminism; his own life and work explored how new relations between men and women changed his identity, his artistic awareness, and his ideas about the formation of modern culture. His question, "Can we build a new civilization on the ruins of the old?" addressed the aftermath of the explosive moment when experiments in art and politics met theories and practices of women's emancipation. When, in other words, would this cultural and psychic experiment stop posing as rebellion and step up to shoulder its responsibility to shape dominant American society?

Dell's plea to his contemporaries was particularly resonant because he had embodied bohemian principles in the 1910s as an influential social critic, editor, and writer. Dell sought to be a hero of modern life, believing that women's struggle for emancipation was part of his own search for a fully realized selfhood and for the transformation of American society as a whole. He wrote extensively about women's emancipation as it was forged in the hotbeds of bohemian experimentation in the 1910s, and his writing in such essays as "Feminism for Men," published in 1914, was particularly acute at revealing how important women's emancipation might be for modern men. Several of his plays produced by the Provincetown Theater staged the difficulties men and women faced in forging equal partnerships, and his second novel, *The Briary Bush,* told in fictional form how his own experiments in modern love had led to the failure of his marriage to Margery Currey in 1911. His ironic, witty, and accessible prose was published in the embattled magazines of the Left, including *The Masses* and *The Liberator,* as well as more mainstream outlets, such as *Vanity Fair.*[3] Dell saw the possibilities of feminism every-

where, from his private trysts with women poets and artists, to his observations of women's behavior and manners on the streets of Greenwich
Village, to his attendance of vaudeville shows. With his sensitive face and
slight frame, his lighthearted, amusing way of bringing together socialism, feminism, and the bohemian dedication to having a good time, Dell
was known, in Sinclair Lewis's phrase, as the "faun at the barricades."[4]

As for many other modernists and feminists, including Isadora Duncan
and Margaret Anderson, World War I was a crossroads for Dell. Political
conservatism brought on by patriotism, the Espionage Act, deportations
of immigrant radicals, and censorship of the mails deeply affected the
cultural production of modernism. While the loose-knit, flexible fabric
of the modernist rebellion had never been harmonious or coherent, the
postwar scene was more rigidly fragmented. Feminists, initially jubilant
to have achieved women's right to vote, soon seemed to be exhausted by
the factions in the women's movement and by the gaps left in their own
pursuit of self-fulfillment. Further, bohemia, the laboratory for modernist experiments in art, life, and politics, seemed to disintegrate: while
some bemoaned that it had been commercialized by middle-class gawkers, others saw that it had been appropriated, disseminated, and woven
into the values of dominant American culture. Dell's ideas in *Intellectual
Vagabondage* and his novel about the "modern woman," titled *Janet
March,* reflected this understanding of bohemia's accommodation with
dominant American culture.

By the 1930s Dell had abandoned his lighthearted, easy tourism of
bohemia's subcultural spaces. His life had settled down. He had a strong
marriage with B. Marie Gage, which had provided two children, and
while he continually struggled for financial security, he had begun to
forge a more authoritative voice on matters of social renewal, publishing
in 1930 a long treatise on modern youth and childrearing titled *Love in
the Machine Age: On the Transition from Patriarchal Capitalism.* His 1933
autobiography explored the personal and political transformations that
had led him from bohemian rebellion to the socially responsible role of
husband, father, and social critic. These texts show how Dell looked back
upon the modernist rebellion with a jaundiced eye. They also are emblematic of the fortunes of American feminism in modernist thought.
While women's independence was almost an aphrodisiac to the earlier,
bohemian Dell, women's dependency became central to his later ideas
about social responsibility, and he himself was eventually sated by the
joys of middle-class domesticity.

Furthermore, the transformation in Dell's thought and life dramatizes a theoretical and historical problem for understanding the role of modernism in the crisis that feminism faced in the twenties. For Dell, the figure of the feminist embodied a link between a redefined heterosexuality and a new American culture. As the figure of the feminist traveled through Dell's writing, from her subcultural representation to hegemonic articulations of men's and women's roles, she gradually became for him suspect, threatening, and unhealthy. Feminism, in its articulation of the meaning of women's emancipation, also was central to the dynamic of modernist rebellion from and accommodation with dominant culture. Dell's call for social responsibility expressed a key aspect of modernist thought: it solidified a more authoritative relation to mass culture that excluded, suppressed, and vilified feminism. While women's struggle to achieve independence had been a crucible of Dell's own desire as a man, by the late twenties, this focus—and especially its connection to an avant-garde spirit of transformation—was excised from his vision.

Feminism in Bohemia

In the prewar years, modernism and feminism were linked by the geography of bohemia. New York City, Chicago, and San Francisco all had distinct neighborhoods that attracted artists, writers, and social activists. Bohemian principles seemed to emerge out of the character of these neighborhoods: New York's Greenwich Village, for example, was characterized by its twisting streets and the hodgepodge of factories, galleries, meeting halls, restaurants, salons, and apartment houses that gave the village an identity with distinct boundaries from the rest of the more grid-like Manhattan.[5] Many innovative projects were housed in Greenwich Village, including Henrietta Rodman's feminist cooperative apartments, the Provincetown Theater's New York productions, the offices of *The Masses* and other little magazines, and Mabel Dodge Luhan's salon, which was one among many gathering places for discussion and debate among a wide array of intellectuals and artists.[6] Within the Village's distinct boundaries, the most important aspect of bohemia was its fluidity: there were no clear lines between political activity, artistic production, or everyday life, in living arrangements, café culture, or work. The geography of bohemia made it fertile ground for the growth of experimental culture.

Bohemia was animated by its inhabitants' desire to create an alternative to middle-class America and rid dominant culture of the vestiges of Victorianism, in large part by opposing "home" and "bohemia." Both modernists and feminists often said that they left their homes to escape

the constraints and traditions of a bourgeois Victorian culture they rejected. While the nineteenth-century ideal of "home" as the haven in a heart-
less world had meant something both emotional and material, "bohemia"
represented the desire among many modernists and feminists to get out
into the world, away from a space they now experienced as confining,
and to experience life in all of its dimensions. Especially because bohemia was either within or near immigrant and working-class neighborhoods, bohemia was a kind of liminal space of class and culture that
allowed modernists to observe the workings of modernity but also to
create alternative modes of living and working.

Feminism was part of this bohemian geography and ethos in the early
twentieth century. As Dell described it, the lure of bohemia and the language of rebellion turned

> what had been perfect pictures of Victorian domestic femininity into (as
> it must have seemed to their fathers and mothers) raging and irrespon-
> sible monsters of modernism, who must forthwith go off to college, out to
> work, into a profession, on to the stage, over to a settlement house, with
> doubtless worse in prospect.[7]

While bohemia did not cause all of these trends in women's independence, it began to represent an ideal of women out in the world, away
from home. The presence of women artists, journalists, actresses, and activists in bohemia was a new phenomenon, distinct from other, older bo-
hemias, such as Paris in the mid-nineteenth century, where the theories
and cultural practices of modernism emerged. Where prostitutes, artist
models, and factory girls were virtually the only public presence of
women in older bohemian environs, now middle-class women were participants in early-twentieth-century bohemia, and thus they were modernist subjects as well as objects of its representation. The writer Djuna
Barnes, for example, started out as a journalist in New York, chronicling
life in the Village, profiling actresses, characters from the Broadway
underworld, and circus performers, as well as reporting on suffrage
demonstrations, including staging her own "force feeding" to describe
what suffragists experienced when they were punished for hunger strikes
while in prison.[8] The sheer range of Barnes's journalistic tourism of life
in New York suggested how women forged new public identities in bohemia, traversing many political and cultural worlds.

Women's presence in bohemia as residents, cultural tourists, or workers
also represented a new development in the history of women's public identities. The feminist partnership with modernism in bohemia undermined

the basic values that had legitimated middle-class women's activities out-side the domestic sphere: their virtue and moral superiority. Women in bohemia were often seen smoking and drinking; they flouted the conven-tions of women's dress, and they often engaged in sexual liaisons outside of marriage. As writers, artists, and poets, they expressed a sensibility of abandoned joy at breaking free from the responsibilities and expectations that had previously guided them. Edna St. Vincent Millay captured this ethos most famously in her poem, "First Fig":

> My candle burns at both ends;
> It will not last the night;
> But ah, my foes, and oh, my friends—
> It gives a lovely light![9]

Through the fashioning of women's behavior, dress, and expressive sensi-bility as irresponsible and therefore free, feminists were often represented as reversing the values women had held in such movements as temper-ance and anti-vice crusades.[10] It was difficult to tell the "good" women from the "bad."

Dell played upon this common duality in literature and social criti-cism about women. While the unattached, independent woman often symbolized moral disorder and social chaos for those who sought to shore up the crumbling foundations of gender in American life, the bo-hemian Dell saw the unfettered woman as a symbol of desire, both for erotic fulfillment and political liberation. He often made his arguments for women's political and economic independence by showing how old-fashioned, crusted prejudice about women presented obstacles to the ful-fillment of men's own desire. He also portrayed feminists as desirable and beautiful, with their independence a centerpiece of their allure and at-tractiveness. These tendencies in his fiction, plays, and essays often de-picted feminists as imaginary characters or literary heroines, vaguely al-luding to "real" women in the village (such as Millay herself, who already had a mythic status among the bohemians) or musing erotically about female performers.[11] Given their imaginative and subjective qualities, Dell's writings from the 1910s were not realistic; rather, they suggested the cultural dimensions of feminism in bohemia.

In discussing the impact of women's independence and new public identities on his own worldview, Dell often used his writing to stage the surprising qualities of the encounter between modernism and feminism. For example, in a 1915 essay titled with perhaps too much double enten-dre, "Enter the Woman," Dell imagined a young woman visiting his office while he wrote an article about feminism. Dell and Max Eastman, his friend and coeditor at *The Masses*, are having a conversation. Max asks Floyd, "What are you going to write about?" Floyd replies, "I'm going to write about the two great theories of woman that have dominated the past." The essay then discusses these predictable and familiar theories for several pages.

Suddenly, the tenor shifts when Dell introduces a new character. A young woman, named only "the girl," bursts into the room, interrupting Floyd's historical and philosophical exposition. Flirtatiously, she complains of a social faux pas: she has two dates for the same evening, and she asks the men for their advice. Max asks her, "Well, what do you *want* to do?" "I'll tell you," she replies. "I want to stay here with you boys and talk about a new book by Havelock Ellis that I've just been reading; and after dinner I want to look over that feminist article you're writing and tell you what's wrong with it." Intrigued, Max responds, "Sit down, put your feet on the desk, and have a cigarette. We will all collaborate on an article entitled 'The Modern Idea of Woman.'"[12]

The scene between the young woman and the two *Masses* editors in this essay was telling for several reasons. Its descriptive and conversational style transformed the desultory, rehearsed quality of Dell's discussion of "woman in the past" into a dynamic and charged encounter.[13] The young woman's entry also suggested that women's agency, their ability to argue, interrupt, and change directions, was central to any cultural portrait of the modern woman: only through the presence of a woman could a truly "modern idea of woman" emerge. Feminism thus meant that women should be able to define themselves as agents of representation rather than exist as passive objects of philosophical speculation. Though the dialogue was indeed framed by Dell's exposition, it sought to dismantle that frame as well.

With Floyd, Max, and "the girl" all working together on an article, the possibility of heterosexual collaboration seemed even more fun than a regular date, and it energized Dell's allegory of modern political and social theory on women. While modernists like Floyd and Max could easily carry on an intellectual discussion of the woman question that surely was feminist in intent, the young woman confidently criticized those who presumed to speak for "woman." In doing so, this character enacted the dismantling of "woman in the past" by embodying the "feminist" of the present. Dell's "girl," then, not only interrupted his conversation, but she interrupted his complacent use of "woman" as trope to reveal the social, political, and intellectual changes feminists wrought when they entered the "room" of modernist theory.

Though Dell's "girl" was imaginary, her dilemmas and her role were not. The themes of dating, sexuality, and modern theory in the essay playfully bridged contemporary manners and mores with more abstract political and aesthetic issues. The "girl's" problem, having two dates on the same night, resonated with popular culture: magazines and fiction often portrayed the dilemmas young men and women faced as traditional courtship rituals eroded. Dell's essay turned the "date" into an alternative and more abstract scene of courtship and sociality between men and women, that of the seductive relationship between modernism and feminism. Like Greenwich Village as a place where boundaries could be crossed, feminism enabled women to circulate more freely in public space, and modernists benefited from the heterosocial pleasures that would result. In this logic, the trope of "woman" in modernism, as the sentimental, domesticated emblem of modernist loathing, would change when, as Dell wrote, "we make room for her as a comrade in our world of adventure and play and effort."[14]

Notwithstanding this groundbreaking reversal, the use of scenarios of courtship and dating to make political and theoretical points had substantial problems. In his essay on "Feminism for Men," for example, Dell conjured up a feminist figure called the "sweetheart," an erotic figure who was not segregated from the activities of men, but who participated in and therefore sexualized them. Despite the fact that most feminists were independent-minded, ambitious, and often highly socially and politically sophisticated, the sweetheart of Dell's fantasy of feminism was always an ingenue, an unformed, empty vessel. In imagining her thus, Dell showed what happened when women broke free of the ideology of "home" and entered "bohemia," albeit escorted by her male bohemian guide. Pointedly referring to the discourse of moral reform that depended on women's roles in the home, Dell wrote, "If she has been brought up with the idea that it is wicked to drink, he will cultivate her taste in cocktails. He will give her lessons in Socialism, poetry, and poker, all with infinite tact and patience."[15] The sweetheart was inducted into bohemian activities, defined within the realm of men's interests, where "vice" became a pleasurable site of seduction. Through this reorientation of vice, pleasure, and women's presence in public space, the walls protecting "respectable" women from the evils of the street were torn down, revealing the "evils" to be merely the amusing activities of the well-rounded bohemian who combines a socialist outlook with a good poker face and an appreciation of poetry.

In addition to its implicit critique of the home as a constraining space associated with a moralizing, cloying ideology of womanhood, Dell's feminism depended upon both the imagined space of bohemia and actual public space, in which the division of spheres of activity based on gender disappeared.

> In the first place, there is the setting, the milieu, the scene of action. This is definite by virtue of its remarkable diversity. One is a sweetheart in the park, in the theatre, in the elevated train, on the front steps, on the fire escape, at soda fountains, at baseball games, in tea shops, in restaurants, in the parlour, in the kitchen, anywhere, everywhere—that is to say, in the world at large.[16]

Dell's outlook resulted from a widening public sphere of leisure, consumer pleasures, and mass entertainment in modern culture. Together, modernists and feminists were cultural tourists, both participants in and observers of public leisure activities, such as going to restaurants, baseball games, and theaters. Along with these activities were the social settings in working-class neighborhoods: the front steps, fire escapes, and parks. In this context, the spaces of "home"—the kitchen and the parlor—were no longer bourgeois cages but places of agreeable sociality.

As if no one ever had to work, Dell imagined bohemia as a fluid world in which men and women could play together and thus create a universe of gender no longer split between home and work, private and public.

> Though one is poor, there are always bus-tops to ride on to nowhere and back under the stars, there are the ferries that slide out into a night of mystery, there are woods to walk in and secluded beaches to lie upon in the darkness, there are picnic fires beside whose embers poetry may be remembered and said.[17]

This interchange between men and women could only take place in a space beyond the old Victorian dualisms—the "nowhere" of secluded beaches, ferries traveling into the night, a night space lit low—that expanded the arenas of courtship and romance and deepened the qualities of those interactions.

In advocating feminism, Dell was much more interested in its value for creating a sexuality based on companionship and passion than the need for women's economic and political equality with men. He enjoyed the play of difference between men and women, not the eradication of gender difference that full equality seemed to portend. Her sexuality, not its absence, was what enabled a sweetheart to enter the public, masculine world, and to be like a man, but not be a man. Such views, however, were more meaningful when read in context, when women's ability to be sexual agents was a major site of struggle and contest with the law. *The Masses*, where Dell initially published many of his feminist essays, was a forum where readers could gain access to information about birth control and other sex-related issues.[18] In part, Dell sought to persuade his readers of the benefits of the struggle for women's sexual independence, in an amusing, not polemical way. Once sex was no longer a question of fear or torment but rather of mutual passion between men and women, he argued, new gender roles would emerge. "Tell me," he asks the sweetheart, "if you lived in a world where you could be, as it were, as much of a boy as you liked, would you not feel freer than you have ever been yet, to be—a girl?"[19]

Feminism thus did not abolish gender difference, which is what many antifeminist men feared, but rather was a way of inhabiting femininity differently. Dell's "feminism for men" paid little attention to what power and privilege men might have to give up in the social world his feminism envisioned. Rather, his fantasy suggested that men would gain much in the way of sexual and emotional gratification. The benefit of feminism, for heterosexual men, was that it would produce better "sweethearts"; feminists, in other words, were sexy.

Dell's fantasy of the "sweetheart" and the "girl" relied upon a symbolic rejection of the "home" by modernists.[20] With romance and self-expression the opposite of domesticity, this partnership between feminism and modernism could not value or even recognize the strength and self-definition women found in the social networks and ideological power of the domestic sphere. Thus while modernists "made room" for feminists, the terms of their admittance did not change the structure of opposition between modernism and the sentimental power associated with domesticity.[21]

Liberation through Mass Culture: Burlesque and the Female Body

Like most "alternatives," bohemian feminism was not and could not be entirely new or outside; it was intertwined with the development of women's activities and representation in mass culture. Dell's imagined portrait of women and men in bohemia was drawn from his observations and experience of how men and women actually behaved in public space, and he appropriated the newly defined public activities of women to make his essays on feminism both lighthearted and current. The trends Dell introduced as "new" for women were already the rage among both middle-class New

Women and working-class Charity Girls.[22] The cultural imagination of bohemia, as a place where liaisons between men and women could flourish and where leisure and consumer pleasure replaced the Victorian emphasis on work and production, was indebted to the growth of mass culture, especially places of public leisure and entertainment.

As a bohemian, Dell prided himself on his ability to traverse both high and low cultural spaces, to discuss poetry and drama in nearly the same breath that he enthused about vaudeville and dance halls. His wide-ranging cultural tastes went hand in hand with the diversity of his political and artistic views. His views of feminism, indeed, traveled with him as he toured urban life. This catholic perspective was particularly evident in his observation of dance and, especially, women's performances as dancers. The cultural figure of the feminist could be identified in what Dell believed to be the transformative effect of watching the female body in dance. In Dell's excitement about Isadora Duncan, the female body was both a symbol for redefinitions of civilization in modernist thought and a site for women's changing sensibilities and power. Duncan was one harbinger of a radical, utopian modernity; another, which Duncan would have violently disputed, was the burlesque show, where highly skilled women performers, often scantily clad, both awoke the viewers' desires and subverted them.[23] While Duncan, for Dell, embodied modernist and feminist ideals of wholeness, the entertainment of burlesque shows was a forum for Dell to project his fantasy of feminism in mass culture.

It was not surprising that Dell took an interest in the culture of dancing. In a broader sense, dance was part of a modernist discourse about liberation from the boundaries of gender and class. As bohemians danced at restaurants, parties, and at the famous Village artists' balls, they expressed and performed heterosocial culture in the Village. But for Dell, there was an even stronger motivation. At a time when dancing was a central form of artistic vision, entertainment, and mingling between men and women, Dell wistfully complained that he was a bohemian who couldn't dance.[24] Perhaps because of the embarrassment he must have suffered as an archetypal bohemian unable to perform one of the most important rituals required of him, Dell wrote about dancing frequently. His play "Sweet and Twenty," for example, presented the troubled courtship between a young man overly dedicated to political work while his lover turned to the pleasure of dancing.[25] Many scenes in his novels and autobiography took place at artists' balls and parties in the Village, as well as at popular dance halls. Dell's interest in burlesque was emblematic of bohemians' appropriation of the new manners and mores found in working-class leisure arenas. His theft, however, like his description of the sweetheart's bohemia, was fuel for Dell's imagining of feminism.

Burlesque shows provided the mass cultural medium onto which Dell projected his fantasy of gender transformation, a fantasy seen through the two parts of the show, the women dancing on the chorus line and the performances of solo dancers. Watching the chorus line was not simply an act of voyeuristic pleasure; it was an act of freeing oneself. Dell imagined the audience seeking relief from the pressures of their daily lives and in a larger sense from the conditions of modern life. Members of the audience could slip into forgetfulness as they experienced the sensual pleasure of gazing upon unfettered female bodies. Dell wrote in 1916,

> The legs burst upon the scene in a blaze of light and sound, a kaleidoscope of calf and ankle, a whirl of soft pink feminine contours, a paradisiac vision of essential Girl: the whole theatre breathes forth a sigh of happiness, and the sons of Adam lean back in the seats, content. The promise is fulfilled.[26]

"Essential Girl" named the power of the female body to not only represent but to produce pleasure, abundance, and fulfillment. These terms had sexual connotations, but they also resonated with the belief that the evolution of the American economy—the increasing use of machines, especially—would release citizens from the need to work and allow them to realize themselves through leisure and play. The display of the chorus line, a collective female body seen through her parts, was a natural machine that produced a revolution in consciousness in the viewer. As Dell wrote, those who attended such shows were no longer "a solid block in the fabric of our sober American civilization"; rather the audience was transported to "a dream-world where all burdens are lifted, all values transvalued."[27] Such a vision was on the order of what bohemians read about in the philosophies of Marx, Nietzsche, or Edward Bellamy but found in homegrown American mass culture. The chorus line literalized modernist notions of freedom, in which sexual pleasure was unfreighted by any concern for virtue or restraint.

But it also remained a heterosexual system in which women were objects of the gaze of primarily male viewers—Dell's "sons of Adam." The chorus line provided a trope of male modernist pleasure, in the form of female bodies, in which repression and neurasthenic anxiety, classic modernist concerns, were purged from the psychological and cultural landscape. Modernists were thus freed from the burdens of capitalism, especially the experiences of alienation and routinization, through the pleasures of dancing female bodies. Because the chorus line expressed a femininity set loose from conventional middle-class moorings, it did not function as a trope of sentimental mushiness that the modernist must resist. Rather, watching the chorus line was a way to achieve liberation. Yet, like the "sweetheart" who passively accepted the teachings of her bohemian pal, the chorus line was a vehicle rather than a fully realized participant.

While Dell described the chorus line as a means to fulfill a viewer's desire, he saw the solo dancer as more specifically feminist; she was "something at once seemingly more and less than woman." Enthusiastically describing solo dancer Edith Day at a burlesque show in 1919 Dell wrote that she was "swift, lithe, foam-like, wind-tossed-spray-like, ever-changing, evanescent, incredible and magical." Similar to Dell's "girl" who burst into the room of modernist theory, the solo dancer was an interruption; she acted as a feminist disruption of both pleasure and the viewers' romantic flight from the psychic alienation of capitalism. The solo dancer was described in metaphorical opposites of the chorus line: while the line was soft, pink, and a whirl of feminine contours, the soloist was hard and machine-like. "Her body was not a body, it was a devilish and fascinating mechanism of cunning wires and delicate swift springs, which did the quaintly impossible in the most wildly graceful manner, and repeated it endlessly and tirelessly when commanded by our applause." Day's body in performance was like a machine, evoking the conditions of modern culture in the present, in contrast to the chorus line's natural paradise, which could only be a romanticized view of the past.[28]

While the chorus line was a gratifying and comforting display of femininity, the solo dancer challenged the viewer's understanding of sexual difference, and thus she introduced feminism at the level of the body, challenging Dell's own desire. The solo dancer defied viewers' voyeuristic pleasure by disrupting their expectations of what a female body should do and be.

> She defies the code of the dream-world in which women burn with the ready fires of miscellaneous invitation; she is remote, unseizable, bewitchingly unsexed. . . . She mocks at desire as she mocks at the law of gravitation; she is beyond sex. Nor is she mere muscle and grace. She has, shining in contrast to this impersonal world of sex, a hint of personality, a will of her own, an existence independent of the wishes of the audience.[29]

By defying desire and exerting a "will of her own," the dancer had an "independent existence" that Dell admitted defined feminism as an aspiration for women. Women's independence, as expressed on the vaudeville stage, thus was necessary to modernist sexual liberation and that which called into question its reliance on sexual difference. Dell's portrait of the solo dancer, nevertheless, was contradictory: her body and movements were like a machine, under the command of the audience; yet she also possessed her own desire, will, and personality. She had no individuality except as it was created by the audience, and yet she was defying that very structure of performer and audience to express a self that was "beyond sex."

Dell's resonant description suggested an analogy between the solo dancer and feminism, the audience and society at large. Women's new-found independence, to move more freely between the public and the private, and to express themselves in new creative ways, was a product of "larger social forces" (as Dell wrote in another essay),[30] and yet women's self-determination undermined these very forces. Dell did not resolve these contradictory impressions of feminism imagined in the context of bohemia. Rather, his uneasiness with feminist defiance of social control foreshadowed his later condemnation of her as socially irresponsible. His own political and personal history also showed how the bohemian persona, always fragile and conflicted, was shaped into a stronger, authoritative voice that found more to accommodate and less to conflict with in dominant culture. In the process of this accommodation, Dell left behind his lyrical representations of the feminist modernist desire to go beyond "home" and its dualisms of gender difference.

The Sexual Politics of Selfhood

Dell's various fantasies of the feminist in bohemia—the "girl," the "sweetheart," and the solo burlesque dancer—reveal how important feminism was for articulations of cultural rebellion. Moreover, Dell's conflicted portrayal of feminist cultural figures bore a remarkable similarity to his description of himself as a conflicted bohemian man. Dell's inability to dance was one symptom of his clumsy, conflicting desires, a self at odds. But there were other, more debilitating symptoms as well, including Dell's difficulty finishing the novel that he considered his most important work and his inability to forge a lasting, mutually fulfilling partnership with a woman in his real life.

Searching for a way to solve these problems, Dell turned to psychoanalysis. Always ahead of the curve of important trends, Dell had read the writings of Freud and his followers in Chicago, just as psychoanalytic teachings and practices began to circulate in the United States. At first, according to Douglas Clayton, Dell was a "facile explainer of Freud," pointing out neurotic symptoms in his friends, finding symbolism in dreams, and playing word-association games at parties.[31] In the context of the fluid world of bohemia, feminism and psychoanalysis were both seen as means to individual and social liberation; both helped cultural radicals to think about liberation from repression into creativity and a fulfilled sexuality. While the new heterosexuality and feminism attempted to break down divisions between home and the wider public world, psychoanalysis attempted to break down divisions between conscious and unconscious, the rational and irrational in the individual psyche. Dell grew more serious about psychoanalysis in 1916, at a moment when he began to feel adrift in his bohemian lifestyle, dissatisfied with the emptiness and casualness of both his writing and his love life. Entering analysis in a more rigorous manner, he did not solve all of his problems, but he discovered through it that his own self-fulfillment did not necessarily match his social and political sympathies.

In its early elaboration in bohemia, psychoanalysis was a theory of individual liberation from repressive social structures and, as a result, it appeared to undermine the need for social revolution—the systemic, institutional overhaul of American society that many socialists advocated. Dell dramatized this problem in his 1920 article, "A Psycho-Analytic Confession," which was a dialogue between his political consciousness and his wayward, lazy, pleasure-loving unconscious. As the illustrations that accompanied the article indicated, Dell's ego believed his unconscious to be "a wayward and cussed thing, always thinking the wrong thoughts. It is always thinking how nice it would be to take a day off and loaf, when your conscious intellect tells you that you must be at the office at nine."[32] His unconscious—burly, robust, and perhaps working-class—clearly overshadows and bullies the frail, dandified ego of the bohemian Dell.

The psychic characterizations presented in Dell's confession posed his unconscious as the foil of the serious socialist Dell attempted to be.

> "You can't fool me," I said bitterly. "You aren't as anxious about the world at large as you pretend to be. You are as selfish as you are depraved. What is it you want? Tell me that, and stop pretending to pity the poor Russians!"
>
> "I," said my Unconscious with shameless candor, "I want a million dollars and a large house, full of children."[33]

Here the facets of the psychoanalytic view of the self—the hard-working conscious and the lazy unconscious always troubling that quest—characterized a conflict between Dell's personal desires and his sense of political

"Ah, Floyd, you know you want a million!"

Floyd Dell and his Unconscious

Floyd Dell bullied by the conflict between personal desire and social responsibility. *"Ah, Floyd, you know you want a million!"* by Floyd Dell, 1920. Courtesy
Floyd Dell Papers, The Newberry Library, Chicago; reprinted by permission.

responsibility. As his character struggled to resolve this conflict, he recognized that he wished to be both productive and happy. Again allegorizing
the bohemian emphasis on self-fulfillment, Dell imagined himself as a
happy artist, playing and laughing, living on a houseboat with a "nice girl
and our children."

I do not wish to wallow in luxury, I wish only to lead a busy and happy and artistic life. . . . I've always wanted to live in a houseboat, with a nice girl and our children, and play in the water most of the time, and not wear any clothes to speak of, and just laze around and talk and laugh and eat and sleep and fool with the kids.[34]

The houseboat, drifting on the waters of cultural change, nevertheless suggested a recuperation of "home": a constraining, monotonous cage no longer, "home" was redefined as the site of self-fulfillment. Though Dell's imagination of himself retained some of its bohemian trappings— the *unfettered* artist at play—it is unmistakably an image of a father in the homey suburban ideal.

This resolution implied something very different for feminism. Although never fully realized or articulated, bohemia's synthesis of women's independence, opposition to home, and commitment to social transformation disintegrated. For feminist critic Alice Beal Parsons, the psychoanalytic turn in American thought neglected a crucial dimension of feminism, its sensibility of defiance and risk-taking. As she wrote in a review of a novel by Dell,

> Gay courage and defiance and the will to martyrdom might not after all be the chief necessities for the social revolution. . . . As the revolution left a good deal of a gap behind it they embraced psychoanalysis with eager fervor and followed its tenuous, guiding string through the wilderness of their own personalities as eagerly as they had once tried to follow Marx's string through the wilderness of social order.[35]

Parsons's ironic history of the shift from Marx to Freud trenchantly traced a change from public contestation to private preoccupations, social structures to the interior of the self.

Taming the Monster: Feminism in the Modernist Odyssey

Dell's redefinition of the meaning of home did not simply indicate one individual's accommodation with dominant cultural ideals. His psychic struggles, and the seeming triumph of personal lifestyle over political commitment that resulted, took place amid a widespread sense of disillusionment among Dell's modernist and feminist generation. While this sensibility took many forms, World War I marked a turning point of both consciousness and political outlook in bohemia. Artists, writers, and activists of the Village experienced the war as a crisis that destroyed the tenuous and never harmonious collaboration among movements, ideas, and experiments that bohemia had symbolized.

While most Americans shared the desire to end the devastating war in Europe, sending U.S. troops and arms had been hotly debated. To achieve consensus, the Wilson government had created prowar propaganda and mobilized a variety of means to suppress political opposition. These tactics included the banning of publications that expressed an antiwar viewpoint from the mails, the indictment of antiwar intellectuals for treason, and deportations of immigrant labor radicals. As cultural historian Leslie Fishbein and others have shown, the U.S. government's routing of political and cultural dissent during and after the war suppressed many of the activities of modernists on the Left, including the stands that many took against the war in the pages of such publications as *The Masses.*

Dell's investigations of modernism and feminism were situated within these changes. His major work of literary criticism, *Intellectual Vagabondage,* had originally come out in the early 1920s as essays in the socialist magazine, *The Liberator,* which was the successor to *The Masses.* Dell continued to be both an editor of and contributor to the new publication. *The Liberator* had replaced *The Masses* in 1918, after *The Masses* had been forced to shut down as a result of its suppression by the Post Office and the indictment of the editors, including Dell, and several contributors under the Espionage Act for articles, poetry, and cartoons that opposed the draft and U.S. entry into World War I. The indicted *Masses* group never went to jail since the juries for the two trials could not agree on whether they were guilty or not. But *The Masses,* unable to recover financially from being banned from the mails, went under. Though the trials gave this group of intellectuals and artists an opportunity to express their views both eloquently and sarcastically, the experience was a "grim joke": as Dell later wrote, "It was like a scene from *Alice in Wonderland* rewritten by Dostoievsky."[36] The Red Scare that followed the war, perhaps even more systematic an instrument of suppression than *The Masses* trials, set the terms for the loss of idealism and a deepening feeling of estrangement from dominant American culture.

While *The Liberator* was founded with similar political principles and its pages were as eclectic as *The Masses,* it did not recapture its circulation because the political and cultural ground of postwar American life had shifted. The loose-knit, flexible fabric of cultural radicalism captured by *The Masses* was torn into an opposition between art and politics, a split that was one of the enduring cultural effects of the war. As the poet Genevieve Taggard wrote in 1925, "[T]he Liberator could not decide whether it wanted to be either a propagandist or an artistic magazine, or both . . . ; what had been masterful was either harassed or sentimental. . . . *[T]he Masses-Liberator* spirit was gone—not so much dead as dispersed and divided."[37] Taggard was making a big point in a lyrical way: *The Liberator* failed because the intellectual optimism it had been founded on was shattered. This dynamic of nostalgic but failed attempts to piece together the shards of an earlier moment of optimistic hope has deeply shaped the character of intellectual life in the twentieth century.[38]

Feminist thought also was affected by the shift from a seductive, revolutionary optimism to a world-weary pessimism after the war. One result of the war, indeed, was the ratification of the Nineteenth Amendment granting American women the right to vote in 1920. For many this watershed in women's political status guaranteed their independence and provided the basis for their economic and legal equality. Cultural currents in feminism, however, did not support this political forecast. In the 1920s the very possibility of progress became a problem for feminist thought. Indeed, "progress" and "women" seemed to go hand in hand: women had won the vote, had reformed working conditions, expanded their educational opportunities, and forged new standards of sexual behavior. Many believed that these developments constituted progress of the most dramatic sort for women.[39]

Despite the signs of progress, feminists focused on failures in women's lives. The tone of their writing was marked by doubt and exhaustion. Even though women had won the vote, a sense of political and cultural unity as women was shattered.[40] Feminists' anxiety could be heard particularly in discussions of a generational divide between women.[41] Where the quest for education and economic independence was a beacon for feminists early in the century, in the 1920s the absence of the other side of the equation—love and domesticity—began to appear as a glaring contradiction that the early feminists had not solved. As they struggled to be both lovers and workers, feminists viewed the combination of career with marriage and motherhood as a double burden. The younger generation seemed to have little interest in carrying the torch their foremothers had borne so long. Instead, they reveled in new styles, youth-oriented activities, a quest for pleasure and sensation of all sorts. The focus of feminism shifted from a celebration of what women had achieved to what they still desired.

With a similar logic, trends in feminist and modernist thought shared a sense of loss, dispersal, and fragmentation. The problems of both, indeed, were intertwined. Dell's work in this period was particularly noteworthy because it paired the dilemmas of the modernist intellectual with the figure of the feminist, addressing the exhaustion of a rebellious spirit and, crucially, calling for a new relation to dominant American culture. While one work, *Intellectual Vagabondage,* was a work of literary criticism, and the other, *Janet March,* was a "modern woman" novel, both attempted to solve the problems his generations faced by arguing for social responsibility, not alienation. Though both works shared this overriding theme, they worked through nostalgia for the past and solutions for the present from different perspectives. Dell's intellectual vagabond returned to the significance of gender for the modernist rebellion, while his archetypal modern woman rewrote the cultural script for women, reconsidering the effects of feminism when women were cut loose from subordination.

Dell's argument in *Intellectual Vagabondage* recapitulated the problem charted by *The Masses/Liberator* shift. The book's elegant and playful style, as critic V. F. Calverton wrote in his review, concealed the seriousness of the questions Dell was posing.[42] The cover of the 1990 reprint paperback edition advertised it, indeed, as a manifesto for artistic awareness: *Intellectual Vagabondage* issued a "challenge to modern literary and intellectual life by one of its most celebrated figures: How should the artist respond in times of great social and economic change, and why is alienation a surrender rather than a solution?" Evoking three genres—the ancient tale of the *Odyssey,* popular children's adventure stories, and the eighteenth-century picaresque, Dell took his reader on an intellectual romp through the literature of modernity. But his challenge to disaffected intellectuals was rooted in the changes of the present, from the prewar bohemian moment to the more conflicted, equivocal climate after the war.[43] Dell criticized a tendency of disaffected retreat among young intellectuals, and this argument was deeply tied to a representation of feminism.

Running throughout Dell's criticism of disaffection and apathy among young intellectuals was the gender politics of rebellion and retreat. The metaphor of vagabondage itself conveyed an escape from the home and the qualities of duty and virtue that women in the home upheld: "We had chafed against the shelter to which the vestigial feudalism of the Home subjected her, and the artificial narrowing of her personality and activities."[44] In their adventures beyond "home," and their quest for experience, they encountered another archetype of women as muses of the sensual dimension of aesthetic experience. Criticizing "a world in which women and wine are a symbol of forgetfulness—a world of dreams,"[45] Dell nevertheless preserved the symbolism of virtue and vice to describe women; once vagabonds escaped the home, and the virtuous and dutiful women within them, they discovered women as decadent or mystical seductresses, feeding their imaginations with pleasure. In this context, Dell refashioned the world of late-nineteenth-century decadence, aestheticism, and Orientalism into ridiculous postures of escapism and isolation; they were not legitimate, in part, because of their representation of women.[46]

A more authentic vagabond appeared, not as a writer or character but as a consumer of the modern drama of Shaw and Ibsen, sympathetic to and inspired by the New Woman. Women's struggles to gain an independent identity in these plays forced modernists to consider the consequences of their own journey. "We had sought escape from intellectual and spiritual struggle in the companionship of the other sex, only to find ourselves involved in a more poignant intellectual and spiritual struggle— the struggle to understand the humanness of women; and we seemed to like it!"[47] In this sense, modernism and feminism were united. "She became like us, like what the world we worked in had made us, for good or ill—more interested in ideas, more honest, and less finicking" (138–39). Indeed, in Dell's intense focus on the significance of the woman question, as both a theme in literature and a dynamic of one's own life, modernism became feminism, in that modernism was in essence dedicated to changing men's and women's relationships with each other.

Modernism and feminism were also entwined in a common language and style. Just as "home" was not only a sphere of influence but the sentimental language that women spoke—what Dell called the "domestic vernacular"—upon leaving the "home," women adopted a modernist rhetoric, which was for Dell a "technical phraseology."

> [I]t was indeed, perhaps, the technical phraseology which we provided, that gave them the courage to denounce their wrongs. For discontents which can only be stated in the domestic vernacular, are, so far as a woman knows, evidences of a peculiar disposition in herself which had best be concealed. But wrongs which have attained the dignity of a technical vocabulary of their own, constitute a Cause. Our feministic terminology was a reputable medium for the utterance of old grudges and new ambitions. (130)

Feminism, then, became a legitimate politics when women's language and identity broke free of the "artificial narrowing" of the tradition of sentimentality. It was the possibility of a shared language that made a new relation between the sexes possible. Moreover, modernists inspired feminist acts of independence and self-expression; it was a "word or two" from the "lips of some young male idealist" who turned dutiful Victorian daughters into the bohemian rebel girls of Dell's fantasy, those who went "off to college, out to work, into a profession, on to the stage, over to a settlement house, with doubtless worse in prospect" (129). Feminists were the "raging and irresponsible monsters of modernism." In defining feminism through a modernist vocabulary, Dell tethered women's articulations of rebellion and independence to a system of representation controlled by men.

But like Frankenstein's tale, the experiment was destroyed when the monster escaped from the cage. Woman's possession of a new language could be used against her creator and master.

> [O]ut of this . . . new honesty . . . came a deep questioning of the validity of our masculine ideas. . . . Perhaps there was not so very much fun in being a modern woman after all. And perhaps it was our fault. When they succeeded at last in making these thoughts articulate, when they battered down our glorious long-term generalizations with immediate prosaic facts—when they pointed out that, no matter what you said, women had the hardest row to hoe, and that we weren't doing a damn thing to make it easier. (141)

Chastened, Dell wrote, "When this happened, our masculine feminism began, sadly, to part company with theirs" (141). Unleashed upon the world from the cage of the home, feminists became truly monstrous when they left their modernist Frankensteins behind and went off on their own.

This narrative provided the framework for Dell's overall critique of the modernist rebellion. All they really wanted, after all, was not a monster who argued and rebelled, but a "glorious playfellow." Growing weary of the adventure, the vagabond returns to find that it was "home" all along where he could find the authentic realization of modernist desire, "the Not Impossible She." As Dell claimed, "We might for a time cease to trouble ourselves about the State; but we could not long remain untroubled concerning Woman. . . . here was a spirit from whose haunting we would never be freed" (157–58). From the old-fashioned domesticity that was the despised opposite of modernism, Dell now understood domesticity as the repressed desire of the modernist. Social responsibility is analogous to being a parent: "He realizes that the essential fact about the Home, the thing which distinguishes it from the hall-bedroom, the garret and the studio, is that it is a place where one's beloved can, and does, bear and bring up children" (164). This conception of the home, distinguished from bohemia's liminal living spaces, transformed feminists into mothers and shut the door upon the feminist modernist acts of rage and irresponsibility. Replacing the "sweetheart" and even the burlesque dancer, a new figure, "mother," now could be set into "the empty frame in which from time to time had been set first one and then another picture of the Not Impossible She" (157). Cropped and firmly placed, the rough, rebellious edges magically obscured, "mother" was the object of male modernist renewal. She anchored the vagabond intellectual to a space that can be called home; she became the image of return and retrenchment. Woman, then, reconstituted the home, which here must be read as a metonymy for Dell's version of "social responsibility." Social responsibility took place through a reconstituted, harmonious relation between the sexes.

In this fantasy of home life, the symbolic mating of modernist and feminist created a new role, the socially responsible parent. It was their generational parenting that would make "living more comprehensible and more enjoyable in its widest sense." Not the adversarial culture both terms had bred and circulated within, "political terms [and the] arts . . . as merely opportunities for irresponsible self-expression," Dell transformed them into "socially acceptable conventions [of the] relations of the sexes" (258). Following this bridge from the bohemian adventure to "home" meant, of course, that young modernists were resolutely to turn their backs on the critique of family ideology bohemia had offered. And it left a feminism grounded in women's independence, "raging and irresponsible," out in the cold.

Dell's call for social responsibility was part of a more general sensibility of reflective self-examination after the war. *Intellectual Vagabondage* was one among many texts that posed the question of where the modernist and feminist experiments were going, including Edmund Wilson's literary history, *Axel's Castle*, Lorine Pruette's psychological portrait of modern women, *Women and Leisure: A Study of Social Waste*, Malcolm Cowley's *Exile's Return*, and Harold Stearn's collection of statements about intellectual alienation, ironically titled *Civilization in the United States*.[48] While these texts offered different perspectives, they shared common questions about the meaning of exile and return, revolt and regeneration, alienation and social commitment that together revealed the links between modernism and feminism that Dell allegorized. For him, the redefinition of womanhood through feminism played a central role in redefining the intellectual's relation to modern culture. In attacking alienation, self-absorption, and marginalization, feminism and modernism were part of the same project. Allegorized in the arc of modernist literary themes, feminism and modernism were locked together in a narrative inflected by postwar alienation and infused with a desire for contentment that only "home" could provide.

Freedom for What? The Problem of Desire in the 1920s

While Dell's *Intellectual Vagabondage* was a grand outline of the social roots of modern literature, he intended his 1923 novel, *Janet March*, to be "an attempt to present a characteristic modern girl truly against her social-historical background."[49] Dell claimed that the social-historical background, meaning "real" experience, and not the fantasies and illusions of bohemia, grounded his portrayal of modern women in this novel. This impulse, like the more theoretical presentation in *Intellectual Vagabondage*, was rooted both in the current times and in historical changes in womanhood and its ideologies.

Dell's novel was one among many portraits of young womanhood in the 1920s: the "modern woman" had become a symbol of mass consumer culture. Popular movies, fiction, and advertising celebrated the image of the flapper, with her lipstick, bobbed hair, and short skirts, as a creature of sexual expressiveness and appealing personality. Out of all the images of New Women that had circulated since the 1890s, the flapper seemed to be the definitive break with the Victorian ideal of chastity and gentility: she was decisively modern.[50] In the dynamic of feminism and modernism, the modern woman as embodied by the flapper seemed to have arrived, fully constituted as modern. She did not need to discover her desire for independence; she did not need to struggle for freedom; she did not need to declare a break with the past; she was the beneficiary of the struggle for progress. Dorothy Day, then a young feminist working at *The Liberator*, conveyed this perspective in her review of Dell's book, "From the time Janet is born she is surrounded by reasonableness, beauty and health. She naturally grows up to be reasonable, beautiful and healthy herself. . . . [S]he doesn't cling to any dream of financial independence. She doesn't want to be free and untrammelled. She just is."[51]

Dell's heroine does not bear a trace of self-sacrifice, nor does she exhibit any of the strains of anger and resistance that ran throughout popular nineteenth-century novels in the sentimental tradition. She did not fit the plot of turn-of-the-century novels about the "new woman," who in discovering her abilities and staking out an independent life resists the lure of marriage, knowing that it would mean her ultimate subordination.[52] Rather, Janet could be recognized by both bohemians and middle-class readers not as the embodiment of an older ideology of womanhood, nor as a rebel against its constraints, but as a symbol of modern culture and the possibility of self-fulfillment it offered to young men and women. In this sense, *Janet March* delivered on the challenge Dell made at the end of *Intellectual Vagabondage,* to provide a younger generation "a literature which . . . will help them to love generously, to work honestly, to think clearly, to fight bravely, to live nobly."[53] As the creator of Janet, moreover, Dell embraced the role of "generational parent," a relation that Day discerned precisely in her only slightly ironic review: "I like your Janet March, and I'm sure you too must have been tremendously fond and proud of her as she walked steadily through your pages."[54]

With a moderately toned, descriptive style and exhaustive attention to social detail, Dell attempted an even-handed approach to manners and mores in the twenties. On one hand, the novel passed no judgment on what conservatives saw as modern women's seemingly wanton and excessive sexuality and behavior. Concurring with sociological studies of behavior and beliefs among youth, the themes of the novel recognized that sexual expressiveness had become a crucible of modern identity.[55] The first edition of the novel depicted Janet having sex with a man she did not intend to marry, and while Dell's metaphors of frolicking kittens and arcadian realms may strike readers now as hopelessly silly, they did convey the thoughts of a woman who understood her experience as pleasurable and not sinful. "Sin?" Janet reflected. "No, sin was something strange and terrible and mysterious. It wasn't sin. What was it, then? It was—freedom." The first edition also included a clear-eyed scene of Janet's visit to an abortionist after she discovers she is pregnant. Dismayed but undaunted, Janet leaves his dirty back-alley office and receives the procedure from a woman doctor in a clean, light-filled clinic.[56] The attempt to present modern, "healthy" ideals of sex nevertheless got Dell into trouble with the censors, not because the novel included discussions of sex but because it did not condemn them as immoral. Rather than fight this battle, Dell and a new publisher issued an expurgated second edition, a decision that earned Dell the contempt of many of his former comrades.[57] Nevertheless, the novel's aim was not to be racy or revolutionary or to create a cause célèbre; *Janet March*, in presenting the dilemmas faced by an ordinary, middle-class girl as told by a sympathetic yet dispassionate narrator, tread the middle ground suggested by Dell's call for health and normality. The novel thus placed Janet in a frame that was neither morally conservative nor sexually radical.

While the novel painstakingly detailed the social conditions of its time, it also was concerned with history, with what made Janet modern, not revolutionary or residually Victorian. Its portrait of young woman-hood thus gains significance when read through a historical compari-son. The name of Dell's title character, Janet March, referenced a story with roots deep in the consciousness of many American readers. The name March, consciously used or not, was associated with Louisa May Alcott's *Little Women,* the extraordinarily popular domestic tale set in post–Civil War America. Even in the 1920s, an era that for many had de-cisively overthrown the Victorian sensibility, *Little Women,* first pub-lished in 1868, continued to be one of the most popular books among schoolchildren.[58] Dell's act of naming his heroine with the March sur-name symbolically associated his novel with readers' familiarity with the nineteenth-century story of the March sisters. Indeed, *Janet March* re-considered the interplay of problems that Alcott's heroines faced in an older era—problems of work and love, independence and familial ties, rebellion and responsibility—in relation to the problems about woman-hood identified by both feminist and modernist thought in the 1920s. The novels at first appeared to be situated in periods that were pro-foundly different, even oppositional, with regard to dominant con-ceptions of womanhood. *Little Women* emphasized work, ideological ac-commodation, and moral certitude about what women were. In contrast, *Janet March* emphasized play, alienation, and doubt about woman-hood.[59] While *Little Women* was about how girls came to accept already received beliefs about women, *Janet March* addressed the problem of how girls discovered what to do and how to live when conventional understandings of womanhood were up in the air.

Intertextually, Janet could be seen as a sleek cousin of rumpled Jo or elegant Amy. Like the March sisters, Janet too was raised by innovative, enlightened parents. But while the 1860s March family was poor, Janet was brought up in wealth, evoking the perception that the problems that middle-class youth faced were ones tied to economic prosperity. Janet does not need to learn to triumph over financial adversity: she already has all the opportunities that the March sisters ever sought and none of their sacrifices are required of her. Further, Janet fits the popular image of young women in the twenties: she is well educated but more athletic than intellectual. She shuns idealism, and instead is pragmatic and fun-loving. Her style in dress and manner is geared to the stark simplicity of the cur-rent fashions, wearing up-to-the-minute sheaths, cloche hats, rolled-down stockings, and low-heeled shoes. She is sexually expressive without having to suffer any of the consequences. She considers various career options yet doesn't really feel compelled to go after any of them, and she isn't ambitious enough to be really exceptional at anything. She is "eman-cipated" without ever having thought that she needed to struggle to achieve that freedom. Through this portrait of Janet as an attractive yet unexceptional young woman, the question the novel posed to the reader is why Janet had to get married and become a mother to achieve true happiness and fulfillment. Reading the novel through this problem al-lows us to explore how "modern women" in the twenties continued to be entrapped by the ideological opposition that *Little Women* portrayed, be-tween the romance of home versus women's quest for public independ-ence. While we can argue that this was and is a false opposition, it was nevertheless crucial to the perception of feminism; it was used to define, to control, and often to vilify feminism even in 1920s texts, including Dell's, that posed as feminist.

Janet's dilemma resonates with the feminist discourse of the 1920s. She goes to college and holds several promising jobs; she meets many in-teresting men, and knows what sexual desire and activity mean. Yet none of these experiences leads her to the fulfillment of her desire for happi-ness. She announces, "But I'm—something. And there must be some real use for me—I mustn't just go to waste. And it isn't enough just being wanted!"[60] What Janet fears is that in a world in which neither independ-ence nor romance can define her, she herself is expendable. Janet wants to "do" something, but she doesn't see that there's anything for her to do. She is desiring, but her dreams have no direction and no object. Her undirected desire is thus tied to the concern shared by feminists and gen-der conservatives alike that middle-class women were leading essentially wasteful lives.[61]

While Janet moans, "I can't just go to waste! I am something!" the fruits of her search for identity lie elsewhere than in the magical synthesis of love and work forged by the nineteenth-century March sisters. While the inveterate tomboy Jo, for example, eventually marries and has chil-dren, her writing and the school she opens continue to be a source of productivity as well as identity for Alcott's heroine. Unlike the ever-widening domestic community of the "Harvest Time" that is the closing chapter of *Little Women,* Janet's harvest is, simply and only, the produc-tion of children. Precisely because the aspirations tied to work and in-dependence were foreclosed in *Janet March*—they simply don't mean anything to her—Dell's Janet discovers that the solution to desire is its fulfillment in motherhood. She discovers that sex itself can be produc-tive, and not wasteful (even if it is pleasurable). *Janet March* ends, then, with the promise of impending motherhood, and Janet defers her own position as an arbiter of the future. "'One has to risk something—create something! All my life I've wanted to do something with myself. Something exciting. And this is one thing I can do. I can—' she hesitated—'I can help create a breed of fierce and athletic girls, new artists, musicians, and singers—.'"[62] Thus in the same gesture that he created the "characteristic" modern woman, Dell deferred her arrival, for Janet understands herself as a eugenic vessel of the future.

These historical resonances reveal both Dell's acceptance of women's roles as mothers, reinvented in a period that had shattered both the inevitability of motherhood for women and women's use of the ideal of motherhood to open a space for their activities in public life. Dell's heroine did not embody the ideals of self-sacrifice, concern over social conditions, or even education. Janet's most important contribution was not to find independence or a public identity, but to move beyond this ending he considered unsatisfying and irresponsible. Rather, the image of a pregnant Janet ideologically redefined the aspirations and identities of middle-class American women; it replaced both the battle for equal rights and the ideology of restraint, temperance, and moral management of the nineteenth century.

Even though Dell's novel was not as successful as he had hoped it would be, its themes were very common. The novel reflected the ascendance of consumer culture as defining women's desire. It placed the problem of women's freedom in the world of leisure and consumption rather than in the world of work and production. Many sexual modernists, including Havelock Ellis and Samuel Schmaulhausen, saw the flapper as a symbol of a sexual revolution as well as the symbol for a new generation of feminists. Women scholars, trained in the newly defined fields of psychology, anthropology, and sociology, looked at the younger generation of women from the vantage point of their expertise, posing more critical, searching questions. To them, the flapper appeared to have inherited the feminist dream of equality and self-fulfillment, but her ambition seemed to be blunted by consumer desire and the very celebration of her as a symbol of the sexual revolution in American mass culture.[63]

Feminist scholars in the twenties believed that cultural and social mores had changed, but they weren't sure that economic and political changes reflected or even allowed the changes to take root in women's identities. For psychologist Lorine Pruette, women wanted too much; their longings and desires seemed to exceed the boundaries of possibility. Because of this emphasis, much of the feminist scholarship in this period grappled not with rights and work but with the meaning of leisure, understood to be suffused with unsatisfiable desires awakened by mass culture. "We appear to feel that if we huddle close to the earth, keep our eyes and our ears closed, like good children, never peeping, always defrauding our various senses of the delights of the passing moment, presently life will come and pop a piece of candy into our open mouths."[64] The economic reality of women's work, sex-segregated and lower paid, meant that women seldom had the means to live independently. Pessimistically, studies of women's prospects concluded that American women were destined to lead contingent lives. *Janet March* did not dismiss this conclusion. Rather it presented marriage and reproductive sex as an end in itself, a totality that neither work nor leisure could produce. Dell's novel thus also reflected a shift in ideas about marriage, from the ideals of chastity, duty, and domesticity in a culture that valued the relations of production, into an institution that could temper and control the excesses of consumption.

Banishing Feminism from Modern Culture: *Love in the Machine Age*

The double burden haunted feminist thought in the late 1920s and early 1930s. Feminists had rejected domesticity ideologically in their pursuit of public work, but many found themselves married with children anyway. Saddled with the constraints of the double burden, they cast about for a critical theory to explain their paradoxical situation. Articles in both Left and mainstream magazines proliferated under such titles as "Still a Man's Game," "Feminism's Awkward Age," and "Confessions of an Ex-Feminist."[65] In 1931, for example, Nancy Evans looked back with a sense of loss at her bohemian days as a feminist, posing a series of questions:

> Freedom versus the home, the home versus freedom—was the change since 1913, since 1923 even, a retrogression? Was the return to convention the result of insufficient will? Or were the home and monogamy the true, deep desires that were inescapable? Or were they merely the best compromise to be found? These and other questions bothered me.[66]

Evans's chronology corresponded to changes in Dell's outlook on feminism, from his bohemian celebration of feminism as a vehicle for modernist freedom to his accommodation with dominant culture. While many feminists agonized over the questions Evans wistfully asked, Dell answered them unequivocally: yes, the home and monogamy were inescapable because they were true desires, not the false consciousness of the rebellious intellectual. Moreover, Dell believed, ironically, that the fulfillment of those desires would achieve the ends of feminism, to end patriarchal society.

Most accounts of early-twentieth-century modernist thought end with the loss of innocence produced by the war.[67] But it was not only the war that changed the tenor of modernism; its subcultural space, bohemia, had dissolved. Greenwich Village, as many of its former inhabitants bemoaned, was being invaded by middle-class gawkers and pretenders, undermining its authenticity and creating the conditions for a commercialism in which bohemia now could be sold and consumed. Just as Dell had chronicled the charms of Village life in its heyday, he also narrated its demise, playing upon the idea of modernist exhaustion and middle-class desire for the new.

> [W]e had something which it seemed all bourgeois America—sick to death of its machine-made efficiency and scared respectability—wistfully desired to share with us. . . . And these fellow-citizens of ours had the money with which to buy, as they fondly hoped, freedom and happiness. And with that golden key they did, indeed, open the door to our citadel.[68]

Though he complained, Dell had benefited from the popularization of bohemia; his first novel, *Moon Calf*, an engaging account of the coming of age of a bohemian, was a bestseller among young, middle-class readers.[69] In the process of drawing young men and women to bohemia, Dell participated in its appropriation.

Moving out of the Village and to Croton-on-Hudson, a suburb outside New York, Dell emigrated from bohemia, leaving the marginal, excessive space that had given his identity the heroism of rebellion and nonconformity. "Could this be because oneself was becoming bourgeois?" he speculated,

> Perhaps! For one could hardly possess a talent and exercise it in the Village for several years without attracting some notice from the outside world and beginning to reap some worldly rewards from it. And gradually one discovered in oneself certain bourgeois traits—the desire for, say, a house in the country, and children, and a settled life—for one becomes tired even of freedom![70]

Dell's writing shows some of the commonalities of the quest for self-fulfillment among both intellectuals and middle-class tourists of rebellion. Intellectual anxiety intersected with cultural retrenchment; in both theory and practice, Dell "went home" from bohemia.

The setting for feminism changed, from the bohemian space that broke down distinctions between public and private spheres and thus the gender system itself, to the increasing centrality of the goal of "home" in mass culture. Dell argued that patriarchal society had stunted the development of healthy heterosexuality. To the extent that feminism emerged from—even as it attacked—patriarchal society, it was associated with an older, residual culture that was holding everyone back, rather than that which was the liberatory force that helped to dismantle Victorianism.[71] Yet to say this is not to retain bohemia as a liminal, utopian space of liberation or transgression. The fantasies of feminism and liberation were part and parcel of a dynamic of cultural appropriation that always limited the possibilities for feminism. Dell's retreat, moreover, was not unusual among his contemporaries in the late 1920s and early 1930s.

Dell's journey took place amidst a general dispersal of the modernist and feminist impulses that had been uneasily but unmistakably present in bohemia. Some American intellectuals expressed disaffection, alienation, and disillusionment with what they sarcastically spurned as "civilization," and others became committed to international revolutionary politics. Others, having become experts in the newly established disciplines of psychology, sociology, and anthropology, became social critics under the auspices of the studies and reports they published. While their strategies and perspectives differed, many artists, writers, and intellectuals viewed dominant American culture in the 1920s with disdain; though some celebrated the potentiality of the institutions of mass consumption—movies, radio, department stores—most vilified the emptiness and hypocrisy of the new middle-class culture.

Many feminists also expressed deep ambivalence about the effects of consumer culture. Some celebrated the revolution in style of the twenties and saw a new freedom in the bared knees and short hair of the flapper. But they often coupled this with criticism. They were ambivalent about the new discourse of liberation because it seemed to replace the emphasis on independence in early feminism. They feared that stylistic play and the new morality were unmoored from a material, economic basis for self-determination. Consumer revelry, they feared, had taken the edge off women's desires for total social transformation.[72] Here was the problem: the more women engaged in a quest for sexual and stylistic pleasure, the more they tended to become ensnared in economic dependency on men and to leave aside their other aspirations.[73]

While modernism is often seen in direct conflict with mass consumer culture, reading Dell across the divide between bohemia and the formation of modern consumer culture allows us to see that the fantasies of heterosexuality imagined in bohemia became prescriptive models to control and contain the rebellious potentialities of feminist independence.

Having lived through the war, the Red Scare, and the dissolution of bohemia, Dell's ideas had solidified into a kind of "family-values heterosexuality." His understanding of feminism retained his bohemian fantasies of sexual liberation but positioned them within prescriptive, dominant cultural models to control modern women and to attack feminism in particular. He did so by emphasizing wife- and motherhood as the most important roles that women could have in a society that Dell actually believed was in "transition from patriarchal capitalism," the subtitle of his 1930 contribution to the mental hygiene movement, *Love in the Machine Age*. While the book received mixed reviews at the time—a former friend from *The Masses* days attacked it, while professional social scientists praised it—the book has since become a classic in the conservative sexology of the period.[74] Dell argued that the transition from patriarchal society would make healthy sex roles possible, free from the dual desires that had defined the struggle of modernist feminism in bohemia.

Love in the Machine Age reworked the themes that had obsessed Dell since the early 1910s, but its style, scale, and ostensible field of expertise were all dramatic departures. Unlike Dell's earlier work, which drew from imaginative literature, here he drew on scholarship in anthropology, psychology, and history. Grounded in "real" social experience, his analysis purported to be about reality rather than the world of imagination and fantasy that his studies of bohemian life had circulated within. This turn to the "real" had a formal effect on Dell's writing. In contrast to his use of a flirtatious style in his earlier essays, Dell adopted a turgid, cumbersome prose style weighed down by long quotations and a repetitive structure. He wrapped *Love in the Machine Age* in the discursive mantle of social scientific authority, repeating his key ideas with each new source. Dell's stance as a writer had changed from the charming Village playboy out to see the sights to the stern and careful social scientist wading into the breach of the chaotic twenties and pointing the way to social reconstruction. He had adopted a hegemonic voice and way of seeing: modern, consumer culture became for Dell, in Richard Fox and Jackson Lears's phrase, "an ethic, a standard of living, and a power structure."[75]

The hegemonic voice and point of view expressed in *Love in the Machine Age* was meaningful especially because Dell continued to support some liberal social and economic goals for women. He argued in *Love in the Machine Age*, for example, that men and women should have equal wages and that all mothers should be able to partake of state-sponsored "social insurance" for the care of children. Certainly, these were (and still are) legitimate feminist goals for women. But crucially, he attacked feminist declarations of independence from the cultural and sexual regimes organized and maintained by men. In the social psychological terms of *Love in the Machine Age,* women's independence was a form of escapism dangerous to the formation of a healthy, normative heterosexuality and thus a stable society.[76] The terms of the woman question thus changed: the "transition" from patriarchal capitalism meant a shift from economic and political rights to the right to have sex.[77] Waged work for women might be necessary now, Dell said, but feminism's insistence on these rights as a gauge of women's freedom or progress was damaging because it robbed "woman" of her "sexual rights."[78]

Though Dell ostensibly advocated feminist social and economic goals, this support didn't really matter because his larger argument foreclosed their importance. Dell associated a feminism that valued work with an older social order, an order that was only incompletely modernized. While the women's movement had emphasized work in a production-oriented ethos under capitalism, Dell believed that the transition from "patriarchal capitalism" would usher in a society of abundance and leisure. For Dell, patriarchy was the social corollary to capitalism: just as the growing use of machines (hence the use of the term *machine age* in the title) would liberate workers from work, break down class distinctions, and promote economic equality, a society beyond patriarchy would allow the family and social relations to be reconstituted. The seeds of that transition were planted not in the world of work, but in the world of consumption, the newly consolidated sites of mass culture in America. In a society of consumption, work could never be a gauge of women's freedom, because labor and production were residual forms. He had found in modern culture the realization of his early bohemian focus on the liberating qualities of pleasure, leisure, and consumption. True change for women, in their long struggle against patriarchy, would take place in the cultural organization of the relations between the sexes.

In pinning much of his critique of patriarchal social forms upon sex segregation, Dell was clearly attacking homosexuality. His examples are familiar, all detailing the effects of intellectual vagabondage and of feminism that took women and men away from healthy matehood. While feminism for men—Dell's old feminism—had been about bringing women and men together, the activism that had brought women into the public sphere, forged in women's colleges, settlement houses, and the suffrage movement itself, did not merely give them the independent spirit that made them the "glorious playfellow" of Dell's play world. Rather, for Dell these activities represented dangerous forms of homosociality, making women not only incapable of but ultimately uninterested in forming attachments with men. Both vagabondage and feminism encouraged the disorders and anxieties of modern life that Dell sought to reorder.

Read in this context, feminism was outmoded and residual, not new and cutting-edge as it had been in bohemia. The effect of Dell's argument was to set up an analogy between feminism and work, modern culture and love. In Dell's caricature the history of feminists' extensive engagement with the problem of work and love in the 1910s and 1920s simply did not exist. "[O]ur civilization will have to realize that work is not the instinctive center of our human lives and that love is; that work gains its chief emotional and practical importance as a means, not of self-support, but of mutual support of those who are joined together in mate-love and family-love" (350). In making this argument, voiced in the tones of rigor and expertise, Dell used the modernist impulse to "break with history" against feminism. Feminism was not a rebellious act in the present; it was part of the past to be destroyed.

It was in modern consumer culture that the real transition from patriarchal society would take place, because it encouraged the bonds of love and established its boundaries. Leisure activities would reestablish the power relations between men and women that allowed love to develop, and for Dell love was about enhancing power, in contrast to the tendency of workplace equality to diminish power. Young love emerged through participating in the mass cultural activities of the 1920s: dancing, the new fashions, and movies. As if in the stentorious tones of a kindly doctor, Dell prescribed these activities as the medicine for a neurotic society. For example, fashions should be designed not to erase sexual difference but to advertise attractiveness; movies were good because of their ability to channel projection and desire into suitable fantasies, allowing young people to "see their crude unconscious fantasies of sexual mating in politely censored form on the screen: they see their dreams come true and they are encouraged" (351). Movies, though censored, were pornographically able to achieve what the censored *Janet March* had not: to create a language for sex that was not based on fear or ignorance. Because modern culture brought young men and women together, there they would be safe from the sex segregation that patriarchal education and work had institutionalized. Leisure culture became the training ground for a new, healthy heterosexuality.

Dancing, again, was Dell's preferred example to represent changes in the organization of gender, changes that required stability rather than fluidity. While burlesque had amusingly confounded Dell's perception of a stable femininity in his Village days, couple dancing now emerged as the medium through which stable gender differences were reestablished. Couple dancing reestablished gender roles because their conventions allowed a man to demand submission from a woman. In an astounding claim for an argument to overthrow patriarchy, Dell argued that dances provided the "only realms in which he may safely display masculine masterfulness for erotic effect and get the results which he expects." In this way, Dell's transformation of patriarchal society reconstituted gendered power relations through a ritualized representation of and expression of heterosexuality:

> [T]hey can find, apart from social and economic realities, in the field of formal play and manners, the symbolic "male" and "female" relation which they desire. . . . [H]e can make all the decisions without asking her whether to turn to the right or left, whether to do this or that; and it is her business to respond automatically to these decisions. . . . [H]e responds to the music only, she to the music as it is expressed through him. And there is no doubt that among all the other emotional satisfactions of all kinds in dancing, this traditional "maleness" and "femaleness" is one satisfaction. It is not a duty but a pleasure. And it does not imply anything as to the world of economic reality. She can be Milton's Eve on the dance-floor without giving up her rights as a sensible and economically capable human being outside. (388–89)

Dancing allowed men and women a free zone to express fantasies of masculine and feminine behavior, which relaxed the strict demands and regimentation of equality elsewhere in "social and economic realities." Dancing was beyond the realm of political and economic equality; it took place in the world of instinct and desire, apart from ambition and choice.

Couple dancing was not as stable a social convention as Dell's characterization of it made it sound. Dell's representation of the couple dancing tended to shore it up as an expression of heterosexuality at a time when many expressed shock and horror at the movements and conventions of popular dancing. One of the criticisms of the Charleston, for example, was that men and women did not dance together; they danced separately and the dance often featured women alone performing its kicks and twists, without the circling embrace and guidance of the masculine partner. Dell's representation of couple dancing thus actively hid the connection to the solo female dancer who represented gender disorder. Dell also suppressed the working-class and African American influence on popular dancing in the twenties, instead emphasizing the white, middle-class respectability of couple dancing as purveyed by such figures as Irene and Vernon Castle.[79]

The promotion of "love" in the culture of leisure and consumption thus reinforced gender difference rather than eradicating it. In distinction to the political and economic realms that stressed equality, in the world of leisure men and women could rediscover in themselves the play of sexual difference. Though leisure activities were forms of relaxation and pleasure, for Dell they were serious pursuits indeed, because it was through leisure that the older order of sex segregation was dismantled.

In this use of mass cultural representations to establish the new heterosexuality, feminism became a conservative parody of what it once had been: the rebellious, independent, and therefore sexy feminist in bohemia was turned into an independent and therefore unsexy figure who was reviled because she could not be brought into the system of heterosexual mastery of men over women. Significantly, however, even in this negative, parodic form that became dominant by 1930, feminism was still circulating as a way to describe the problem of modern culture for women.

Conclusion: The "Comforting Arms" of "Home"

The response of his contemporaries to Dell's embrace of rigor and expertise in *Love in the Machine Age* revealed the politics of nostalgia and irony that characterized both modernist and feminist thought in the twenties. Both former cultural radicals and modern feminists noticed that Dell had abandoned his Village bohemian pose. Max Eastman, Dell's former colleague at *The Masses,* wrote that Dell not only had turned his back on sex radicalism but that his embrace of social science had led him to accept the terms of normality. Eastman parodied Dell's pose of detachment from his past as a champion of cultural radicalism.

> The attempt to break loose from the grip of patriarchal customs, and get free to enact the "general higher mammalian mating pattern" . . . leads people to invent all sorts of wild sex ideals, extravagant programs and red radical theories and notions about sex. . . . These radical theories, most all of which Floyd Dell has acted on and championed at some point in his career, are now dismissed as "ideological over-compensations"—attempts, that is, to make up with a foolish fancy for your incapacity to walk straight out of the meshes of the patriarchal custom.[80]

However arch Eastman's parody was, in the end it missed the point, for, despite Dell's changing perspective as well as his changing discourse, his was an attempt to see in modern culture the possibilities forged in bohemia. Though Dell's specific prescriptions for heterosexuality were condemned by his former comrades, the impetus to adopt a position of social responsibility characterized broader intellectual trends.

Feminist psychologist Lorine Pruette, on the other hand, saw the continuities in Dell's preoccupation with love, marriage, and patriarchal custom, and she noticed as well the shift in genre and style that marked *Love in the Machine Age.* "And now the novelist lays aside his puppets, however engaging, to grapple directly with the problems which have so long held his attention, love and marriage, and living in a strange, new civilization."[81] Pruette placed Dell's turn in a broader context than the demise of prewar bohemia, and instead wrote with wry observation about the cycles of cultural critique that formed the context for the changes in Dell's perspective:

> It is clear, from this book and from many other indications, that a new old trend is making itself felt. What price futility and smart cynicism? The war is going out in a blaze of war books; we are arriving at a demobilization of the literary war generation; humanism is upon us and romance is just around the corner; in five years we may all be leading lives with a purpose.[82]

Pruette saw that Dell's project was not simply one of renunciation but of recognizing the extent to which prewar feminism and sex radicalism had become woven into the fabric of dominant culture. Moreover, Dell's call for social responsibility would become in a larger sense a political imperative. The Left turn in the thirties would pose the same question: "What price futility and smart cynicism?" Communists and fellow travelers, too, would criticize the pose of alienated disaffection among the intellectuals and turn to a form of romantic humanism and appeal to "middle-class" values that rejected sex radicalism. While Dell's appropriation of a discourse of normality to counter the upheavals of feminism and modernism can now be clearly seen as a disturbing harbinger of the rise of middle-class heterosexual consumerism, it must also be read as a precursor to the gender conservatism in the cultural politics of the decade to follow.

In his autobiography, significantly titled *Homecoming,* Dell told the story of his experiences as a man struggling to find his mate and how he achieved a "norm," a position that was not different, not exceptional, just normal. Because of this insistence on normality, though it chronicles

Dell's life from his early boyhood to his present in the early thirties, the work is almost antiautobiographical. Dell was not interested in conveying what made his experience unique; rather, he sought to convey what made him "like everyone else." He built his ego out of the materials he had discarded when he was a bohemian, a cultural radical, and a feminist, and *Homecoming* reads as if it is establishing a paradigm for that strong, healthy ego, which Dell believed would free everyone from patriarchal society.

Homecoming tells the story of Dell's own liberation from the wondering, wandering stance of the vagabond.

> From my point of view, the remarkable thing about Floyd Dell is that he actually could do, and finally did do, most of the things that other people do. This will be the story of, first, how he got into that fix of not getting the ordinary satisfactions out of life—getting instead some valuable artistic and intellectual satisfactions; and then the story of how he triumphantly got most of the commonplace everyday satisfactions, without surrendering all the others—though some of them had to go by the board in the process.[83]

Floundering in a sea of difference, Dell discovers that by becoming the same as everyone else, he can stay afloat. What in Dell's eyes is most "remarkable" about his life is his ability to achieve the pinnacle of unremarkability.

Finally anchoring the drifting houseboat of his familial desire, *Homecoming* staked his call for social responsibility to his own success at becoming normal.

> I did want to find "common things at last.". . . . I wanted to be married to a girl who would not put her career before children—or even before me, hideously reactionary as that thought would have seemed a few years ago. One artist in the family, I was convinced, was enough. And since all intellectual and artistically creative young women seemed . . . hell-bent upon careers, perhaps it was only with a girl as simple and natural as a South-sea islander that I could find the kind of permanent happiness I wanted.[84]

Once again, Dell appropriates "woman" as a vehicle for his fantasies, here using anthropology to fantasize about the primitive other woman who, like the sweetheart, would present no obstacles to his vision of perfectly normal heterosexuality. At the same time, it also reveals how far Dell had to go to make a good mother out of the monstrous modern woman and to assert his masculinity in the context of the conflicting desires of his intellectual stance.

The comforting arms of the imagined South Sea islander shielded Dell from the conflicts of gender, but they did not keep him from falling into the trap of irony. His appeal to primitivism as a structure of family life sheds light on the difficulty of actually achieving an untroubled heterosexuality in the modern world. Dell's partner was, after all, just such an intellectual and artistically creative young woman he claimed to have left behind. His metaphor of the perfect mate found in the arms of the "primitive other" of the South Sea islander was still a fantasy, despite his claim of having gotten to the real. He believed that his achievement of becoming just like everyone else, because it was achieved and not natural or inevitable, made him a responsible parent and a role model for a younger generation in danger of falling prey to the seductive lures of vagabondage. But his fantasy of his place in the real, everyday world—the middle-class husband and father—turned out to be just as estranged as the rebellious feminist modernists he thought he had thrown overboard.

Studies of modernism have typically praised the resistant potential of cultural radicals or demonstrated how their failed projects ultimately served hegemonic ends. A richer understanding of these issues would result from recognizing how modernists offered both at different moments. This survey of Dell's shift from insouciant bohemian to stern "social scientist" of normality suggests that it is important not only to recover feminism in its avant-garde moment but also in its reified, negative formulation. It is particularly important to look at how modernists interpreted, appropriated, celebrated, and rejected feminism between 1910 and 1940, a period that uneasily shifted from adversarial beliefs in liberation to cultural disaffection to outright conservatism. Especially because feminism is increasingly seen as a repressive cultural formation in our own time, the revision of modernism ought to include as one of its most pressing questions why feminism was both a privileged way of representing modernist views of freedom and how it was made "other."

CHAPTER 4

In Search of a Usable Past

Josephine Herbst on

the Margins of History

J osephine Herbst was one of many American journalists and intellectu-als who went to Spain to cover the civil war, but more often than not during her sojourn in 1937 she was holed up in a hotel in Madrid with-out the resources of good contacts, a car, and food, which were needed to get to the countryside where the international brigades of soldiers were fighting and where the villagers and farmers lived. The bombing of Madrid frightened her, and the increasing splits among the anarchists, communists, and socialist factions composing the republican govern-ment deeply troubled her. She picked her way through the rubble-strewn streets of Madrid with dust in her hair and grit in her clothing, hungrily staring at empty shop windows or watching Marlene Dietrich movies at a theater where a sign advertising Charlie Chaplin's *Modern Times* was blown to bits. "Everyone knew where he was going, what he was doing, except me,"[1] she recalled plaintively. Herbst felt like an outsider in a struggle she desperately wanted to participate in. Like many others, she was inspired by the commitment of the Spanish people and of the inter-national brigades to preserve the republic. As a radical intellectual, she saw the Spanish civil war as the final attempt to combat fascism from the Left: "It was one of the great social revolutions which have swept through the world and among which we live."[2] But she found it extremely difficult to discover the "real" Spain she was supposed to write about.

Herbst contrasted her experience in Spain with that of her friend Ernest

Hemingway, who was there making the documentary *The Spanish Earth.* Hemingway, she reported, strode around purposefully in shiny boots and a uniform, with two cars at his disposal and a wardrobe full of food in his hotel room. While Herbst felt that she could barely write, Hemingway, she said, was "annexing new realms of experience." Parodying Hemingway's simple prose style to convey the ease of his political and artistic stance, Herbst wrote, "[H]e wanted to be *the* war writer of his age, and he knew it and went toward it. . . . What was the deepest reality . . . was in an extreme form *here*, and to get it he had to be in it, and he knew it." Hemingway knew what he thought, the depth of his commitment was clear, and he fully believed that he had a significant role to play as a writer and filmmaker in support of the republic. In contrast to Hemingway's unproblematic political commitment and artistic empowerment, Herbst was incapacitated. "I didn't believe that I could write anything deathless or even sway to any appreciable extent the rigidities that made for the fantastic nonintervention pact."[3] Herbst described herself as powerless and silent in order to say what everyone now knows to be the truth: that intellectuals did little to change the events that led to the devastation wrought by World War II.

In transforming her experience in Spain into the historical insights of her memoirs, Herbst used a politics of gender. She characterized Hemingway as pompous and manly in order to claim that his very centrality as a writer had little influence on events in retrospect. In contrast, she associated her inability to write with a forlorn, hungry femininity, evoking an extreme marginality that now seems a truer characterization of the fate of intellectual engagement with "modern times" in the thirties. Herbst's story of her experience in Spain suggests a larger dynamic in feminist and modernist thought and action. As modernists confronted the wrenching crises of the international economic depression and political suppression, feminism—that which sought to represent and to change the language of gender—expressed hidden dynamics in that movement. Even as modernists sought action, they became enmeshed in a paralyzing process of factionalization and betrayal; Herbst's language of gender expressed this paradox of modern intellectual life.

Herbst kept returning to scenarios of the possibilities and impossibilities of the role of intellectuals in times of crisis, a return that took significant shape in her memoirs first published as separate essays in the 1960s but only recently as a book. These long essays broadly covered the sources and circumstances that led intellectuals of Herbst's generation from experiments in form and a sense of detachment from dominant culture to expressions of social and political commitment. In contrast to the silence and intellectual paralysis Herbst experienced at the time, the memoirs achieved a historical perspective that submitted neither to a politics of apology nor to orthodoxy: they are brilliant and evocative portraits of the art and politics of the interwar period. Herbst wrote, "There was one thing you couldn't do when you came back from Spain. You couldn't begin to talk in terms of contradictions. . . . If I didn't write, if I didn't speak, it wasn't that I felt ignorant. But it may have seemed to me that what I had brought back was too appallingly diffuse."[4] This explanation of her silence upon her return from Spain indicated her retrospective viewpoint more generally. Herbst's memoirs were built around the contradictions of her experience, not the "authoritative answer" from someone who was "there." They explored why she thought it was important to be able to speak in terms of contradictions in order to write about the past.

Herbst was a typical member of her intellectual generation, and the outline of her activities and writing makes this clear. Steeped in the political disillusionment and cultural alienation of the twenties, she published two coolly cynical novels. But with the Depression, Herbst began to be more politically committed, and, like many, she was a fellow traveler with the Communist Party. Her novels and reportage in the thirties reflected this commitment; working in the style of documentary realism, she produced a trilogy of novels that traced a generational history of her family from the 1870s to the Depression in relation to a dialectical analysis of the failure of American capitalism.

Herbst also was a journalist who covered many of the major events of the decade, part of the movement of writers toward direct contact with wrenching social experience during the Depression in the United States and the growth of fascism internationally. In her reports for such publications as *Scribner's,* the *New Masses,* and the *New York Post,* she covered many theaters of activism and crisis that directly shaped intellectual life in the thirties: in addition to the Spanish civil war, she wrote about a writers' congress in Russia in 1930, the farmers' strikes in the Midwest, the Scottsboro trials, workers struggling against the plantation system in Cuba, and Germany during the rise of Nazism. Herbst participated in the struggles and wrote in the genres we associate with intellectuals in the interwar period, and she knew many major writers, including Hemingway, John Dos Passos, Nathanael West, and Katherine Anne Porter.[5] In contrast to the other figures in this book, Herbst did not retreat from historical crisis; rather, she was a full-scale participant in the modernist rebellion against innocence.

Though Herbst's intellectual biography suggests her centrality to the period, her reputation as a writer speaks more to a dynamic of marginality. Herbst is not considered a major novelist of the Depression era (though her work is discussed extensively in important recent work on Depression Era women novelists and cited frequently in a major cultural history of the period).[6] Her reputation and ongoing work suffered first as a result of the wave of anticommunism that swept aside the contributions of leftist writers in the 1950s; her fate is thus an important example of the cultural politics of repression that went hand in hand with the political tactics of McCarthyism. Perhaps even more important for this study, Herbst's legacy as a writer was not completely restored by the recuperation of the literary Left that began to take place in the 1960s. As Herbst herself understood, the tendency to label thirties writing as "proletarian literature" and the focus of criticism on the heroic, manly worker made her own work marginal. Herbst's attention to gender encourages a view of modernism that goes beyond the dichotomies drawn between aesthetic experiment and social realism, femininity and manliness.

One of the enduring effects of the economic crisis was a backlash against women's economic and cultural independence. The increase in women working, especially married women, was blamed for the mass unemployment of men. Accompanying the attitudes toward women's work was anxiety and uncertainty about gender roles: the figuration of women as the avatars of the sexual revolution in the twenties was displaced into widespread concern about traditional family arrangements in the context of the economic upheavals and dispossession that so many families faced in the thirties. This anxiety was also expressed in the cultural representation of the period. The public art of the New Deal, for example, often portrayed women in nostalgic terms as the helpmeets of men in order to shore up the social order in the midst of economic devastation and political fear, quite a contrast to the independent flapper as the embodiment of modern life before the Crash. While feminists continued to articulate the need for women both to gain economic power and to be afforded protection specific to women's situation in the workplace, the idea of feminism as a utopian ideal of modernity in twentieth-century America eroded.[7]

And yet feminism persisted as a form of critical insight into the period, especially in the context of a more general turn to history among modernists. Herbst's memoirs were feminist, not only because they addressed women's concerns and experiences, but because they disturbed a complacent gender-based view of history. As the historian Nancy Hewitt said in another context for assessing the importance of marginality as a critical question in women's history, "It is only by remembering our own fragmented and fissured development that we will open up the possibility of a decentered future. Then, the transformative power of exploring the margins will remain, or regain, its rightful place, displacing any hierarchy of women's histories."[8] Herbst used expressions of femininity and marginality to represent the cultural politics of the twenties and the thirties. The concept of the usable past was also a critical tool to represent a feminist modernist self in a history that made that position marginal. Herbst's interest in history recapitulates and elaborates upon the problem that this book seeks to address as a whole: the language and representational power of history, she recognized, was indeed treacherous, and she sought to show how and why history had entrapped her. In this sense, Herbst's perspective on the "usable past" helps us to see, in literary scholar Susan Stanford Friedman's evocative formulation, "a modernism of the margins, a modernism based on an identification with those left out of the cultural mainstream."[9]

Detachment: The Rejection of History in the Twenties

The 1920s and 1930s have often been described in terms of opposition, between a modernism of aesthetic detachment and a social realism that dedicated art to political ends. For Herbst this opposition was inaccurate and damaging: it was a contradiction that characterized the modernist impulse itself, but which was difficult if not impossible to articulate in those times. Perhaps because Herbst was sought out as a source of knowledge by literary critics and social historians in the 1960s, her memoirs deflected easy answers. Avant-garde in spirit, they were a stone thrown at the scholarly barricades erected against exploring the problems of radicalism, the impulses behind the development of revolutionary literature, and the formalist treatment of modernism that emptied it of political meaning. She thus wrote as a witness to and participant in the cultural politics of the interwar period and as someone intervening in how this period was being understood in the fifties and sixties.

Keenly attuned to the way that history had begun to assess her own contributions to American literature, Herbst described the twenties and her participation in its artistic, cultural, and political movements in terms of its attitude toward history. By the 1950s the twenties had become known as the era of "high modernism." Among other aspects of the process of canonization of writers like Fitzgerald, Hemingway, and Eliot was the belief that modernism had attained aesthetic excellence as its art became disinterested in politics.[10] In addition to the tremendous movement to recover and reconsider the work and lives of minority, women, and radical writers and artists, recent revisions of modernism have challenged this way of understanding the purity of artistic concerns.[11] Revisionary criticism of modernism has argued that the claim that modernism became *the* art of the early twentieth century served to veil its political significance as an art of rebellion, connected to the desire to effect social change.

Herbst's discussion of the twenties was hinged on her belief that radical politics and aesthetic experiment were not divided from each other but were part of the same cultural moment. Her memoir about the year 1927, "A Year of Disgrace," challenged prevailing notions of the decade as the era of high modernism and an art of political detachment. "The twenties was not at all the museum piece it has since become, where our literary curators have posed on elevated pedestals a few busts of the eminent," she wrote. "It was all flux and change, with artistic movements evolving into political crises."[12]

> Two young people writing in different styles, using different materials, could afford hospitality to one another's work. Those who had socialist inclinations, those who ran gaily down the stairs with a manuscript no one would ever print, those who liked to read "The Waste Land" aloud to a girl, . . . all mingled in a sort of ridiculous, gorgeous, open-house limbo.[13]

Herbst challenged the "museum piece" history of the twenties by arguing that the lines drawn between the politics of "socialist inclinations" and the art of "The Wasteland" were false boundaries. Though Herbst's characterization of the "gorgeous limbo" in which writers, political activists, and artists mingled runs counter to the cultural despair, retreat, and pessimism that an older generation expressed about American culture after the First World War, including Floyd Dell, Margaret Anderson, and Isadora Duncan, a spirit of rebellion and countercultural exuberation persisted, even remade itself in the terms that the twenties offered: a sense of alienation from middle-class cultural expectations and yet a headlong rush to "experience" that resonated with the consumer abandon of the period. Despite the cries that bohemia had died, Herbst's characterization of the twenties testified to the power of bohemia to emerge again in the sensibilities and spirit of a younger group. Moreover the period's hospitality to competing artistic forms and political inclinations were, to Herbst, the conditions upon which the assessment of modernist alienation toward dominant culture must be made. The themes of this historical critique included a rejection of the exalted idea of progress, skepticism of consumer culture, a jaundiced attitude toward the sexual revolution, and an immersion in the politics of style—including the modernist suspicion of sentimentality and its seemingly uncritical celebration of the "machine age." It was in this context that a feminist examination of women's emancipation and progress emerged and was articulated, an examination that was deeply critical.

Herbst's novels and social criticism in the twenties addressed all of these themes. The two novels she published in the late twenties were hard-edged and cynical; no positive relation to the past, let alone the present, was allowed to surface in these examinations of manners and mores among the middle class and the rebellious youth that Progressive Era America had spawned. In rebellion from her girlhood in the Midwest, Herbst's view of history stemmed from the paucity of imagination and the pious complacency she experienced growing up as a middle-class girl in Iowa. Herbst felt alienated from that culture; her detached prose style expressed the attempt to escape from the past.

In this sense, the constraints of femininity were intertwined with cynicism toward the past. Though she saw that relations between men and women had dramatically changed in the early twentieth century, for her this was no revolution. Her two early novels pessimistically exposed the dynamics of the sexual revolution by dissecting both small-town, middle-class life and bohemian subculture. Her prose also was a form of rebellion from the gendering of literary style: Herbst's tough, colloquial language in these novels was compared to that of male writers such as Sherwood Anderson, Ernest Hemingway, and Nathanael West. Unlike other women writers of the period such as Djuna Barnes and Virginia Woolf, whose experimentation conveyed women's interior consciousness and thus subverted gender conventions, for Herbst gender was a determining force to which her characters responded like marionettes to jerks on their strings.[14]

In the flux and change that characterized the twenties, Herbst emphasized a current of disillusionment, noting that her pleasure as a writer came from "mocking and criticizing."[15] Though the present allowed little optimism, a return to the past was no solution either, for it was cloaked in the layers of a culture she had sought to escape. Women's constraining, heavy clothing at the turn of the century provided the terms of her rejection of the past in the 1920s:

Though we had put distance between ourselves and our origins, . . . we bore the stigmata of an early upbringing. It would take years to value the long shadows on the grass, the smell of homemade bread, the hum of telegraph wires in the winds of an empty prairie. Now we chose to remember the rustling long skirts, the heavily flowered hats, of mothers or older sisters whose tiny pinched waists had betrayed the stays of a cruel medieval corset.[16]

In recalling the heaviness and cruelty of long skirts and corset stays, Herbst suggested that her generation remembered the turn of the century only in terms of repression and constraint; as a result, this was a past that had little to offer them.[17]

Her reading of women's emancipation—which had flowered as a result of the social movement of women decades before—reinforced this pervasive sense of disillusionment with the past.

Who believed in the vote? Women had been given the vote, but if they were now "emancipated," it was not through suffrage but by jobs, birth control, even Prohibition. If a fine martial spirit existed between the sexes, it was a tonic and a splendor after so much sticky intermingling and backboneless worship of family and domesticated bliss.[18]

Unlike the vote, in which Herbst had little interest, the social relations of the sexes, the new heterosociality, and the expansion of women into the public sphere fundamentally shaped her sense of detachment from her parents' sensibility, and she shared these concerns with her contemporaries in her attempt to come to terms with the twenties. Herbst's perspective thus resonated with a history of feminism in which the twenties have been viewed as a period when young women both inherited and forsook the legacy of women's long struggle for political and economic rights. Herbst expressed a younger generation's rebellion from their foremothers, yet she forged a critique of any women's history that insisted on a narrow view of political rights as determining women's freedom.

Having come of age after World War I, Herbst was generally disenchanted with the ideals that had animated the spirit of reform among progressives, including feminists. But she did not uncritically accept the cultural trends of consumerism and mass media that made progressivism appear anachronistic. Her modernist generation, indeed, levied an even more acute critique of dominant culture. Disappointed with the idea of social and material progress, Herbst and her contemporaries saw that "progress" had become more identified with commodity culture, the worship of goods and things. She wrote in an essay published in the late 1950s,

> The illiberalism of the post-Wilsonian period had deepened the trough of what looked like incurable swinishness. The appalling inertia of human nature struck at those hopefuls who had counted on a different kind of progress than that signified by a headlong race from autos to radios to electric refrigerators to Tom Thumb golf courses.[19]

Criticizing a mistaken faith in modernization among progressive intellectuals and mocking the commodity culture that parodied their vision of abundance and social order, Herbst generalized this position of detachment in her memoir to convey generational rebellion: "'The lovely and the beautiful' became for our generation a term of contempt, the grounds for complacency held by the parents, despised."[20] Through this analysis, Herbst wrote within and not beyond a modernism that vilified commodity culture, including its gender politics that associated women with unproductive consumption.

In her novels, appropriately titled *Nothing Is Sacred* and *Money for Love,* Herbst created an arid world that focused on greed and hypocrisy among the middle class as well as on the inability of young people to find liberation in the new manners and mores for relationships, sexual behavior, and marriage. While *Nothing Is Sacred* (1928) gestured nostalgically toward an older set of values such as self-reliance and family dedication, modern culture made it impossible to sustain such values, and the characters Herbst created wander aimlessly, lacking a moral center. Leisure and prosperity, the hallmarks of modern America in the twenties, did not solve or even offer an escape from the alienation the progressives had fought so hard to overcome. Clearly, Herbst's themes evoked the failures of modern life after World War I.[21]

In her critique of the alienating effect of leisure on middle-class women's lives, she argued that women had lost the power of productivity. In a 1926 magazine article Herbst criticized women's consumption of literature as a symptom of a more general problem for women's freedom when it was defined as consumption.

> Half-baked knowledge has dulled rather than sharpened the Iowa female brain. The old pioneer types are gone. The shrill squeak of radios is in the land; automobiles race over perfect roads; new fangled lamps sprout from the floor. Everywhere the home is up-to-date, and everywhere the inhabitants are making the fight of the modern pioneers—a burlesqued,

impoverished fight against nothing more exciting than futility, meaning-less, ennui. With the bigger share of freedom in their hands, the women lead. But where they are going, none know.[22]

For her, commodity culture had severed women from a productive pio-neer ethos. Herbst's characterization of the frontier was romantic and nostalgic, with no hint of the potential uses of that past. In contrast to women settlers on the frontier, women living in the cities and suburbs of the now-prosperous, settled Middle West had the leisure to become "cul-tured," but their consumption of literature, like their consumption of lamps, left them predictably both bored and unproductive.

Herbst's critique of consumer culture was rooted in an avant-garde fear of appropriation: no matter how subversive the rebellious modernist writ-ers on the literary frontier of the teens and twenties considered themselves to be, their work could be and was brought into the leisured, unproductive world of consumer culture and middle-class life. Herbst's rebellion from women's culture in Iowa and her invention of herself as a bohemian woman writer thus was analogous to a more general spirit of retreat among her contemporaries. Unlike the clubwomen in Iowa who lost their productive power in being freed from domestic labor, Herbst redefined the terms of "being productive" by writing novels. In them, she developed a writing style that resisted recuperation by bourgeois culture; indeed, her style was considered a threat to the novel form itself. In this, Herbst's rebel-lion from conventional understanding of gender and the cultural practices of women were linked to her sense of herself as an avant-garde writer.

Herbst's second novel, *Money for Love,* situated a group of young people in bohemia "under the hard edge of metropolitan economic life," as critic Clifton Fadiman put it.[23] The novel's characters are burdened by thwarted aspirations; pessimistic about the present, they also disavow the past and are paralyzed by the thought of the future. Though Herbst's *Money for Love* addressed many of the issues of other "modern woman" novels, including women's quest for independence and newly refashioned definitions of sexuality, it shared none of the optimistic hope invested in characters such as Floyd Dell's Janet March. Herbst's story replaced the romance plot of novels like Dell's with a different anatomy of the New Morality. Its doleful consequences were not freedom, but, rather, in-fidelity, abortion, and extortion. As the title indicated, the new sexual freedom for women, to Herbst, was reducible to an economic exchange.

Despite Herbst's determination to resist appropriation by critiquing women's habits, the reception of her writing was nevertheless affected by the gender politics of modernism and sentimentalism. The themes of *Money for Love* did not disturb reviewers as much as Herbst's detached style did. Herbst related her tale of men's and women's inability to find love and happiness in prose that offered little psychological insight or descriptive texture. Fadiman wrote in *The Nation*:

> If her books can be said to celebrate anything it is the extinction of the heroic. The emotions of all her characters are, as it were, stepped down, reduced several degrees. Love is not transformed into lust (for that is a romantic transformation) but minimized into a kind of weary attraction. The impulse of pleasure never blackens to viciousness but grays to a dull desire for the simpler anodynes: cheap liquor, superficial literary culture, banal . . . conversations.[24]

The problem for reviewers was not that the story itself was degraded and shallow—they all understood Herbst's point about "the dismal unimportance of most American lives."[25] Rather, the reviews articulated anxiety over a literary style that so closely approximated the banality and smallness of commonplace lives. For the *New York Times* reviewer, the colorless prose matched the dullness of the characters so well that the novel could not be considered literature at all, for it failed to provide "those truly enriching and permeative effects which constitute—unacademically—the real province of creative art."[26] Herbst conveyed so successfully a sense of detachment that it suffused the reading experience itself and threatened the category of art. The reviewer for the *Bookman* stated the problem clearly: "This is the type of book that makes one wish with a fanatic's fervor for some law to protect the novel form."[27]

Herbst's jaundiced focus on the economics of sexual relationships but especially the style of her "colorless prose" placed her in what was considered both a masculine and a modernist "school of austere detachment" that cut her off from a tradition of women's writing that celebrated female consciousness. Herbst was accused of imitating Ernest Hemingway in both her subject and style but criticized for not doing it as well as him. As one reviewer wrote, "Miss Herbst's simple sentences are so colorless they become monotonous; she has nothing of Hemingway's raciness or bite."[28] Behind this question of style, however, was the problem of gender, which is at stake when raciness turns into sordidness.

Condemned for writing "like a man" but not as well, Herbst responded to the reviews of *Money for Love* in an essay published in the *New Masses*. The essay was significant for its expression of anger and brutal irony, but even more so, astonishing for the precision with which it identified how women's writing suffered under gendered distinctions between modernism and sentimentalism. In the essay Herbst disputed the insidious belief that writing novels with nurturing and civilizing uses was cultural work that naturally fell to women. And it argued against the idea that women's writing must convey emotional intensity. Written in the style of avant-garde manifestos, the essay used an experimental style to convey anger and irony. It also parodied the voice of reviewers, exposing their tone of condescension and moral uplift.

> Now your stories are too bitter, what they need is more emotion as if this country wasn't already rotten with emoting authors. You have fine characterization but more tenderness is what you need. Page the *Ladies' Home Journal* and that tender button, the *Bookman*. . . . What we need today is EMOTION AND TENDERNESS AND MOTHER LOVE. Especially a return of that and of the more wholesome things. And the next thing you do, why not try to make it less—well, less sordid. . . . But really, you are too hard. For a woman, you are too, shall I say, bitter about life. . . . People do have good times you know, and look at the happy couples you see around you![29]

Herbst's parody showed that while she may have detached herself from genres such as the domestic novel or the romance, the culture at large was still wedded to them, a dynamic that limited her as a woman as well as a modernist writer.

Despite Herbst's anger toward those reviewers and critics who sought to contain her art within narrow, preestablished roles for women writers, her intense focus on the bankruptcy of modern life provided no hint that new genres would be any more hospitable to writing by women. Instead, her themes and style displayed her detached disaffection regarding celebrations of the supposed freedom and liberation that modern women experienced in the twenties. Herbst's fiction in the twenties cast a disquieting light on the figure of the modern woman in both style and substance. Her work showed little interest in the independence, romance, sense of adventure, and equal partnership with men as both lovers and comrades that modern women gained with the new cultural mores. Herbst's early fiction thus not only cut the modern woman off from history, it also gave little critical force to the act of emancipation itself. Stylistically, as one reviewer wrote, Herbst's stories were "emptied of glamour and meaning," leaving the reader with a "pretty acute feeling of spiritual nausea."[30]

Herbst herself did not remember the twenties with glamour, as her comments on the trim, streamlined styles of fashion make clear: "Hats with brims became helmets out of which the face pressed, egglike, from a nest too tight."[31] But these critiques of women's fashions in clothing and in writing were part of a larger critique of the signs of rebellion and liberation in the twenties. The gendered aspects, both in the constraints Herbst experienced as a woman writer experimenting in a rigid, austere prose that was understood as both masculine and modernist, and her belief that futility and alienation had accompanied women's "emancipation," were signs of a more general untenability of cultural politics.

Disenchantment with the "Shock of the New"

In turning to this period in her memoirs, Herbst addressed the rejection of both history and dominant culture that she herself had expressed in the twenties. She criticized the attempt by bohemians, including herself, to escape from rather than reconstitute American life. Archetypally bohemian as a young writer in the twenties, Herbst lived in cold-water flats in New York and in a dilapidated farmhouse nearby in Connecticut. "If we had abandoned the safe lives our parents had fancied so valuable, we seemed to have gained an insight into the creative fissures of the world" (73). Yet her representation of the life of bohemian abandonment did not escape the tendency to "mock and criticize" that informed her historical outlook. The city was indeed a site of liberation from complacent bourgeois life, but it was also the site of dissipation and meaningless play in the midst of a drifting moral order. The countryside offered a respite from modernity that deferred social or political action. The "creative fissures of the world" thus also revealed a political pessimism, a blurry response to changing social mores and a cacophony of competing voices striving to define the avant-garde.

When Herbst looked back at the period in her memoirs, she felt that the revolution in language she herself had participated in was empty of meaning and that its wavering positions on the political status of art and its efficacy as a political tool demanded "sterner answers." She wrote, citing one of the little magazines that had produced the "revolution of the word": "[T]hough you might snatch at a new transition as a member of an underground might pore over a secret leaflet for a possible direction to action, [you could not] always respond with a throb of conviction. There was a scatterbrained diffusiveness about some of these outpourings that aroused suspicion" (82). Her essay titled "A Year of Disgrace" thus focused on a shift in sensibility among her generation that also marked a distinct change in the culture of modernism, from the privileging of aesthetic and social detachment to the subsumption of "art" to the commitment to radical social change.

On one level, "A Year of Disgrace" described one year in Herbst's own life—1927—spent writing in rural Connecticut, working in New York, and sailing in Maine: it evoked the pleasures of a bohemian life. Yet on another level the essay addressed a more abstract problem: were there limits to the bohemian dedication to art and to aesthetic experience? Herbst accused herself and her generation of a kind of irresponsibility, of blinding themselves to social conditions outside themselves. In order to make this claim, however, Herbst evoked and provoked nostalgia for this period, its freshness, vitality, and experimental drive. Even though Herbst sought to show the 1920s as a period in which art and politics were intermixed, her perspective was inflected by her later convictions; she couldn't resist the attempt to knock down the "fetish" of the alienated artist. The essay revealed that the artistic declaration of detachment from the realm of politics was itself a political act. Moreover, the detachment of writers and artists from their social and cultural conditions prevented an assessment of the very consequences of this act of false detachment.

Herbst's use of her own persona and activities in this memoir was also significant as a historical act, because she focused on her sense of marginality and estrangement from the spirit of the times. Such a stance can dislodge our own complacent understanding of the very difference between the twenties and the thirties. In order to evoke the shifting sensibilities among modernists, she juxtaposed her response to two powerful events from that year, the premier of experimental composer George Antheil's "Ballet Mecanique" and the executions of Sacco and Vanzetti. Antheil's "Ballet Mecanique" used music and dance to imitate the sounds and movements of machines; in a larger sense, it performed the modernist fascination with the machine age. Herbst used the event of the noisy, riotous concert to identify the moment when "the revolution of the word" became an "idolatrous symbol of the inane" (82). Like her contrast of herself with Hemingway in Spain, Herbst felt the outsider at this "conclusive event." Having rushed to the concert with no time to change her clothes, she stood at the back of the hall as a witness to the event with messy hair and a coffee-stained sweater. In reconstructing the event forty years later, Herbst expressed her suspicion of the general mood of celebration among the modernists and their contempt for those conventional art lovers who walked huffily out of Antheil's experiment.

> What did the music mean? I longed to be moved . . . but it seemed to me I had heard no more than a hallelujah to the very forces I feared. My longing for a still, small voice, for a spokesman not for the crash of breakers on

the rock but for the currents, down under, that no eye could see, made me feel alone but not an alien. . . . Was Antheil to be the symbol of an opposition to the Philistine? In a corner of my heart a slow movement of the pulse began to turn my attention elsewhere. (84)

Herbst saw the event of the "Ballet Mecanique" as an extreme example of a dubious, uncritical celebration of the machine by modernists who joyously dismantled artistic convention without considering the loss of human consciousness that such a celebration entailed. Her suspicion of the machine age future produced a need to turn back to what had been forgotten about the past.

If the Antheil concert represented the failure of artistic representations of modernity, the parallel example in this essay was about modern politics. It considered the debilitating failure of the coalition of artists, writers, and radicals to gain the pardon of the anarchists Nicola Sacco and Bartolomeo Vanzetti, convicted, many thought falsely, of murder in 1920 and sentenced to death in 1921. Their case had been widely publicized in leftist magazines, and many of Herbst's contemporaries had been arrested in demonstrations at the Massachusetts prison where they were held. When the long-delayed executions finally occurred in 1927, many intellectuals ceased to believe that reform of the current American system was possible or even desirable. However, the suppression of political dissent that their case had come to symbolize convinced many that revolution was necessary. For cultural history, the executions of Sacco and Vanzetti signaled more than the failure of an intellectual generation to save them from powerful state forces; it illustrated the failure of a detached, alienated posture toward social and political conditions. Yet rather than assign a single, determining meaning to their death and the failure it signified, Herbst used her experience of this event to reveal a transitional moment that included exhaustion and despair as well as hope and regeneration.

> All that I knew was that a conclusive event had happened. What it meant I couldn't have defined. Looking back from this distance, I might add explanations that would signify. But I don't want to do that. I want to try to keep it the way it was, back there, on the early morning of August 23, 1927 . . . a kind of shuddering premonition of a world to come. But what it was to be we could never have foreseen. (97)

Constructing the concert and the execution as the moments that defined the end of the twenties, rather than the more conventional focus on the crash of the stock exchange, Herbst actually tried to show the continuities between the twenties and the thirties. Though the chronology reiterated a distinction between art and politics, the memoirs as a whole continually return to the debate, thus demonstrating the importance of both for defining American modernism.

This juxtaposition shed light on Herbst's own position in the twenties as one who had worked within a style that effaced human agency and will in a machine-like method of austere detachment. It also suggested in a more tangential way that Herbst began to change her attitude toward "the past," to relinquish her tendency to "mock and criticize," which influenced her understanding of gender relations. At the root of her alienation from both avant-garde and dominant culture was the sense that it was not usable, no longer generative as either an artistic medium for her writing or as a coherent social vision. But by precisely dating the end of the twenties in this way, Herbst established in her memoirs the terms of the transition from "the twenties" and its detachment from history to "the thirties" and its engagement with the past.

Herbst ended her interpretation of these events in 1927 by saying, "It would be three years before we took down a volume of Kuntsgeschichte from our shelves, to be replaced by a thin narrow book in red entitled *What Is to Be Done?*, by V. I. Lenin." Political action, in other words, supplanted artistic exploration in the crisis of the 1930s. This change was not as easy to make as such a simple swap would suggest. While the position of detachment gave little critical force to Herbst's reversal of gender conventions in her writing of the twenties, the political turn sharpened her gender analysis, including the stakes of "writing like a man" and the evocation of women's experiences.

The Gender Politics of the Usable Past

Just as Herbst infused the modernist twenties with political sympathies and currents, her discussion of the thirties encourages us to view the "red decade" as a continuation of modernist concerns. By broadly defining *modernism* as a historical culture, it becomes clear that the alienation from American culture after World War I and the rediscovery of America during the Depression era expressed the dialectical quality of modernist thought and art. The distinction between art and politics as analogous to the difference between the "twenties" and the "thirties" thus was not as extreme or superficial as Herbst's changing library appeared. Nevertheless, there was a crucial change in attitude: after decades of proclaiming that they had rejected history and its hold upon them, modernists turned back to the past in order to explain the crisis of the present. This new relation to history deeply informed Herbst's major work of the period. Her trilogy of novels, *Pity Is Not Enough* (1933), *The Executioner Waits* (1934), and *Rope of Gold* (1939), expressed the modernism forged in the Depression era, what Michael Denning has called "the extraordinary flowering of the historical imagination in Popular Front fiction, film, music, and art."[32]

The search for a usable past was part of what cultural historian Warren Susman has called "the culture of commitment."[33] Based in part on Van Wyck Brooks's 1918 interpretation of early America, the usable past was an idea about finding a purpose for history in the present, an impulse that became acute in the growing crisis of the Great Depression. In order to heal the economic ills of the nation, many argued, the idea of America itself had to be rediscovered and communicated anew. The impulse to communicate what was "usable" about the past could be seen in a wide array of artistic mediums; it was encouraged in the public art projects initiated under Roosevelt's New Deal programs; it informed major trends in documentary photography and literature; and it fueled anthropology, especially the collection of interviews with former slaves and efforts to preserve mountain folkways.[34] Broadly defined, the search for a usable past was an effort to recover the sources of and to give meaning to the experiences of the marginal and the dispossessed of the Depression, to embrace a more populist style of the vernacular and the folk with an unsentimental view of the effects of social and economic conditions on the lives of a wide array of people. This was not only a question of shifting the focus of cultural expression from the upper class to the working class, but a question of value and meaning as well; looking at the past from the bottom up also meant valuing a different social order in the present. For modernists, including Herbst, who stood for a radical transformation of American society, then, the usable past was an idea that helped them redefine their relation to modernity in the crisis of the Depression.[35]

The "past," however, was not a placid reservoir of events and trends; in discovering the past, the meaning of the present was destabilized. Herbst wrote, evoking a mythic structure for history: "[S]ome of us pried open the Pandora box of the past to see what had once lived there."[36] Characterizing the widespread movement to "rediscover America" as a historical awakening that included both outward exploration and an inward process of remembering, she elaborated in another essay:

> The writers did pry the lids off old cesspools; they did explore old roads, little streams, forsaken meadows. Their awakened sense of America helped

to recover a tradition and a heritage that had been lost track of; in seeking a spirituality that might prevail for their day. They turned with a guilty recollection to a heritage that had been too long neglected.[37]

The "they" of Herbst's collective representation might as well have been "I." What distinguished her early fiction in the twenties from the series of novels Herbst began in the early thirties was her idea to use the novel form to infuse contemporary events with historical resonance. While a turn to history is often understood as abandoning experiment in favor of documenting reality and truth, in documentary realism these two impulses were often conjoined. Often compared to John Dos Passos's USA, Herbst's "Trexler trilogy" did not abandon experimentation with literary form. The trilogy used an array of narrative devices, including multiple points of view, letters and newspaper clippings, episodic narratives, and bits of "found writing," to tell a central story about the failure of American capitalism to fulfill middle-class aspirations. Instead of providing an overarching moral center in one character, Herbst's novels strove for a more documentary effect; they blended the thoughts and concerns of ordinary people with the authority and structure that real facts and events imparted. These fictions thus resembled a history written from the bottom up; they engaged with the social and material conditions of ordinary people and included both public demonstrations of political struggle and private dramas of family conflict.

The turn to history in documentary novels attempted to infuse the past with the fissures of modernity, intertwining modernist concerns with fragmentation with the imperative of revealing the dislocations of the economic crisis. Herbst's trilogy mapped the experience of its characters onto the landscape of economic crisis, both past and present. Its central themes were the economic and psychological failures that revealed the contradictions in the drive for success—the ideology of American middle-class life that Herbst saw plague her own family and that she hoped to escape. While separate characters prosper or sink into poverty, the melange of stories in the trilogy works to convince the reader that capitalism as both an economic system and a social organization has failed to provide either material abundance or a moral and psychological anchor in a world of crisis and depletion.

In contrast to the static qualities of alienation that characterized her earlier work, the evidence that Herbst assembled in the trilogy enacted a dialectic between the failure of a social order and the emergence of the consciousness necessary to change those conditions. Her polemical posture in 1936 reflected the change. "All of the qualities that we term 'American' are rich and useful—the marvelous idiom, the variegated pattern of events almost overpowering in their diversity. America to me is a country that has never fulfilled itself; it will only do so through the processes of revolution."[38] In this manner, Herbst designed the novels to take the reader through those processes of revolution.

The trilogy documented a family legacy of records, diaries, and letters and connected these quotidian sources to the more abstract concept of the usable past. It thus told a version of American history from the post–Civil War period to the late 1930s, but from the point of view of people who were rather commonplace citizens. Herbst explained,

> My family provided me with an extensive laboratory record of American life. The first of my people had a grant of land from William Penn long before the American Revolution. The family were inveterate letter-writers and diary-keepers. They left a fine chain of written evidence. . . . The duty toward political life before the Civil War turned to cynicism and get-what-you-can after the war. Darwin was discussed, the Haymarket murders put a mark on them all.[39]

Because her family's story was long, tangled, and yet unexceptional, it was inextricable from touchstones of historical consciousness in the nineteenth century: the successive crises of the post–Civil War era, social Darwinism, and the violent labor battles symbolized by the hanging of the anarchists in Chicago in 1887. These events represented the cultural formation and economic upheaval wrought during the Gilded Age, the crucible of American modernity.

Just as she understood the events of her own time—the Antheil concert, the executions of Sacco and Vanzetti—as unstable, Herbst's worldview was situated within a sense of the ambiguity of meaning in historical events, and the novels attempted to reflect that in their structure. Herbst, then, did not use the family past to provide a glimpse of a classless society, nor to simply mirror the material conditions of the "actual" world. Rather, she used the past to establish continuity with an embattled present, to make sense of the struggles of her characters, both to record their psychic legacies and to speculate on what could rouse them to change their lives.

Though Herbst was widely respected in the thirties as a writer who helped shape the genre of documentary realism and who employed the idea of the usable past, she continued to face the gendering of style and marginality. Ironically, her work was often left out of literary history.[40] Acutely identifying this problem, critic and novelist Harvey Swados wrote,

Of all the imaginative and rebellious writers of the depression decade, Josephine Herbst . . . has been perhaps the most seriously underestimated and surely the most actively adventurous. Like a legendary reporter, she had the knack of being in the significant place at the crucial moment, and of being on a footing of comradely equality with many of the most important figures of the day. With the exception of John Dos Passos, no other writer at work in the thirties had ever attempted a fictional reconstruction of American life as sweeping and ambitious as Josephine Herbst's trilogy, *Pity Is Not Enough, The Executioner Waits* and *Rope of Gold.*[41]

Despite Swados's intention to restore Herbst to visibility, he actually articulated the problem that many women writers faced, especially when situating them in the period meant creating an analogy between the person and the period. Herbst was "like the thirties" because she wrote "like" Dos Passos, and was on a "footing of comradely equality" with the central figures of the day. As he went on to discuss specific elements of Herbst's writing, Swados used examples from her trilogy that describe male comradeship during a farmers' strike.

The "recovery" of Herbst recapitulated the gender dynamics in the reception of her novels in the thirties. Reviewers often attributed a masculine quality to the large scale of Herbst's historical canvas, the use of a vernacular prose style, and an unsentimental view of the effects of social and economic conditions on the lives of a wide array of characters. The reviewer for the *New York Times* commented, "Miss Herbst writes . . . with a fierce, masculine virility that does not falter at the language of the beer joint and the lavatory."[42] In a change from the reception of her twenties novels, critics asserted that she actually wrote better than men in this gendered space and language:

> "Rope of Gold" . . . is better written than any of Dos Passos's novels, and depends little on tricks. . . . No one, not even Hemingway or Lewis, has a surer sense and command of the vernacular, and . . . it might be added that Miss Herbst yields nothing to Dos Passos or Hemingway scatologically.[43]

Herbst was often lauded for being better than a man at being able to convey with a "cold exactitude" the class struggle during the Depression.[44] Since this exactitude and earthy expression were precisely what was desired as illustrations of the rediscovery of America, Herbst was admitted "like a man" to the genre of documentary realism, becoming a writer of the people and not a decadent aesthete.

Despite their appreciation for the authenticity of expression in the novels, reviewers were confused by the elaborate tapestry of details woven into the long novels. "Miss Herbst's pattern is elaborate, but one could admire its careful intricacy more whole-heartedly if only there were a key to the labyrinth."[45] Indeed, the attention to the details of daily life in a wide array of characters and narrative voices was aesthetically rich, but it denied the reader's pleasure in locating a revolutionary purpose through identification with one character, as reviewer after reviewer pointed out. "In spite of this rich picture of social movement, the novel is not dramatic; it has no powerful, pointed scenes . . . no clash of resolute wills."[46] One reviewer wrote that he was not convinced by the necessity for revolution because "revolutionary longing" was not located in any single character.[47] Herbst's novels did not seem to achieve their didactic purpose: readers were supposed to be aroused to revolution, but they weren't sure which character's story to follow. The novels thus failed to teach their readers what was "usable" about the past.

Assumptions about gender infused this critical theme in the reception of Herbst's novels; it was difficult if not impossible to disentangle "revolutionary longing" from masculine ideals about the heroic worker so common in the literary and visual art of the period. The tension between the panoramic scope of the trilogy and the absence of a "revolutionary" plot and character was also a problem of gender; it originated from Herbst's inclusion of domestic space and female characters. Her rediscovery of the past explicitly framed the larger historical canvas of the novels, but it was filtered through her mother's family lore and personal documents composing the family history, including letters and diaries. Using a common device in documentary fiction, Herbst inserted interchapters between the narratives that form the bulk of the novels; these tell how a daughter, named Victoria Wendel, recollected and retold her mother's stories. A central narrator emerges, then, literally in the margins of the work, but the interchapters nevertheless are history told from a woman's point of view. Victoria Wendel is also a modernist and feminist, significant identities since she shapes the reader's understanding of the events of the past. Herbst's focus on family history from a feminist modernist point of view—one that expressed great longing, but sadly, no revolution—destabilized but ultimately enriched the concept of the usable past.

The first volume of the Trexler trilogy begins in the early twentieth century with Victoria's mother, Anne, and her four daughters weathering a cyclone in Iowa huddled in the basement of their house. Anne tells bits and pieces of family lore to distract the girls, but her tales nevertheless are an allegory of the crisis outside. "She made a little island of her past and climbed aboard with all her dead and gone and took us children too, clinging and listening, fascinated and scared."[48] Later, the stories gain a crucial material dimension for the daughters in the family heirlooms and bags and boxes of letters, diaries, and newspaper clippings stored in disarray in the attic of the family house. The documents and heirlooms enable Victoria to take hold of the past and to give it her own meaning. Family documents were also central to Herbst's sense of history. "The first inkling I had of the complexity and significance of people in relation to each other and to the world came from these documents. . . . Living seemed constantly fertilized and damned by the tragic burden one generation passed to the next."[49] In the fictional framework Victoria's act of giving meaning to the documents is the story the trilogy has to tell, from the island of the mother's memory to the complexity and interrelations of the daughter's sense of history.

Significantly, the letters and artifacts tell the family's story through their effects on the women who receive and keep them. The men set out to make their fortunes, and their letters home, the diaries they keep, the newspaper accounts of their successes and their troubles comprise the family records. The reader understands the story through the documents' effects on the women who stay at home.

> She collected all of her father's diaries and old letters and began reading them. . . . She felt like a nun, closed in and shut tight from the world. She was earning her living, helping the family, went to church, wrote to relatives, and while she had been puttering with the past, digging up old names, Aaron had been living. . . . Sometimes lately she had no desire to go to Sunday school and stayed home instead cutting out clippings from papers about duty and the home and womenly women.[50]

This passage conveys a dynamic of gender in history: Victoria's uncles ventured forth to pursue their fortunes while her aunts waited and worried at home, while maintaining the routines and patterns of domestic life to which the men return. This dynamic not only imparts a subjective dimension and everyday texture to women's perspectives but sheds light on the secret destructiveness of men's desires to "make a fortune." Instead of celebrating women's lives in the nineteenth and early twentieth centuries, Herbst applied the concept of a usable past to the structures and psychic legacies that constricted those lives.

Victoria's experience is shaped by and rooted in these events, even as she attempts to escape from the cycle of thwarted desire. The storehouse of family history, then, is both a treasure and a dangerous burden that

Victoria both assesses and negotiates. Should those in the present destroy the past, ignore it, or attempt to come to terms with it? Victoria and her sister repeatedly attempt to destroy the family record, thinking that by burning the record of the past they could free themselves from it.

> The two younger girls . . . thought it was about time some of the old papers were burned instead of cluttering up bags and boxes. Somehow they began to read one old letter and then another and for hours they sat there piecing together the dead and gone. . . . The two girls had come to burn, now they wrapped the old papers together, tied them and dusted their hands. They knew the papers would go with them and wondered how far. (201)

As Victoria comes of age, she pieces together the family's struggles with the historical events that enable her to connect with a radical tradition.

> The Wendel girls . . . came on a yellowed newspaper with an account of the Haymarket Riot and the hanging of the anarchists and their silent defense. . . . The words carried over the years, they suddenly wondered what that paper had meant to Uncle Joe and they began to talk about him and to feel that the paper had a relation to themselves. . . . [I]n their thoughts this dead uncle was not the successful man who had bought silver and fine clothes but a man who pretty thoroughly failed. Now in their bones the Wendel girls felt alive and as if they had a clue to living. They were ready to burn all the old papers but Victoria said it would be a shame to do that to poor Joe. (189–90)

The family documents also convey the mother's desire for her daughters to break away from being "womenly women." Anne Wendel tells Victoria, "'Don't be stupid and shut your eyes and imagine that the only things in life worth while come from men and what people call romance,' she used to say when she . . . tried to find ways to tell her girls how best to live" (80). Like her uncles, Victoria embarks on her own adventure, not to make "her fortune" but to get out into the world, to "live." When Victoria does marry, the mother sends as a wedding present some of the family letters: "Perhaps in her daughter's life all the wrongs that the Trexlers had suffered would be made right." Victoria, however, did not accept their lesson: "She did not have her mother's glorified ideas of the past. . . . [S]he was tired of pity . . . All their good generous qualities were in danger of trapping them, not helping them, in a world where the plums went to the biggest thieves."[51] Even as she became a free-thinking bohemian and worked as a journalist, the letters nevertheless tied her to the womanly past.

The documents in *Rope of Gold* are the lens through which Victoria understands her own life. "[T]he past had a way of tolling, like some bell. It could bring you to a dead stop in the middle of the day." Without the power to transcend her history, her eventual marriage to a writer named Jonathan Chance could not survive the heavy weight of both this domestic history and the necessity to change a world they see rushing toward catastrophe. While Jonathan follows the conventional path of the masculine intellectual, Victoria's path is more difficult to recognize. She at first occupies that marginal place assigned to women in the movement as the wife of a man who sloughs off his identity as a writer to become a communist organizer. The novel places Victoria in the central locations of intellectual life and activism during the thirties, but she is repeatedly characterized as "being completely cut off from the people around her."[52]

This characterization of Victoria thus injects a critical note into the "rediscovery" of America; as a marginal figure she observes the downside of the new radicalism—the armchair dogma of urban leftists, the tension between farmers in crisis and the reporters roaming the countryside eager to document them, the hypocrisy of organizers who forsake personal responsibility for the public engagement with class struggle. Victoria is stuck in the position of an agonizing observer who chronicles the problems but cannot get beyond them. Victoria embraces and refuses to give up a radical view of the world, but she is equivocal, passive, and unhappy. Herbst invested hope in Victoria Chance's name—the "chance" to escape an older model of femininity symbolized by the English queen—but this did not come to fruition in her drawing of the character. The character inherits the past and thus is the conscience of the trilogy, but her ambivalence does not allow the reader to assimilate her vision of history into a morally resolute position; she is neither a revolutionary hero nor does she show why the idea of a revolutionary hero in a historical novel devoted to women's lives would be wrong. The problem lies in the documentary genre's approach to history, which attempts to let real and varied voices speak about events but also to leave the reader with a definite opinion about what to think about those events. Herbst's trilogy is devoted to an objective, materialist rendering of implacable historical forces, but that project conflicts with letting Victoria's point of view surface.

Victoria's marginality in her own story mirrors Herbst's own position in the literary culture of the thirties. While this long work of fiction may have represented the dynamic forces of history and women as subjects of history, the figure of Victoria was only one model of femininity that Herbst imagined. Reading Victoria through Herbst's other female characters makes it possible to see how Herbst located the difficulty of actually using the past in the dilemmas of writing and political action in the present. In this way, Herbst's movement toward documenting and changing the situation of Americans mired in the Depression was double, an inward movement toward reconfiguring her relation to the past, and an outward movement into the sites of struggle in the present as an activist striving to capture the "real" in the documentary imagination. This reflection on history and immersion in the present moment of crisis and confrontation was characteristic in a larger sense of the dynamics of feminism and modernism.

Reportage and the Uses of Femininity

The search for a usable past was a rationalization for action in the present. Thus while Herbst presented her interpretation of the past in the trilogy, she also used her experiences as a journalist both to report on important events and to make them usable in the context of radical politics in the thirties. This activity broadly was known as *reportage,* which blended journalism and the storytelling devices of fiction, often making real events into inspiring examples for future political action. Reportage elevated the events of workers' uprisings, revolutions, and other acts of resistance into influential models. As Charlotte Nekola and Paula Rabinowitz explain, "It was the ideal form of writing for revolutionary and proletarian aesthetic: it was 'true,' without the distortions or excess of bourgeois individualistic fiction; it used the individual in the service of the mass; it raised political consciousness by linking one person with larger political movements; it replaced private despair with mass action."[53] Thus the perspective of the reporter was central: the reporter possessed authenticity by participating in the fray and authority by taking those events into the larger arena of political thought. As the Hungarian modernist Georg Lukacs wrote, "Genuine reportage is in no way content simply to depict the facts: its descriptions always present a connection, disclose causes and propose consequences."[54] Herbst covered many events as a reporter, including the agricultural crisis in the Midwest in the midthirties, the Kharkov Writers' Congress in Russia in 1930, the Scottsboro trials, and the rise of Nazi Germany.

The attempt by Cuban farmers to establish a sugarcane soviet in 1935 inspired Herbst to write several pieces of reportage. Herbst went to Cuba on an assignment for the *New Masses* to report on the soviet, known as Realengo 18. While she was in Havana, a student uprising was violently suppressed by Batista's government. The *New Masses* published "A Passport to Realengo 18" in July 1935, and it was often reprinted, becoming the most successful of all of her works of journalism. Her experience in Cuba also formed the basis for a short story, "The Enemy," as well as a long section in *Rope of Gold*. The situation in Cuba represented a microcosm of both the possibilities and the costs of struggling for economic and political freedom, and it in turn provoked Herbst to consider her role as a modern woman engaged in this struggle as both a radical and a reporter. Taken together, her writings about Cuba revealed the problematic tightrope act that reportage entailed for women: how could one write both as a woman and as a voice for political protest?

In covering these events, Herbst had entered spaces still considered untraditional for women; that novelty forced a confrontation between sexual politics and revolutionary politics. Herbst used the problem of femininity to explore the dilemmas of political action itself, and in doing so she raised important questions about writing, femininity, and the basis for political action, questions that challenge the masculinist ideology predominant in thirties writing. Herbst showed how useful femininity was in a political arena, but also that consciousness of sex was unstable as a source for both ideological and experiential knowledge.

The Cuba section in *Rope of Gold* reveals how private despair was mitigated by the political act of reportage. As in many novels of the Depression era, economic and political crisis lead to romantic crisis in *Rope of Gold,* and Cuba is the setting for the disintegration of Victoria's marriage. "It's no good," Victoria says to Jonathan, "if it always comes back to whether I love you or not. I love you all right. . . . The trouble is the earth's shaking and we stand here talking about love."[55] Victoria is caught by irreconcilable demands that pit her activities as a reporter against the survival of her marriage. In the novel, however, Herbst emphasized the private arena; Cuba is merely a backdrop for Victoria's romantic anguish.

As Victoria sits in a hotel room in Havana trying to write Jonathan a letter, Batista's troops are violently suppressing a student rebellion in the streets.

The words looked bloated and deformed with her tears. If there were something she could send him to remind him so he would speak again. . . . She reached for the scissors and pulling up her skirts cut quickly. The letter felt springy and soft; she took it downstairs to mail quickly. . . . As she stepped out to the street, a shrill "Don't go out, Señora" made her hesitate but she walked firmly to the corner, dropped the letter in the box and returning heard the hotel clerk's angry voice, "Lady, there's shooting. Do you want to get killed?"[56]

Without language, Victoria sent a bodily reminder of their marriage, risking physical danger to do so but ignoring the violence around her.

In contrast to sending a demonstrative yet inarticulate love letter, Victoria's reporting gives her another language to express her despair. Discovering upon her return from Cuba that Jonathan has left her, Victoria suffers as if she is a casualty of a war. She survives her private ordeal, however, by appropriating the political language of the Cuban resistance.

> A terrible pounding shook her body and she must hurry for fear something should break inside and she might drown in blood. She sat down and began hammering the typewriter keys. It was like an antidote to poison, the harder she struck the keys, the quieter she became. She pushed back everything, way back, and as if this might be the last deed she would ever do, as if the guns had already been mounted and were training upon that very room, she finished, stuffed the long envelope, put on the airmail stamp and dropped it in the box.[57]

This section of the novel reiterates but cannot transcend the split between politics and love, public and private that runs throughout reportage; political writing and not love letters enable Victoria to survive. She reestablishes her connection to the world by reaffirming her commitment to public, political activity. *Rope of Gold* demonstrates the liberating effect reportage has for Victoria—yet it stops short of showing how reportage itself enacts gender roles.

This private, interior rendering of the act of reportage was displaced in the actual story Herbst filed for the *New Masses*. Herbst's consciousness of sex disappears in "Passport to Realengo 18," and instead she casts herself as an observing stranger who could either be a man or a woman. In contrast to the white suits of the sugar agents, she wrote, "I am a stranger in a pair of overalls and a blue workshirt sitting astride a very bony and mangy horse."[58] By describing herself not as a woman but as a sympathetic stranger attempting to blend in with the workers she was visiting, Herbst's voice attains the objective authenticity valued in reportage. The barriers of language and national identity that stood between the reporter and the Cuban farmers were overcome by a common international perspective. "Passport" was a classic example of reportage expressly because Herbst emphasized her sense of commonality with the people whose story she was reporting rather than her difference from them.

Realengo 18 is a small spot on a small island and we have been discussing the problems of this island, its relation to the world. Every person in the room has been weighed down with the great bulk of the United States pressing from above on that map drawn upon the floor. We have been looking at the map and feeling the powers that are against this small island in its battle for freedom. The visa is a kind of magic that restores everyone.[59]

The reader of the *New Masses* was encouraged to appreciate the achievements of the sugarcane farmers through the connections Herbst established between their struggle and the U.S. struggle. Herbst again was on a footing of "comradely equality," marked by the absence of any discussion of her role as a woman and by her clear identification with the male leaders of the soviet. Despite the hardships the Cuban farmers faced, Realengo 18 was represented as a utopian, free space in which the female reporter could androgynously blend as both an ambassador and writer, helping to transmit the message of Realengo 18 beyond the island.

As a result, while Victoria is circumscribed within private language and bodily tokens of femininity in *Rope of Gold*, "Passport" effaces the reporter's consciousness of sex in order to carry an international message beyond the private sphere. The fact that the reporter could not be seen and heard as a woman, read here as symptomatic of the problem of women's participation in the modernist turn to effecting political change, has been read elsewhere as exactly its strength: "Passport" has been reprinted and cited as an excellent example of reportage partly because gender does not "get in the way" of its expression of revolutionary identity.

Herbst's 1936 short story, "The Enemy," however, confronts these concerns by focusing on the multiple roles of the female reporter, exploring both private consciousness and public displays of commitment. As an example of reportage fiction, "The Enemy" explores the position of the woman reporter in Cuba that Herbst did not reveal in the piece for the *New Masses*. It neither effaces femininity nor traps its expression within private despair.[60] Rather, the story makes gender visible and thus usable in the genre of reportage. "The Enemy" intertwines the discourses of sexuality, language and political action, placing the narrator's consciousness of herself as a woman at the center of the story. In the process, the story destabilizes the dichotomy between the femininity of romantic love and the masculinity of political action that was so frequently asserted in thirties modernism.[61]

Again the setting is the revolutionary movement in Cuba, which a woman reporter is covering for a radical magazine in the United States. The protagonist of "The Enemy," Mrs. Sidney, uses both the conventions of reportage and different expressions of femininity to survive an evening of bloodshed and subterfuge during a strike. In order to get her story, Mrs. Sidney wears two different masks of the "other": the American tourist and the Anglo bourgeois woman. She is a tourist for the voyeurs on the street and in the hotels: "To keep herself free and above suspicion she must continue to walk, to look aimless, to buy foolish souvenirs, stare at the capital like a tourist and be indifferent to death."[62] At the same time, she is a sob sister in the eyes of the sugar company officials, "a little sentimental about the poor and oppressed but then she was a woman with a woman's heart and the administration had no wish to antagonize such people. . . . She put a smiling face on like a mask, turning soft and feminine" (97, 99). To the rebels who are her main contacts she is a hard-hitting and canny sympathizer.

> In dreams those Cubans saw their story liberated . . . and they fancied that such long passionate pieces would appear in headlines in New York papers. . . . And underneath this phantasy . . . , the head heads that counted cynically on organization only to achieve their purpose allowed themselves to hoard a tiny hope that she might really stir up sympathy for their cause. (98)

Playing multiple roles, the story dramatizes femininity as a series of personas that enable the protagonist to negotiate the revolutionary situation in Cuba. Through its use of these different personas and masks, the story parodies the necessity of a single revolutionary identity, a demand common in Left rhetoric of the period. "Trouble is, you're a bourgeois pessimist," a character known as "the man" tells Mrs. Sidney when she informs him that a student strike surely would be suppressed. Mrs. Sidney rejects this label even as she had played the role of a middle-class North American woman: "'Don't throw that word at me. Don't I can't stand it. A goddamned label. When am I going to get rid of it? What must I do?' She had her hands over her ears, looking at him furiously" (104). Though Mrs. Sidney angrily tries to cast off the label, her identification as a "bourgeois pessimist" shows the extent to which it was reserved for women who dared to express a critical relation to the tactics and aims of revolutionary movements. Yet through Mrs. Sidney's adoption of masks and roles, she undermines the possibility of a stable revolutionary identity. In a larger sense, the story dramatizes the problem of reportage as a synthesis of writing and action, using gender dynamics to expose the limitations of revolutionary ideology.

Ripping Holes in Ideology

The different approaches to gender in reportage reveal limitations for Herbst as a woman writer as well; Herbst's larger body of journalistic work in the thirties confirms that reportage required her either to erase any consciousness of sex or to assign the multiple roles of femininity to mere bourgeois pessimism. Thus, even as the act of reportage, as a synthesis of participation, sympathy, and writing within revolutionary situations, brought such a figure as Herbst to the center of struggle in the 1930s, it also recreated the terms of her own marginality. These difficult negotiations of femininity in the context of reportage about larger sites of struggle formed the foundation for her investigation of the usable past when she turned to writing her memoirs in the 1950s and 1960s. Her experiences as a reporter and a novelist in the thirties placed her at the center of major questions about the role of art and political commitment, but as the preceding discussions of the Trexler trilogy and her reportage demonstrate, these questions cannot be addressed without a consideration of gender politics. In her memoirs, Herbst took up the category of gendered experience as a tool to pry open both the ideology of the period and the reconstruction of literary and radical politics in scholarship on the thirties. The dynamic of political participation and feminine marginality, indeed, became what Herbst had to explain about the past, which she could only enact but not escape at the time.

Herbst's rendering of femininity as a position of marginality raised questions about ideology, the myths, symbols, and images of revolutionary change created in the culture of commitment. Though these emblems changed throughout the period—from the heroic worker, to the "people" as a figure of mass appeal, to the estranged social and political critic of Stalinism—they were always masculine emblems. Herbst was marginalized on both sides of the divide between the culture of commitment in the thirties and the forceful suppression of that culture in the forties and the fifties, on the one side because she was a woman, and on the other because she was a radical.

Herbst, thus, was in a significant position to challenge the cultural memory of literary radicalism; she was a sophisticated intellectual with wide knowledge of the period and yet had experienced marginality as a woman who was outside the myths, symbols, and images of literary ideology. Her experiences were eminently usable for a critique of the period. However, she did not use her own experience to claim that the ideologies were wrong or exclusive, but rather to explore the ways in which the function of ideology itself had marginalized her as a writer and an intellectual. All memoirs and autobiographies mold the flux of the past into a significant shape, for as gender historian Joan Scott has discussed, experience and its representation are inextricably connected: "It is a question of social categories, personal understanding, and language, all of which are connected, none of which are or can be a direct reflection of the others."[63] Herbst's memoirs express a particular consciousness about the stakes of that act; they not only tell us about the period of the twenties and the thirties now, but they render experience as a representational act. She wrote about the difficult, protracted process of writing her memoirs:

> For there are . . . problems to solve and technical devices to invent which will allow me to use the material I have to use, some of which is so painful that I can't do it directly but have to find its metaphor. . . . I can't even explain some things to myself—they are just there—and yet by relating them, by being able to see them in a concrete context . . . another dimension unfolds. And what I was interested in was the mutations, and then to ask, what central core, what dynamo keeps the whole business going.[64]

This passage meditated on the mechanics and devices used to create the product of historical narrative. In doing so it exposed the extent to which this act was a series of mutations and metaphors that prevented the revelation of naive, uncompromised "experience."

The representation of "experience" was not only a formal concern within the problem of autobiography as a genre; it was also at the heart of cultural politics of modernism from the late thirties through the fifties, a period in which anticommunism deeply shaped American intellectual life. The atmosphere of suspicion and accusation during World War II and the Cold War, as well as the blacklists and graylists that punished dissenting citizens across the country in many walks of life, affected Herbst on many levels. Her job opportunities were restricted, and she was accused of "Stalinism" by anticommunist intellectuals. In a more general sense the conservative climate made a writer like Herbst seem anachronistic. These factors contributed to a dynamic that the literary historian Cary Nelson has termed the repression of "cultural memory," in which the radical currents in art and literature were suppressed, forgotten, or neglected.[65] Astonishingly aware of this cultural process, Herbst's memoirs both show the mechanisms of that repression and attempt to allow radical experience to resurface and to become, again, usable.

Her memoirs address the interrelations of ideology and experience by returning to the themes of sexuality, language, and the desire for revolution, which were the themes she had struggled with as a writer and that shaped the experience for most women activists and intellectuals during the thirties. She began her memoir, "Yesterday's Road," with the moment at which her experience was constituted as an ideology, her investigation by the Civil Service Commission in 1943. She recognized that from the government's perspective there was very little gap between her experiences and activities and their expression as ideology. Unable to make a living as a writer and inspired to combat fascism and Nazism, Herbst had taken a government job in Washington, D.C., as a translator of American propaganda efforts against the Germans. She soon was fired, however, because she was suspected of being a communist, suspicions that had also prompted the investigation of her.[66] Interviewed by Civil Service investigators, whom Herbst called her "interlocutors," she was confronted by a series of statements that always began with the phrase "It is reported . . ." and then divulged evidence about her activities and affiliations in the thirties. The statements established an ideological fabric of incrimination, and Herbst, in turn, used the essay to rip holes in that fabric and to weave in her own perspective, retelling the stories behind the statements and describing what was at stake in those experiences. Little by little, Herbst wrenched her memory from the construction of her experience as subversive or treacherous.

While it was tempting to situate her interrogation as an example of governmental suppression of a more authentic political experience, for Herbst ideology cut both ways: modernists on the Left had also built a complex ideological structure for political truth. Herbst's memoirs thus refused to claim that she escaped ideology in the thirties. "Often I had miscalculated and misfired; often engaged in internal combat while in combat without."[67] Moreover, Herbst recognized that her activities and affiliations were in many ways representative of the radical experience in the thirties. As Swados said, "She had the knack of being in the significant place at the crucial moment," and Herbst used that knack as a point of departure to ask questions that her interlocutors' statements left out.[68] She speculated, then, on the meaning of her experiences during the thirties, in relation to their ideological construction both by the Left and by the government. Though Herbst examined different angles in this essay, she never resolved the question of the authority of what was "real," the interpretation of her experience as incriminating evidence or as expressions of her commitment to a radical vision.

Herbst's experience of marginality as a woman was a central theme in her speculation. She, indeed, had been fired from her post as a German translator when she laughed at the propaganda the intelligence office was using against the Germans. Their propaganda was intended to undermine German confidence by playing upon their fears of sexual immorality and marital infidelity.

> As a woman, I felt a certain conceit in my awareness of the violent potentials simmering within situations and human beings. This stuff was silly. Hunger would have made more sense: older Germans remembered its pangs from the First World War; younger ones from the rickety legs of kids during the inflation. But sex—if I knew what I was talking about, damaged goods would have more appeal than empty arms, and the women knew it, the men knew it, and would be more likely to laugh than to weep at our piety. Sex—to Germans, who were pulverizing Jews and politicals by the million![69]

Despite her hearty contempt for this tactic against the Germans, Herbst was still bound by the conventions of gender during the investigation. As she sat with her interlocutors, she realized that the listing of political evidence against her also incriminated her respectability as a woman, a dynamic that made her lose confidence in her own memory and beliefs. "The very politeness of my Interlocutors unhinged me, made me regard trivialities with concern. I noted with alarm one ink-stained finger of my gloves; another finger was ripped. A bit more of this, and I would begin to simper, 'Shall I pour the tea?'"[70] "Yesterday's Road" led to a complex exchange between her interpellation by anticommunism and the contradictions Herbst saw in her own experience as a radical and a woman. She was uncomfortable in both roles, and her expression of this discomfort exposed the gender politics of both anticommunist suppression and of Left orthodoxy.

In the essay, Herbst disrupted a stable interpretation of her interrogation as a series of indisputable facts by going back into her own experience and asking different questions of it.

> But what is a fact? Who is to interpret it? What ideas ride on its back? And a protean Me wanted to break the cords that bind, and to soar, if only back to my attic, where there was some hope of getting to the source of things. . . . Nothing within except a bunch of love letters, some tied together with a ribbon, others with a string or a busted rubber band; or in ink, or pencil, or typed; addressed Madam, Mme., Mlle., Fraulein, Senorita, Mrs., or Miss. One clawed with a stern warning: Destroy.[71]

By telling us that she had marked a bunch of love letters "Destroy," Herbst commented on her desire to write her own history, not to apologize for her sexual and political history.[72] Unlike the interrogators with their long list of "facts," Herbst was not interested in telling the reader everything. The stories she did tell intervened in the implacable naming of the events she participated in, the places she went, and the manifestos she signed.

Herbst's memoirs also challenged the literary history written in the 1960s that focused on the institutions and intellectual circles of the thirties Left to the exclusion of the various work that was produced.[73] Herbst was in an important position to make this intervention, since she was often sought out as a source of knowledge about the interwar period by scholars. Literary historian David Madden, for example, asked Herbst to contribute an essay to an anthology titled *Proletarian Writers of the Thirties*.[74] Herbst, however, refused, writing Madden a long letter explaining her decision. Madden quoted the letter so extensively in his introduction that it almost became a "contribution" to the anthology anyway; by weaving the letter into the introduction, however, Madden defused the autonomy and power of her critique.

Herbst's criticism was that "proletarian literature" was a narrow term that did not describe her writing, nor that of most writers of her generation. While Madden's framework reiterated the dichotomy between art and politics—the aesthetics of detachment and the turn to social experience and commitment—that limited most discussions of the thirties, Herbst sought to undo that opposition. For example, in "Yesterday's Road," she focused on the polemical limitations of proletarian literature at the 1930 Kharkov Writers' Congress, which brought an international array of radical writers to the Soviet Union to discuss the role and purpose of revolutionary literature. Rather than recapitulating the endless debates over workers' literature—Was it really literature? Were all writers and intellectuals bourgeois pessimists and therefore to be dismissed? Isn't workers' writing the only true revolutionary literature because it is produced by those at the cutting edge of the struggle against oppression?—Herbst identified the moments in which the renunciation of "aesthetics" and "literature" for political purity became untenable.

After discussing her own frustration with the discussion at this conference, Herbst recounted a speech by a Russian woman government official that cut through the layers of polemic and impassioned rhetoric to remind the participants of their own cultural history:

[W]hen the handsome woman from the Comintern looked down at us, she seemed to understand the more that was at stake. She reminded the stubborn group, who sat stiff-faced, that the . . . favorite author of Marx had been Balzac. By the time the workers had mastered the work they were to make, what would the term proletariat mean? . . . But why was it, in reports written by the Faithful and printed back home, I never once heard mention of that speech or her name?[75]

The "more" that Herbst alluded to was not a recuperation of bourgeois literature, but rather the danger of suppressing the historical connections between modernism and revolutionary politics. Significantly, the person who identified the problem was the nameless, nearly forgotten "handsome woman." The danger of ideological suppression thus was expressed by women's marginal presence at the conference and its place in history.

Herbst played a role similar to the "handsome woman from the Comintern" in Madden's book, as the upholder of a more expansive, historical tradition than scholarship had created for thirties literature. While proletarian literature in the United States sought to establish the genre as the literature of social change in America, Herbst rejected the ideological cast of the label because it excluded the writing marginal to its dominant masculinized myths and symbols. "Proletarian" was a short-lived description, according to Herbst, one laden with the ideology of the John Reed Clubs and the New Masses, radical organizations of writers with which she was often at odds. For her the more accurate term was "revolutionary literature" because it more precisely identified the much broader attempt by many radical writers to capture and to mold a new consciousness and to efface the boundaries separating the production of art from the social world. Herbst accurately identified the effect of the former term on historical perceptions of the era: "proletarian" had been tainted by McCarthyism.

Who made the demarcations for the works you put into this category? It seems to me arbitrary. I have felt that my own work has been considerably damaged by the category and that the term since the Second World War has been used more as blackmail than as a definitive term with any valid meaning. I think the whole thing needs a more fundamental approach. Where are the roots to the writing in the thirties? Was it all political?[76]

For Herbst political categories tended to efface the differences among and within literary practices. Ironically, it has been precisely through the category of proletarian literature that Herbst's work as a writer has been

recuperated.[77] She herself cautioned, however, that the effort to catego-
rize thirties literature effaced its artistic subtlety and its connection to
historical traditions of both radicalism and innovation. And while Herbst's
massive trilogy is still difficult and cumbersome to read even with that
appreciation, her insistence on its literariness, not only its political
vision, was central to her consideration of history and the usable past.

Her emphasis on literary qualities was also connected to her awareness of how sexuality and gender affected the assessment of the past.
Herbst argued, indeed, that the term *proletarian* excluded writing by
women from its definition, since the proletariat was an ideological emblem of the industrial worker, almost always identified as a man. The
term itself thus was metaphorically associated with a masculinist politics
of representation. As she wrote to Madden, "Language—sex, the exalted
role of the body—the confluence of so many diverse elements—how can
it be nailed down to Marx or to an angled proletarian?" For Herbst sex
and language were central not only to her ideas about radical politics but
how those politics should be engendered in history. "Language played a
role in the revolution, as in sex, preceded the social revolution in this
country at least."[78] A more flexible, dynamic literary criticism would recognize, then, the tangled relationship between experience and its representation, bodies and words. "No head versus heart, mind versus flesh,
here. Words, too, are carnal."[79]

Fragments of "Experience"

Her memoirs were a more subtle yet devastating rejoinder to the literary
criticism of the 1960s: Herbst sought to write a "carnal" memoir of the
thirties, to give texture and specificity to the marginal experiences left out
of institutional histories. "The Starched Blue Sky of Spain" section paid
attention not only to the dynamics of centrality and marginality, as she
characterized the difference between Hemingway and herself, but also to
the relationship between words and the experiential body. Even though
she had read most of the major studies of the Spanish civil war and was
considered an expert on the subject, in order to make the past usable
Herbst rejected the revisionist history of the civil war as a model for
revolutionary politics in favor of an experiential one.[80] She claimed
polemically, "I don't know anything really about Spain except what came
through me and my skin."[81]

At the same time that Herbst laid claim to the category of "experience," she made no attempt to express the truth about the war based on
that experience. Herbst acknowledged her confusion, her discomfort, her

desires, her jealousy, her awe, and her conflicts as elements of the political and the personal dimensions of her sojourn in Spain. In this way, Herbst's metaphor of detachment and marginality became an ethic of social and personal criticism. From this perspective, linked to her position as one of the only women reporters there, Herbst was often sarcastic and biting, noting both her own failure to get out into the "real" Spain mythologized in ideology as well as the thinly veiled career aspirations of the other reporters. She also alluded to, but did not judge, the moral quandaries that beset many intellectuals as they watched the factionalization and betrayals of the republic's coalition.[82]

Herbst's ethic of experience functioned in tension with and collaboration with the ideologies, language, and representation that channeled and shaped experience into political expression and action. As she wrote in another essay, "Even the most inner experience is a response to some outside."[83] Here again, the complex, contradictory dilemmas of representing "experience" were what was actually usable about it in the present. As if trying to warn the student activists of the 1960s deeply involved with creating their own political movement and language of rebellion, Herbst wrote about her own contemporaries:

> An entire young generation had been swept up in a violent protest against the realities of events. But the answers were numbing. The slogans were pieces of twine throttling something that was struggling. Phrases like "the toiling masses" did not answer terrible questions. There were always people, real people, each of them an individual spirit with its own peculiar past.[84]

Fearing the "slogans" would compromise her ability to report on what was actually going on, Herbst sought to discover the "real" of a magical, enchanted Spain. This desire, of course, did not mean that she could escape from the power of ideology to determine experience, but in expressing it she created an alternative that included her and other "real people, each of them an individual spirit with its own peculiar past." Herbst forsook traditional political analysis in favor of the literariness of her cultural memory, its "peculiarity" and "individual spirit." The literary elements, those elements that emphasized her sense of estrangement from dominant ideology, made it possible for her to privilege the gendered aspects of history.

In this essay, the partial, local qualities of her perspective, not its universality—evoked by the very title of the memoir, "The Starched Blue Sky of Spain"—were what was in the end usable. Here we can see the articulation of a feminist modernism that had broken through the desire for wholeness that had so deeply shaped a figure like Isadora Duncan and her intellectual generation. In the midst of historical crisis, through which the dream of harmony and integration was irrevocably shattered, Herbst recognized that she longed for a unity between her self and the world she sought to repair. But her experience could only be revealed through fragmentation, a series of disjunctures between her body, a confused, disjointed sense of reality, and dangerous politics under wartime conditions. Describing her life in the hotel where she stayed while covering the Spanish civil war, Herbst evoked her sense of marginality as not simply a cultural location, but a bodily, subjective sensation:

> As I think of the Hotel Florida [in Madrid] now, I can see it only as a misty sort of unreality. I never seemed to be there, even when I was actually there. Something inside seemed to be suspended outside, waiting. Or listening. Or hovering around, in places where I had managed to be or in places that I heard of and to which I hoped to go. There was a disembodiment about my own entity, which didn't even disturb me. I soon got used to it. There was a kind of distinct core inside me, around which the disembodied elements might cluster as around a magnet, and they came and went around that magnet, sometimes swarming and buzzing. (137)

Herbst's sense of her body as broken up and in different places marked her sense of detachment from her surroundings in a Spain that was itself a divided political body. Struggling to put her self and the nation back together held out the possibilities of "real" moments of engagement and connection. But to be honest, retrospectively, the only thing real about her experience there was the elusiveness of those moments of connection. The "reality" Herbst sought was mediated by her position as a woman reporter, which she characterized as a "disembodied" persona with a fragmented quality of vision. Significantly, such a self-characterization both anticipated and criticized postmodern theories of the decentered self that have been a key to cultural scholarship of the last two decades.

Though such theories have been attacked because they seem to endanger the possibility of human agency and action, Herbst's description actually conveyed the frailty and difficulty of the attempt to change the course of history. In "The Starched Blue Sky of Spain," Herbst used her position of detachment and her self-conscious characterization of herself as a plaintive, often lost observer to inject a sense of confusion and ambivalence in the scenes of life on the front. Running across an open, unprotected hilltop to get to the trenches on a visit to soldiers, Herbst wrote, her presence as a woman interrupted the battle.

I never saw this hilltop as a whole scene, but saw only its parts as they met the hurrying eye, because it took all of one's concentrated energy to get across this emptied space. The birds had deserted it. You could hear distinctly the rattle of a machine gun, then the olive tree near you shivered in a gust of wind. A bullet had passed by. Some leaves fell lightly. . . . To have a newcomer, not a soldier but a woman, suddenly pounce down into the dugout was a refinement of warfare they hadn't expected. (143)

The essay thus interpreted the war from a woman's point of view; it disturbed the scene of war as the site of virility and violence to emphasize the vulnerability and fragility of the soldiers. In a later scene, Herbst sat and smoked a cigarette while the soldiers lined up for typhoid shots. Her own masquerade as a brave reporter enabled her to see their masquerade as soldiers:

The men were ordered to take off their tunics, strip to the waist, and the pale cage of their ribs looked pathetically vulnerable. . . . It seemed to me the clothes were a masquerade. . . . The cinnamon-colored uniform gave his body an appearance of health; underneath the skin shivered with a kind of phosphorescent light. (145)

Herbst's essay insisted that her marginality heightened rather than diminished her power to characterize the struggle in Spain from a woman's perspective. Her experiential, gendered vision redefined the meaning of the international struggle in Spain as a moment of communion and collectivity in which differences were bridged but not eradicated, and thus at certain moments held out the possibility of including the marginal, the lost, and the dispossessed. During a night of celebration between the soldiers and the villagers, the masquerade turns into a carnival atmosphere in which the order of things, including gender, is turned upside down. In the atmosphere of carnival, masquerade, and celebration that one night, Herbst was emboldened, and she wrote her memoir of Spain as a series of reversals in which staking out a vulnerable and confusing position on the margins of cultural politics was actually a good, if scary, thing to do. Even though this position cost her a "disembodied entity" and a thirty-year silence, her evocative tale provided a feminist approach to the usable past that shaped modernist thought at the brink of the Second World War.

Conclusion: Feminism and the Usable Past

Herbst used her painful experience in Spain and in the culture of commitment wrought by American intellectuals in the thirties to get underneath

the ideological expressions of the era. But hers was not a naive or innocent experience posited against the danger of suppression posed by Left
or anticommunist ideology. As Herbst herself reflected on the process of
writing her memoirs, she transformed her experiences into metaphors
that intervened in the making of ideology. In doing so, she created an alternative ideology that accounted for the experience of marginality, the
usable past, and the critique of masculinist emblems of representation
in the thirties. Her memoirs avoided the simple identification with the
poor and oppressed (which her fiction and reportage of the period came
perilously close to doing); instead, she used her experiences to focus on
intellectual marginality, on those things that the ideology left out, for a
broader analysis of the intellectual culture of modernism. In so doing,
this study of Herbst suggests, the usable past endured as a crucial concept
from the thirties.

Herbst's perspective on the usable past was broader than its use as a
structure for her novels in the thirties. The concept is also useful as a way
to think about both women's history and a more general notion of historical narrative itself. The impulse in much feminist history is to find a
usable past for women; what has been deemed "usable" is the origins of
the women's movement and the political basis on which women changed
their lives. Modernist women have been described as cut off from this tradition and thus are not a part of the "usable past" for feminism. Herbst's
early fiction from the twenties certainly represents that loss. However, her
turn to documentary realism in the thirties led her to look again at the
sources of her own life, and she connected the marginality of her family
history to her own sense of marginality as both a radical modernist and a
modern woman. As both a novelist and a reporter, she challenged the
gender dichotomy that arose in so much documentary fiction and reportage of the thirties between the femininity of romantic love and the
masculinity of political action. Women's culture was a central theme in
her fiction, and her mother's stories were central documents in Herbst's
excavation of what was usable in the usable past.

As has been shown for each of the figures in this book, women modernists often desired to break from the contexts established for them.
Strategies of engaging the past allowed them to articulate different relations to the present as it was being understood in its historical moment.
Herbst acted in many of the most important arenas of thirties radicalism,
but she also often saw herself as an outsider. Her sense of detachment can
be considered a critical relation to the cultural politics of the twenties
and the thirties.

The usable past, then, was an idea that traveled with Herbst from its flowering in the expressive culture of the thirties to what she had to explain about the history of her own marginality, as a woman, a writer, and as a political subject. This interpretation of the usable past dislodges an entrenched reading of women in the culture of commitment, in which those women failed to focus on gender politics in making a commitment to revolutionary literature and thus either succumbed to the ideology of literary radicalism or were forced to celebrate its gendered archetypes. In addition, Herbst should not be seen as a martyr to a later feminist movement compelled to resurrect and reinterpret the heroines of women's art and activism, nor should she be seen as an apologist for a failed radicalism, as the conservative modernist critic Hilton Kramer characterized her legacy.[85] Such a perspective is damaging for many reasons, not least among them its antifeminism and antiradicalism. But it recapitulates the problem that this book as a whole has sought to address: feminism and the cultural politics of modernism were not separated, but rather deeply intertwined in the lives, thought, and most important in the subjective cultural analysis of the early twentieth century. Herbst's fiction and reportage paid significant attention to the politics of gender, exploring the difficult, multiple positions women assumed in activist struggle and cultural imagination. The contradictions and marginality that Herbst articulated also raised questions about the status of feminism in this period of literary radicalism for modernist culture. Because women were the figures who spoke about the untenability of an ideology that lashed art to political ends, Herbst's use of experience as a category characterized by femininity, marginality, and silence resembles the use of "woman" as the figure for the gaps, blind spots, and silences of modernism, especially in its failure to provide a coherent theory of art and politics.[86]

On the other hand, the literariness of her "experiences"—the choices of them, their mutation into metaphor—in Herbst's effort to make the past usable emphasized narrative complexity and patterns of relating event to fact, experience, and interpretation. At a later moment, from the retrospective distance of the 1960s, the language of historical representation did not betray her. The past was treacherous, but Herbst understood both her complicity and her marginality. Such a perspective is eminently useful for feminist history, especially in interpreting a period when "feminism" no longer flourished as a wide-ranging articulation of women's goals and aspirations. Herbst's struggles as a writer in the thirties and the more general struggle into which she made them in her memoirs suggest there is not a single use of "experience" to create a usable past for modern

Conclusion

The Loss of the
Coming of an Age

The many articulations of feminism as a "semantic claim to female modernism" represent a lost opportunity in American culture that has yet to be fully recovered in history or regained in the present. The bold and creative steps many New Women took toward independence, artistic invention, and social freedom were understood as symbols of the emancipating possibilities of modern American culture itself. And yet the fissures of that culture—the heavy toll that modernity took on so many modernists—also trapped feminism in a view of the past marked by betrayal and marginality. Returning to the dynamics traced in the preceding portraits allows us to see what was significant about the link between women's freedom and independence and the "shock of the new" in modernism. Furthermore, by addressing modernism's privileged authority to represent modernity itself, we also can see the constraints faced by feminist modernists and the limitations they themselves expressed.

Elegantly encapsulating the tensions in this dynamic, Floyd Dell once again revealed the possibility that feminism provoked in modernism and the loss of that moment of cultural transformation. In his 1931 autobiography, Dell recounted his experience sitting for a woman sculptor. The artist's gaze fastened upon him as she modeled his bust, and he was drawn into the drama of being looked at.

> I shall never forget the sensation of sitting on a model stand and being stared at by a handsome sculptress. A man is used to having a prolonged

159

meeting of his eyes with a girl's mean something; and it is hard to get used to meeting a girl's wide-eyed, impersonal stare. Her liquid, starry gaze embarrassed me. And as the gaze continued, piercing me, probing me, seeing me with calm indifference, I became uneasy and almost afraid—I wanted to look away, but that seemed cowardly and evasive, so I kept on staring back, until those grey eyes of hers seemed profound gulfs over which I hung, dizzy, tottering, about to drown. And then, saying "MM," she would turn to the clay head, and put a tiny pellet of clay on the end of the nose. She had not been searching my soul, but only considering just how long my nose was.[1]

The typical gender roles of the masculine artist who looks upon the feminine pose and transforms her image into art were reversed. Not merely passive, Dell articulated the difficulties of the posing subject, especially the feeling of drowning and the unsettling feeling of being under examination. Struggling to assert himself, Dell wondered if he could turn this exchange of looks into an erotic encounter, but the artist resisted him with her indifference to his attempt to return her look; her gaze remained an "impersonal stare." Neither adoration nor attempted seduction, her look possessed the rigor of aesthetic contemplation. Disoriented and dizzy, Dell's gender expectations in this artistic encounter were turned upside down. Women's artistic work, independent and self-motivated, could not be reduced to a romance.

Dell's explanation of this moment could have been emblematic of the subjective transformations wrought by women's entrance into modernism, articulated by a man who had championed women's emancipation, tried to live in equal partnerships with his female companions, and written extensively about how feminism would change men and expand women's independence. But it was not. At this moment, on the brink of articulating how completely women's independence and artistry had disrupted his expectations and led into the not-yet-known, Dell retreated. Sounding more like a curmudgeon than a willing player as he recapped the encounter, Dell sputtered, "So this is what we are coming to, with all this modernism!" In this moment of historical reckoning, Dell linked women's independence to modernism and yet neutralized and trivialized its significance.

While this moment represented the perspective of a man looking back upon his youth with a jaundiced eye, it also portrayed a more general foreclosure of the possibilities women found in modernist culture. The preceding portraits each have traced a history that charts this dynamic across the period in which modernism played a significant role in the shaping of modern American culture, between the early twentieth century and the end of the 1930s. This claim is both indebted to and a contribution to a conception of modernism's historical culture. This study is linked to others that have shown a dynamic relationship between modernism—a distinct and changing constellation of art and ideas among a diverse group of artists and thinkers—and popular culture, racial and sexual identities, and political history. My research into the lives of these figures and the more general tendencies they represented suggests first that articulations of feminism were key elements of modernism, and that the field of cultural representation offered feminists ways to reinvent a critique of constraints and exclusion based on gender.

Isadora Duncan's ability to project and instill the experience of wholeness resonated with broader modernist beliefs that one of their central acts was to heal the Victorian divisions of class, race, and sex in its establishment of "civilization." The female body was an emblem of that attempt: a whole female body, in contrast to a body debilitated by Victorian division, was substituted for more general ideas about freedom and liberation. Stripped of the conventions of Victorian dress, moving lyrically and expressively alone on a spare stage, Duncan made a cultural leap from the old to the new. The exceptional and dramatic qualities of Duncan's performances and personal style led many to see her as a literal embodiment of modernist dreams of liberation. Duncan's act of baring her breast, and explaining to an audience that tended to fetishize and eroticize the female body rather than to see in it a natural wholeness, "This is truth! This is beauty!" represented that appeal.

Margaret Anderson was like Dell's woman sculptor, seeing in artistic endeavor not an erotic encounter but her own attempt at becoming modern. Through her acts of self-expression, Anderson allied herself with a more general avant-garde cultural rebellion against genteel American culture. Modernists insistently challenged hegemonic culture through their calls for a new language of expression. For example, the manifesto of the "Revolution of the Word" first published in the little magazine *transition* in 1929 proclaimed, "Narrative is not mere anecdote, but the projection of a metamorphosis of reality. The literary creator has the right to disintegrate the primal matter of words imposed on him by textbook and dictionaries. The writer expresses. He does not communicate. The plain reader be damned."[2] Anderson's editorship of the *Little Review* paved the way for this claim, in which cultural resistance was linked to self-expression. Insisting on an expression detached from "reality," modernists distanced themselves from a shared, dominant culture. By damning a common language, they showed that dominant culture enforced its view of reality through the narrative power of history and the defining power of language. Indicated by "the word" were not only literary and poetic texts, but also the language of visual representation, the vocabulary of the body's movement through time and space, and bohemian experiments in living and working.

Through this modernist conception of cultural independence, Anderson was able to express a lesbian identity that resisted rather than understood itself through heterosexual gender conventions of romance. In refusing to be a muse or vessel of artistic inspiration, and by declaring herself immune from "reality," Anderson became a symbol of the outlaw status of the modernists and their attempt to remake culture. Her belief in self-expression also enacted her resistance to dominant meanings of womanhood: Anderson sought not to live for and through others but to live for herself. In doing so, she went "beyond the ending," Rachel Blau DuPlessis's powerful phrase, of traditional narratives for women, including romance, self-sacrifice, and the frayed ideal of sisterhood itself.[3]

As a young writer in the late 1920s, Josephine Herbst entered a literary and artistic world in which modernism and an artistic, rebellious life for women were established trends. To her, "true literature" was "not about life. It *was* life, as authentic as bread and salt, an essence that passed into your blood and filled your lungs with the air you breathed. It was the differentiating power, to separate this from that and to shake you out of the notion that the straight and narrow was the only way."[4] Her own literature linked this exhilarating life to women's independence. In the spirited words of her fictional mother: "Don't be stupid and shut your eyes and imagine that the only things in life worth while come from men and what people call romance."[5] Such independence, however, was impossible to sustain in the wider culture. Herbst angrily confronted a literary world that continued to distinguish between men's writing as modernist and therefore authentic and women's writing as not modernist, imitative, and inauthentic. Further, Herbst's life and work were emblematic of the sexual revolution's failure to create a fulfilling place for women in modern American culture. By delineating her own marginality, Herbst revealed the larger marginalization of feminism to be one of modernism's most debilitating blind spots.

The cultural politics of wholeness, self-expression, social responsibility, and revolutionary desire that these figures articulated seem ever more part of the past. Modernism, which had been a declaration of the present, the "now," has become a historical concept, indicated by our designation of ourselves as "post-," or beyond, modernity. Yet by making modernism part of the past, we risk ignoring its own relation to history. Each of these portraits reveals a persistent historical tendency suggested by my title, *The Secret Treachery of Words*. While the "word" became a symbol of a revolution in representation itself, the multitude of texts and visual representation this revolution produced also became "history," how the past was written into a narrative with authority and coherence. For each of these figures, modernism's historical representation of feminism was treacherous.

Modernists have had a privileged role in representing the nature of twentieth-century modernity. Their project, in part, was to write a history of how American artists, thinkers, and writers slipped the noose of a repressive and stultifying Victorianism for the freedoms and complexities of modern American society. Their many declarations of this break have since become the accepted story of the transition from Victorianism to modernism.[6] Despite their desire to reinvent an expressive language, however, modernists did not escape the tendency of representation to create meaning through the symbolic power of gender difference. The modernist narrative was also a story about gender: heroic men rescued American culture from the clutches of Victorian matriarchs and, in doing so, created a cosmopolitan alternative that broke down nineteenth-century dualistic views of class, sex, and race. This now-ubiquitous vision of that transition is both inaccurate and emblematic of the troubled fortunes of American feminism. In representing modernism as breaking with the past, male modernists—the ones who have been canonized and who have had their vision of history enshrined as "fact"—relied on the suppression of feminism as part of modernism.

Though it continues to be powerful, this story misrepresents the cultural moment in which modernism and feminism were intertwined declarations of the "new." Modernists celebrated women's refashioned public identities as a harbinger of what was positive about modernity, often likening women's independence to the forces of the industrial revolution itself. Conversely, critics of what became known as the "machine age" pointed to the modern woman as the quintessence of modernity's problems. As Dell phrased it, "The two great riddles of the world to-day are machinery and woman. . . . In them lie hidden the possibilities of failure or happiness for the human race. What the future will be, depends on these two things—machinery and women."[7] Women's very modernity was both enthusiastically celebrated as a symbol of the new century's possibilities and vigorously denounced as a threat to an older moral order. Editor Baker Brownell's sonorous pronouncement was typical: "The modern woman breaks the past, like an old platter on the floor, and seeks new ways.... [Modern women] are products among the other huge productions of this day, but industrialism has made in them the critics of its own system."[8] The preceding chapters have attempted to reveal this logic: feminist modernists were both products of modernity and critics of its own system. Thus they became privileged emblems of the renunciation of Victorianism and a harbinger of the future modernists sought to create.

Modernist feminists were part of the revolt against a feminine Victorianism; they endeavored to find a way out of the dead end that reformist women's activism had reached. Feminist modernists sought to think, write, and act their way out of the world from which they came. Duncan, for example, used ancient Greek motifs in her costumes, movements, and music to retrieve ideas about harmony, timelessness, and above all wholeness. But crucially, she also used Hellenism to criticize an oppressive late-nineteenth-century view of "civilization." For Duncan, this was not an archaeological quest, but an effort to become modern. In a moment of self-definition, Duncan wrote that on a journey to Greece in 1902 she realized her search for truth among the ruins would remain elusive, lost in a culture that could not be fully recovered. She wrote, "Suddenly it seemed to me as if all our dreams burst like a glorious bubble, and we were not, nor ever could be, other than moderns. We could not have the feeling of the Ancient Greeks."[9] Duncan realized that there was no romantic escape from modernity. Emulating ancient forms as a way to remind late Victorians of what they had forgotten or suppressed about the body, she believed that her performances actually enacted a vision of modernity that gave women's liberation a central place.

The modernist narrative of its break from Victorianism erased feminist modernists like the ones studied here, and obscured the fact that many declarations of feminism were in essence a modernist stance. Initially hostile to the world the reform-oriented progressives had made, Herbst's creative work in the 1920s was consistent with the modernist penchant for "mocking and criticizing." The devastating conditions wrought by the Depression changed all that. Chastened by her denunciation of the past and nurtured in the broad context of the documentary impulse that shaped artists and writers of the liberal New Deal and the more radical revolutionary movement, Herbst began to search for what was usable in the shards of the Victorian world now decisively shattered. In her historical novels written in the 1930s, Herbst furiously condemned the destructive results of the modernization wrought by capitalism. And yet their effects on women were marginal to the larger, complex story she told. It was only by turning back, not to the nineteenth century, but to the historical representation of modernism itself as it was being understood in the 1950s and 1960s, that Herbst was able to forge a voice that showed feminism as a key voice of critical insight and revision. In doing so, Herbst forecast new ways of thinking about both modernism and feminism.

One of the ways we must then interpret the significance of feminism is through the history of its marginalization and exclusion as modernists hardened up their story of cultural formation. Duncan, for example, became an emblem of the limitations of prewar cultural radicalism. The more Duncan seemed unable to come to grips with the development of popular culture that made her project appear anachronistic, the more "of the past" she became. Duncan began to be seen as a residual figure who had not quite made the leap to modernism, clinging to a kind of sentimentality and antique idealism, instead. Such representations led to the monumentalization that made Duncan part of the past, rather than the dynamic and radical present that modernists sought to engage. The process of monumentalizing Duncan had the effect of neutralizing her gestures and philosophy of liberation. As Duncan turned to a divisive and corrosive racism that underwrote her attack on popular culture, the limitations of the desire for wholeness were revealed. Monumentalizing Duncan has prevented us from seeing how key this move was for her, and for other modernists who also turned to rhetorics of race and nationalism to shore up their cultural influence and to express their increasing hostility to the modern world.[10]

The process by which artists and texts were elevated over the cultural practices that supported them reflected a more general gender politics that was difficult to escape. The negative construction of Margaret Anderson as a dilettante, consumer, and aesthete was deeply connected to the process of the canonization of high modernism. Anderson's subsequent retreat from the cultural moment of the avant-garde under the pressure of wartime conservatism and the *Ulysses* trial allowed her to preserve herself, but it also tended to suppress the wider cultural and political meanings of acts of self-expression that gave both her pranks and her self-fashioning such bite.

Nowhere was historical representation more treacherous than for the writers of the thirties Left, who inherited modernism and reshaped it to directly engage their desire to document the Depression, and dedicated their art to the belief that social and political revolution were necessary.

With this turn, however, new polemical postures indicted feminism, which was branded a form of middle-class individualism that had no place in the revolution. Gone were the more experimental feminist claims that challenged the nature of "reality" and dominant culture's language of gender difference. Moreover, the nostalgic gestures to women's traditional roles in the cultural representation of the 1930s tended to enshrine women in a romanticized past. These twin dynamics undermined women writers' desire to promote a transformation of gender relations as a key part of what needed to be changed in American culture.

As recent revisions of modernism have shown, the cultural politics of the Red Scare hardened still further a narrative of modernism as an art and literature divorced from any claims to political and social change. By the 1950s modernism came to be understood as an artistic movement detached from social context itself. Yet significantly, the dialectic of feminism's historical entrapment continued into the 1960s as the Old Left of the thirties was remembered and recovered by a new generation of politically conscious scholars of literature and history. Despite its very intention to retrieve those lost to political slander and suppression, this movement hardened the concept of the masculine proletarian and the opposition between art and politics. In doing so, it effectively excluded the diversity of writing that was actually produced, suppressing our access to the dynamics of marginality and cultural critique that women writers expressed. The politics of cultural representation forced Herbst, along with other women writers, into positions of marginality. But this very position also led her to critical and representational dissent. Seeing modernism anew in the fields of intellectual history and cultural theory, then, has meant seeing the deep connections between experimental art and social and political currents. Through this revision we can begin to see again the significance of feminism.

These portraits show that feminists were key participants in the historical culture of modernism. But they were betrayed by the process of historical representation that detached a conception of modernism from its social and political context. This study has attempted to capture the richness of both modernism and feminism, and their paradoxical relationship, through the method of intellectual portraiture. These portraits have sought to show the interaction of text and context, life and work, general cultural tendencies and the exceptional qualities of individuals. While Duncan, Anderson, Dell, and Herbst worked in distinct arenas, taken collectively their stories show the significance of feminism across a broad spectrum of cultural politics. Like Herbst's reflections on the process of writing her memoirs, the pressing and shaping of these lives, thought, and work tell us, almost as allegories, of the possibilities and limitations of their cultural moments and the history that has been written about them.

Finally, the subjects of these portraits revealed their own complicity in the process of historical representation. Their autobiographies, especially, articulate their desire to position themselves in history, and thus they are subjective contributions to the larger narrative of modernism and feminism. Each attempted to think their way into the modern world, but they also were enmeshed in the cultural politics of their time: Duncan's reliance on a narrative of racial and national superiority, Anderson's surrender to a detached aestheticism, and Dell's journey from bohemian experiment to suburban normality all follow a modernist trajectory in which feminism was attenuated rather than fully developed. Perhaps because Herbst was doubly betrayed by both the conservative politics of the Red Scare and by the very movement that sought to give voice and legitimacy to her experience, her memoirs were more able to articulate the limits of a modernism that could not fully break free of the exclusions and oppositions it nevertheless attacked. Dizzy and drowning in modernity, modern men and women clung to what they already knew but had longed to escape.

Notes

Introduction

1. Dorothy Dunbar Bromley, "Feminist—New Style," *Harper's* (October 1927): 560.

2. Describing the moment around 1910 when *feminism* began to be used as a term to describe a complex constellation of ideas and practices of women's emancipation, Nancy Cott wrote that feminism was "a semantic claim to female modernism" (*The Grounding of Modern Feminism* [New Haven: Yale University Press, 1987], 10). Sandra Gilbert and Susan Gubar have argued that modernist writing was profoundly shaped by, even found its origins in, a reaction against feminism and the increasing social, political, and artistic power of women since the 1870s (*No Man's Land: The Place of the Woman Writer in the Twentieth Century*, vol. 1 of *The War of the Words* [New Haven: Yale University Press, 1988]). Marianne DeKoven has traced both a feminist and socialist political unconscious in even the most abstract and experimental modernist writing (*Rich and Strange: Gender, History, Modernism* [Princeton: Princeton University Press, 1991]). In "Mass Culture as Woman: Modernism's Other," Andreas Huyssen theorized that women's roles as mass cultural consumers made them "modernism's other," raising questions about the meaning of feminist challenges to this status quo (Huyssen, *After the Great Divide: Modernism, Mass Culture, Postmodernism* [Bloomington: Indiana University Press, 1986]).

3. Clement Greenberg, "Avant-Garde and Kitsch," in *The Partisan Reader, Ten Years of Partisan Review, 1934–1944: An Anthology,* ed. William Phillips and Philip Rahv (New York: Dial Press, 1946), 378–92; Max Horkheimer and Theodor Adorno, "The Culture Industry: Enlightenment as Mass Deception," in Horkheimer and Adorno, *The Dialectic of Enlightenment* (New York: Seabury Press, 1972), 120–67. For

one of the most important critiques of the opposition between modernism and mass culture, see Fredric Jameson, "Reification and Utopia in Mass Culture," *Social Text* (Winter 1979): 130–48.

4. Feminist analyses of consumer culture and the dilemmas for modern womanhood include: V. F. Calverton and Samuel Schmalhausen, eds., *Sex in Civilization* (Garden City, N.Y.: Garden City Publishing, 1929); V. F. Calverton and Samuel Schmalhausen, eds., *Woman's Coming of Age* (New York: Liveright, 1931); Freda Kirchwey, ed., *Our Changing Morality* (New York: Albert and Charles Boni, 1924); Suzanne La Follette, *Concerning Women* (New York: Albert and Charles Boni, 1926); Alice Beal Parsons, *Woman's Dilemma* (New York: Crowell, 1926); and Lorine Pruette, *Women and Leisure: A Study of Social Waste* (New York: E. P. Dutton, 1924).

5. Pruette, *Women and Leisure*, 205.

6. Rayna Rapp and Ellen Ross, "The Twenties Backlash: Compulsory Heterosexuality, the Consumer Family, and the Waning of Feminism," in *Class, Race, and Sex: The Dynamics of Control*, ed. A. Swerdlow and H. Lessinger (Boston: G. K. Hall, 1983), 93–107.

7. Susan Ware, ed., *Modern American Women: A Documentary History* (New York: McGraw-Hill, 1996), 146. Ware's statement represents a consensus of opinion about feminism in the 1920s, especially regarding how women's history is generally taught. However, Cott, in *The Grounding of Modern Feminism*, argues persuasively for the need to distinguish feminism from the "woman movement" in the nineteenth century and the loose coalition of women's groups in the early twentieth century. Though Cott goes on to argue that the perceived decline of the women's movement was actually the early struggle of modern feminism, the backlash model remains strong. See Estelle Freedman, "Separatism as Strategy: Female Institution-Building and American Feminism," *Feminist Studies* (Fall 1979): 512–79; and Christina Simmons, "Companionate Marriage and the Lesbian Threat," *Frontiers* 4, no. 3 (1979): 54–59.

8. Rita Felski, *The Gender of Modernity* (Cambridge: Harvard University Press, 1995), 16.

9. Cott, *Grounding of Modern Feminism*; and Mari Jo Buhle, *Women and American Socialism, 1870–1920* (Urbana: University of Illinois Press, 1981).

10. Judith Schwarz, *Radical Feminists of Heterodoxy: Greenwich Village, 1912–1940* (Norwich: New Victoria Publishers, 1986), 7.

11. Marie Jenney Howe, "Feminism," *The New Review* 2, no. 8 (August 1914): 441. See also Louise Newman, "Critical Theory and the History of Women: What's at Stake in Deconstructing Women's History," *Journal of Women's History* (Winter 1991): 58–68.

12. Virginia Woolf, "Mr. Bennett and Mrs. Brown," in *The Virginia Woolf Reader*, ed. Mitchell A. Leaska (New York: Harcourt, Brace, Jovanovich, 1984), 194.

13. Christina Simmons, "Modern Sexuality and the Myth of Victorian Repression," in *Gender and American History Since 1890*, ed. Barbara Melosh (New York: Routledge, 1993), 18.

14. Ann Douglas, *Terrible Honesty: Mongrel Manhattan in the 1920s* (New York: Farrar, Straus and Giroux, 1995), 6, 295.

15. Suzanne Clark, *Sentimental Modernism: Women Writers and the Revolution of the Word* (Bloomington: Indiana University Press, 1991), 33.

16. Emma Goldman, "The Tragedy of Woman's Emancipation," in her *Anarchism and Other Essays* (1917; reprint, New York: Dover Publications, 1969), 214, 215.

17. Carolyn Burke, "The New Poetry and the New Woman: Mina Loy," in *Coming to Light: American Women Poets in the Twentieth Century,* ed. Diane Wood Middlebrook and Marilyn Yalom (Ann Arbor: University of Michigan Press, 1985), 47.

18. Mina Loy, "Feminist Manifesto," in *The Last Lunar Baedeker,* ed. Roger L. Conover (Manchester, England: Carcanet Press, 1982), 269.

19. My perspective is influenced by Denise Riley's theoretical and historical account of the effects of women acting on behalf of "woman" in *Am I That Name? Feminism and the Category of Women in History* (Minneapolis: University of Minnesota Press, 1988).

20. Their critique could be found especially in discussions of prostitution, birth control, and their own battles against censorship and the Comstock laws. See William L. O'Neill, ed., *Echoes of Revolt: The Masses, 1911–1917* (Chicago: Ivan R. Dee, 1989); and Leslie Fishbein, *Rebels in Bohemia: The Radicals of The Masses, 1911–1917* (Chapel Hill: University of North Carolina Press, 1982). In a later period, even Bromley's tamer doctrine of feminist individualism departed from a discourse of reform, though it too depends upon a middle-class definition of independence that obscured what is possible or even desirable for other women.

21. Daniel Joseph Singal, "Towards a Definition of American Modernism," in *Modernist Culture in America,* ed. Singal (Belmont, Mass.: Wadsworth, 1991), 1–27.

22. The process of cultural formation can be seen vividly in anthologies of cultural criticism. For early studies of modernism and mass culture, see Irving Howe, ed., *The Idea of the Modern in Literature and the Arts* (New York: Horizon Press, 1967); and Bernard Rosenberg and David Manning White, eds., *Mass Culture: The Popular Arts in America* (New York: Free Press, 1957). For more recent approaches in cultural history, see Richard Wightman Fox and T. J. Jackson Lears, eds., *The Culture of Consumption: Critical Essays in American History, 1880–1980* (New York: Pantheon Books, 1983), and Fox and Lears, eds., *The Power of Culture: Critical Essays in American History* (Chicago: University of Chicago Press, 1993).

23. Cary Nelson, *Repression and Recovery: Modern American Poetry and the Politics of Cultural Memory, 1910–1945* (Madison: University of Wisconsin Press, 1989). See also Walter Kalaidjian, *American Culture Between the Wars: Revisionary Modernism and Postmodern Critique* (New York: Columbia University Press, 1993).

24. See Paul Gilroy, *The Black Atlantic: Modernity and Double Consciousness* (Cambridge: Harvard University Press, 1993), and Douglas, *Terrible Honesty.* The recovery of the radical stream in modernist culture and the establishment of the centrality of the cultural production of marginalized groups in modernism has not necessarily been compatible with feminist analyses. For an important feminist approach that looks at antiracism in modernism, see Susan Stanford Friedman, "Modernism of the 'Scattered Remnant': Race and Politics in H.D.'s Development," in *Feminist Issues*

in Literary Scholarship, ed. Shari Benstock (Bloomington: Indiana University Press, 1987), 208–31.

25. For important studies of the representation of gender in the thirties, see Paula Rabinowitz, *Labor and Desire: Women's Revolutionary Fiction in Depression America* (Chapel Hill: University of North Carolina Press, 1991); and Barbara Melosh, *Engendering Culture: Manhood and Womanhood in the New Deal Public Art and Theater* (Washington, D.C.: Smithsonian Institution Press, 1991).

26. For studies that see continuities between the teens, twenties, and the thirties, see Marcus Klein, *Foreigners: The Making of American Literature, 1900–1940* (Chicago: University of Chicago Press, 1981); and Kalaidjian, *American Culture Between the Wars.*

27. The film starring Vanessa Redgrave as Duncan is especially indicative of her as a harbinger of the sexual revolution. See Karel Reisz, dir., *The Loves of Isadora* (1969).

28. See Ann Daly, *"Done Into Dance": Isadora Duncan in America* (Bloomington: Indiana University Press, 1995); and Deborah Jowitt, *Time and the Dancing Image* (New York: William Morrow, 1988).

29. Jerrold Seigel, *Bohemian Paris: Culture, Politics, and the Boundaries of Bourgeois Life, 1830–1930* (New York: Penguin Books, 1986).

30. Shari Benstock, *Women of the Left Bank: Paris, 1900–1940* (Austin: University of Texas Press, 1986).

31. See Hills's long introduction to the recent publication of Anderson's novel, *Forbidden Fires* (Tallahassee: Naiad Press, 1996).

32. Jessica Feldman has written a fascinating account of the gender politics of such posing in *Gender on the Divide: The Dandy in Modernist Literature* (Ithaca, N.Y.: Cornell University Press, 1993).

33. See especially Kathy Peiss, *Cheap Amusements: Working Women and Leisure in Turn of the Century New York* (Philadelphia: Temple University Press, 1986); and Joanne Meyerowitz, *Women Adrift: Independent Wage Earners in Chicago, 1880–1930* (Chicago: University of Chicago Press, 1988).

34. For the former, see Fishbein and Ellen Kay Trimberger, "Feminism, Men, and Modern Love: Greenwich Village, 1900–1925," in *Powers of Desire: The Politics of Sexuality,* ed. Ann Snitow, Christine Stansell, and Sharon Thompson (New York: Monthly Review Press, 1983), 131–52. For the latter, see Simmons, "Modern Sexuality and the Myth of Victorian Repression"; and Pamela S. Haag, "In Search of 'the Real Thing': Ideologies of Love, Modern Romance, and Women's Sexual Subjectivity in the United States, 1920–1940," *Journal of the History of Sexuality* 2 (April 1992): 547–77.

35. As Kalaidjian has pointed out, however, most artistic movements in the Depression call upon earlier modernist styles.

1. From Event to Monument

1. Mabel Dodge Luhan, *Movers and Shakers,* vol. 1 of *Intimate Memories* (New York: Harcourt, Brace, 1936), 322, 325, 327.

2. Ibid., 328.

3. Quoted in ibid., 331.

4. Lewis Mumford, *My Works and Days: A Personal Chronicle* (New York: Harcourt Brace Jovanovich, 1979), 22.

5. Charlotte Perkins Gilman, "The Dancing of Isadora Duncan," *The Forerunner* 6, no. 4 (April 1915): 101; Jean Garrigue, "On the Legends of a Dancer," in Garrigue, *Country without Maps* (New York: Macmillan, 1964).

6. Luhan, *Movers and Shakers*, 319.

7. See Vanity Fair's retrospective on the magazine's early years in *Vanity Fair* (March 1999): 146–90; and the Pembroke College Archives, Providence, Rhode Island.

8. Karel Reisz's 1969 film, *The Loves of Isadora*, starring Vanessa Redgrave, characterizes Duncan as a swinger; critic Patricia Meyer Spacks and philosopher Simone de Beauvoir focus on Duncan's autobiography, *My Life*, to talk about Duncan's view of herself as a lover, mother, and artist. These classic feminist explorations of womanhood focus almost exclusively on Duncan's "private" life. See Simone de Beauvoir, *The Second Sex* (New York: Vintage Books, 1953); and Patricia Meyer Spacks, *The Female Imagination* (New York: Avon Books, 1972).

9. Max Eastman, "Isadora Duncan Is Dead," *The Nation* 125 (September 28, 1927): 310.

10. Paul David Magriel, ed., *Isadora Duncan* (New York: H. Holt and Co., 1947), 53.

11. Max Eastman, "Heroism Plus Heroics: Difficulties in Worshiping Isadora Duncan," *Heroes I Have Known: Twelve Who Lived Great Lives* (New York: Simon and Schuster, 1942), 86.

12. For a good introduction to the desire for wholeness among American modernists, see the special issue of *American Quarterly* (Spring 1987), especially Singal, "Towards a Definition of American Modernism," 7–26.

13. Floyd Dell, *Women as World Builders* (Chicago: Forbes and Co., 1913), 48.

14. Ann Daly, "Dance History and Feminist Theory: Reconsidering Isadora Duncan and the Male Gaze," in *Gender in Performance: The Presentation of Difference in the Performing Arts*, ed. Laurence Senelick (Hanover, N.H.: University Press of New England, 1992), 239–59. For other descriptions of Duncan's costume, see Norma Adler, "Reconstructing the Dances of Isadora Duncan in the United States," *The Drama Review* 28 (Fall 1984): 59–66.

15. Duncan quoted in *Isadora Speaks*, ed. Franklin Rosemont (San Francisco: City Lights Books, 1981), 48.

16. Michael Gold, "The Loves of Isadora," *New Masses* 4 (March 1929): 20.

17. Duncan, "The Dance of the Greeks," in *The Art of the Dance*, ed. Sheldon Cheney (New York: Theater Arts, 1928), 96.

18. Duncan, "Movement Is Life," in ibid., 79.

19. Duncan didn't reject all female performance, however. She idolized two famous actresses of the period: Ellen Terry and Eleonora Duse.

20. She also condemned the bourgeois and the rich audiences who attended these theaters, instead valuing artists, intellectuals, and students as the best viewers. Duncan

attempted to make her performances financially accessible for working-class immigrants on the Lower East Side during her American tour in 1915–17. She often wanted to deny that her performances took place in a theater at all, and claimed not to want to charge money. This is one of the reasons she gave for leaving the Soviet Union in 1922: the Revolution was moving so slowly and hardship was so extreme that the government could not support a free theater.

21. Quoted in "Isadora Duncan's Triumphs and Tragedies," *Literary Digest* 95 (October 8, 1927): 51.

22. For a description of Duncan's stage design, music, and movement vocabulary, see Daly, *"Done Into Dance,"* and Deborah Jowitt, "The Search for Motion," in *Time and the Dancing Image* (New York: William Morrow, 1988).

23. Quoted in Rosemont, ed., *Isadora Speaks*, 53, 118.

24. Isadora Duncan, *My Life* (New York: Boni and Liveright, 1927), 17.

25. Ibid., 18.

26. Quoted in *Isadora Duncan*, ed. Magriel, 46.

27. Duncan, *My Life*, 241.

28. Ibid., 254.

29. Quoted in Rosemont, ed., *Isadora Speaks*, 118.

30. Duncan, "The Dance of the Future," in *Art of the Dance*, ed. Cheney, 62.

31. Victor Elyitch Seroff, *The Real Isadora* (New York: Dial Press, 1971), 327.

32. Historians have tended to read the above in terms of its shock value and in terms of the invective, anger, and outrage it evoked from Duncan's audience. But reading it outside of that, for what she is saying for and against women's sexuality, Duncan's rhetoric is as controlling and regulating as Comstock's. Nevertheless, Duncan was held up as the symbolic antithesis of Comstock.

33. Margaret R. Miles, "The Virgin's One Bare Breast: Female Nudity and Religious Meaning in Tuscan Early Renaissance Culture," in *The Female Body in Western Culture: Contemporary Perspectives*, ed. Susan R. Suleiman (Cambridge: Harvard University Press, 1985), 204.

34. For a fuller analysis of women's representation in art history, see Griselda Pollock, "Modernity and the Spaces of Femininity," in Pollock, *Vision and Difference: Femininity, Feminism and Histories of Art* (New York: Routledge, 1988).

35. Fishbein, *Rebels in Bohemia*; see also Tom Quelch, "The New Paganism," *The New Review* (June 1913): 593–95.

36. Duncan, *My Life*, 156.

37. Eastman, "Heroism plus Heroics," 72.

38. Floyd Dell, "Who Said That Beauty Passes Like a Dream?" in his *Looking at Life* (New York: Knopf, 1924), 48–49.

39. Abraham Walkowitz, quoted in William Innes Homer, *Alfred Stieglitz and the American Avant-Garde* (Boston: New York Graphics Society, 1977), 140. Homer explains that Walkowitz produced "spirited, linear sketches, accented with color, in the tradition of Rodin's drawings of the moving model, which helped to establish Walkowtiz's reputation as an American artist of some consequence."

40. "To Isadora Duncan: A Tribute from a Young Student," *Touchstone* 7 (1920): 308.

41. Duncan, "Dance of the Future," 61.

42. Quoted in Rowland Elzea, *John Sloan's Oil Paintings: A Catalogue Raisonné* (Newark: University of Delaware Press, 1991), 109.

43. Paul Padgette, ed., *The Dance Writings of Carl Van Vechten* (New York: Dance Horizons, 1974), 24.

44. Quoted in Francis Steegmuller, *"Your Isadora": The Love Story of Isadora Duncan and Gordon Craig* (New York: Random House and The New York Public Library, 1974), 386.

45. André Levinson, "André Levinson on Isadora Duncan," ed. Jill Silverman, *Ballet Review* 6, no. 4 (1977–78): 11.

46. On the problem of modernity for European and American intellectuals, see Jackson Lears, *No Place of Grace: Antimodernism and the Transformation of American Culture, 1880–1920* (New York: Pantheon, 1981); Stephen Kern, *The Culture of Time and Space, 1880–1918* (Cambridge: Harvard University Press, 1983); and Marshall Berman, *All That Is Solid Melts Into Air: The Experience of Modernity* (New York: Viking Penguin, 1988).

47. Duncan, *My Life*, 325.

48. Naomi Schor's analysis in "Decadence: Wey, Loos, Lukács," in Schor, *Reading in Detail: Aesthetics and the Feminine* (New York: Methuen, 1987), offers a helpful approach to the problem of the detail for modernists.

49. Duncan, "Depth," in *Art of the Dance*, ed. Cheney, 100.

50. Luhan offers a good description of these qualities of Duncan's persona in *Movers and Shakers*, 320–39.

51. Duncan, "Movement Is Life," 78.

52. For an account of the different but interrelated meanings of modernity and modernization, see Berman, *All That Is Solid Melts Into Air*.

53. On the desire to preserve the aura of wholeness and integrity in the work of art, see Walter Benjamin, "The Work of Art in the Age of Mechanical Reproduction," in *Illuminations*, ed. Hannah Arendt (New York: Schocken Books, 1969).

54. Arnold Genthe, *As I Remember* (New York: Reynal and Hitchcock, 1936), 199; and Adler, "Reconstructing the Dances of Isadora Duncan," 59.

55. Quoted in Steegmuller, *"Your Isadora,"* 346. Gordon Craig was also the son of the Edwardian British actress Ellen Terry, who figures in Duncan's autobiography as a model for women artists.

56. Gertrude Stein, "Orta or One Dancing," in *Two: Gertrude Stein and Her Brother, and Other Early Portraits 1908–1912*, vol. 1 of *The Yale Edition of the Unpublished Writings of Gertrude Stein*, ed. Carl Van Vechten (New Haven: Yale University Press, 1951), 304.

57. Duncan, *My Life*, 75. This idea of an inner unity was characteristic of appeals to totality. See Martin Jay, "The Discourse of Totality Before Western Marxism," in Jay, *Marxism and Totality: The Adventures of a Concept from Lukàcs to Habermas* (Berkeley: University of California Press, 1984), 21–80.

58. Duncan, *My Life*, 224.

59. Duncan, "The Dance of the Greeks," in *Art of the Dance*, ed. Cheney, 96.

60. Duncan, "Depth," 99.

61. Gold, "The Loves of Isadora," 21.

62. Luhan, *Movers and Shakers*, 333.

63. Duncan, *My Life*, 136, 144.

64. Duncan, "Dance of the Future," 63.

65. Duncan, "The Art of the Dance," in *Art of the Dance*, ed. Cheney, 62. Duncan's autobiography and the speeches and other writings in Rosemont, ed., *Isadora Speaks*, also are good sources for Duncan's often impassioned stand for women's liberation.

66. Dell, "Olive Schreiner and Isadora Duncan," in *Women as World Builders*, 41, 44.

67. Eastman, "Heroism Plus Heroics," 73.

68. Janet Flanner, "Isadora Duncan, 1878–1927," in *Paris Was Yesterday, 1925–1939*, ed. Irving Drutman (New York: Viking Press, 1972), 30.

69. Duncan, "Dancing in Relation to Religion and Love," in *Art of the Dance*, ed. Cheney, 126.

70. Duncan, *My Life*, 340.

71. Claude McKay, *A Long Way from Home* (New York: Lee Furman, 1937), 212.

72. Levinson, "André Levinson on Isadora Duncan," 7, 16.

73. Duncan, "Dance of the Future," 61.

74. Duncan, "Dancing in Relation to Religion and Love," 126.

75. Ibid.

76. The practice of lynching, especially, punished African American men for perceived threats to white women. The ideological underpinnings of lynching, especially its intertwining of racial and gender understandings, are explored in many studies, including Gail Bederman, *Manliness and Civilization: A Cultural History of Gender and Race* (Chicago: University of Chicago Press, 1995); Angela Y. Davis, *Women, Race and Class* (New York: Vintage Books, 1983); and Jacquelyn Dowd Hall, "'The Mind That Burns in Each Body': Women, Rape, and Racial Violence," in *Powers of Desire: The Politics of Sexuality*, ed. Snitow, Stansell, and Thompson, 328–49.

77. Duncan, "Dancing in Relation to Religion and Love," 125.

78. Duncan, *My Life*, 358.

79. Ibid., 341.

80. Ibid., 340–41.

81. Eastman, "Isadora Duncan Is Dead."

82. See Kathleen Woodward, *Aging and Its Discontents* (Bloomington: Indiana University Press, 1991).

83. Levinson, "André Levinson on Isadora Duncan," 15.

84. Seroff, *The Real Isadora*, 350.

85. Eastman, "Isadora Duncan Is Dead," 310.

86. "To Isadora Duncan," 307.

87. Duncan, 1921 interview, quoted in *Art of the Dance*, ed. Cheney, 134.

88. Duncan, *My Life*, 323.

89. There have been efforts, however, to reconstruct her dances and there are small groups of Duncan dancers who perform according to these reconstructions.

90. Duncan, "Fragments and Thoughts," in *Art of the Dance*, ed. Cheney, 143.

91. Duncan, *My Life*, 344.

92. Seroff, *The Real Isadora*, 332.

93. Eastman, "Heroism Plus Heroics," 69.

94. Millicent Dillon, *After Egypt: Isadora Duncan and Mary Cassat* (New York: Dutton, 1990), 256.

95. Margaret Anderson, "Isadora Duncan's Misfortune," *Little Review* (April 1917): 7.

96. Flanner, "Isadora Duncan," 28.

97. Eastman, "Heroism Plus Heroics," 70.

2. A Battle with "Reality"

1. "Greenwich Girl Editors in Court," *Chicago Examiner*, February 15, 1921, 8.

2. Margaret Anderson, *My Thirty Years' War: An Autobiography* (1930; reprint, New York: Horizon Press, 1969), 222.

3. Matthew Josephson, "The War for Modern Art," *The Nation* 130 (June 18, 1930): 707.

4. Women's work as editors, publishers, and patrons has been a significant arena for recovering women's contributions to modernist culture. See especially Benstock, *Women of the Left Bank*; Gillian Hanscombe and Virginia L. Smyers, *Writing for Their Lives: The Modernist Women, 1910–1940* (Boston: Northeastern University Press, 1987); and Jayne Marek, *Women Editing Modernism: "Little" Magazines and Literary History* (Lexington: University Press of Kentucky, 1995).

5. Of course, this set of ideas about women was a principle of division among women throughout the period in which the cult of true womanhood held sway. Many women were excluded from its purview, especially slave women, prostitutes, and working-class or poor women who could not or refused to conform to the ideology of moral purity and self-sacrifice. Indeed, the cult of true womanhood gained strength as it excluded women from it, and should be understood as a principle of contrast and division between women. See Shirley Samuels, ed., *The Culture of Sentiment: Race, Gender, and Sentimentality in 19th-Century America* (New York: Oxford University Press, 1992); and Nancy A. Hewitt, "Beyond the Search for Sisterhood: American Women's History in the 1980s," in *Unequal Sisters*, ed. Vicki L. Ruiz and Ellen Carol DuBois (New York: Routledge, 1994), 1–19.

6. Elizabeth Stuyvesant, "Staying Free," in *These Modern Women: Autobiographical Essays from the Twenties*, ed. Elaine Showalter (New York: Feminist Press, 1978), 96.

7. Malcolm Cowley, *Exile's Return* (New York: Penguin Books, 1934), 60.

8. Anderson, *My Thirty Years' War*, 9, 13.

9. Margaret Anderson, "To the Innermost," *Little Review* 1 (October 1914): 4.

10. Anderson, *My Thirty Years' War*, 12.

11. Ibid., 31.

12. For discussions of the flâneur, see Seigel, *Bohemian Paris;* Charles Baudelaire, *The Painter of Modern Life and Other Essays,* trans. and ed. Jonathan Mayne (New York: Da Capo Press, 1964); Walter Benjamin, "On Some Motifs in Baudelaire," in *Illuminations,* ed. Arendt, 155–200; T. J. Clarke, *The Painting of Modern Life* (Princeton: Princeton University Press, 1984); and Keith Tester, ed., *The Flâneur* (New York: Routledge, 1994).

13. Anderson, *My Thirty Years' War,* 33. Anderson's conflation of class and an identity as a female flâneur represents a different model than that suggested by cultural theorist Janet Wolff in *Resident Alien: Feminist Cultural Criticism* (New Haven: Yale University Press, 1995).

14. See Meyerowitz, *Women Adrift.*

15. See Bernard Duffey, *The Chicago Renaissance in American Letters: A Critical History* (East Lansing: Michigan State University Press, 1956); and Dale Kramer, *Chicago Renaissance: The Literary Life in the Midwest, 1900–1930* (New York: Appleton-Century, 1966).

16. Floyd Dell, *Homecoming: An Autobiography* (Port Washington, N.Y.: Kennikat Press, 1969), 228.

17. *Sister Carrie* was first published in 1900, and Anderson says she discussed it in 1912. Why Anderson would review a book twelve years after it was published is mysterious, except that it was an excellent way to tell her story in retrospect.

18. Anderson, *My Thirty Years' War,* 34.

19. Duffey, *Chicago Renaissance in American Letters;* and Douglas Clayton, *Floyd Dell: The Life and Times of an American Rebel* (Chicago: Ivan R. Dee, 1994), 86.

20. The history of little magazines and the *Little Review* specifically has been an important component of an adversarial and canonical modernism. See Marilyn Atlas, "Harriet Monroe, Margaret Anderson, and the Spirit of the Chicago Renaissance," *Midwestern Miscellany* 9 (1981): 43–53; Frederic J. Hoffman, Charles Allen, and Carolyn F. Ulrich, *The Little Magazine: A History and Bibliography* (Princeton: Princeton University Press, 1946); Thomas L. Scott, Melvin Friedman, and Jackson Bryer, eds., *Pound/The Little Review: The Letters of Ezra Pound to Margaret Anderson: The Little Review Correspondence* (New York: New Directions, 1988); Jackson Robert Bryer, "A Trial Track for Racers: Margaret Anderson and the *Little Review,*" Ph.D. diss., University of Wisconsin, 1965; David D. Anderson, "The *Little Review* and Sherwood Anderson," *Midwestern Miscellany* 8 (1980): 28–38; Abby Ann Arthur Johnson, "The Personal Magazine: Margaret C. Anderson and the *Little Review,* 1914–1929," *South Atlantic Quarterly* 75 (Summer 1976): 351–63.

21. Margaret Anderson, "Our First Year," *Little Review* 1 (February 1915): 1.

22. Sherwood Anderson, "The New Note," *Little Review* 1 (March 1914): 23.

23. "Armageddon," *Little Review* 1 (September 1914): 4.

24. Maxwell Bodenheim, "The Inner Hermit," *New Review* (January–February 1931): 64.

25. See Seigel *(Bohemian Paris),* who offers an alternative to the anecdotal characterizations of the work of little magazines in relation to the production of mod-

ernism. In theorizing bohemia as a set of subcultural practices that not only supported artistic production and provided its central motifs, Seigel argues that bohemia can
only be understood in relation to dominant bourgeois culture.

26. Anderson, "The Artist in Life," *Little Review* 2 (June–July 1915): 20.

27. Anderson, *My Thirty Years' War*, 13.

28. Anderson, "Our First Year," 5–6.

29. Anderson, *My Thirty Years' War*, 15; Robert Sage, "Anderson's War of Independence," in *The Left Bank Revisited: Selections from the Paris Tribune, 1917–1934*, ed.
Hugh Ford (University Park: Pennsylvania State University Press, 1972), 69.

30. Discussed in June Sochen, *The New Woman: Feminism in Greenwich Village,
1910–1920* (New York: Quadrangle Books, 1972); and Matthew Josephson, *Life
Among the Surrealists* (New York: Holt, Rinehart, and Winston, 1962).

31. Margaret Anderson, "Incense and Splendor," *Little Review* 1 (June 1914): 2.

32. Don Darnell, "Martie," *Chicago Tribune Magazine*, January 20, 1991, 20–23.

33. Eunice Tietjens, *The World at My Shoulder* (New York: Macmillan, 1938), 64.

34. Ben Hecht, *A Child of the Century* (New York: Donald I. Fine, 1954), 233.

35. Ibid., 235.

36. Sherwood Anderson, "Real-Unreal," *New Republic* 63 (June 11, 1930): 4.

37. Anderson, *My Thirty Years' War*, 227–28.

38. See especially the discussion of Djuna Barnes and Nina Hammett in Bridget J.
Elliot and Jo Ann Wallace, *Women Artists and Writers: Modernist (Im)positionings*
(New York: Routledge, 1994), 122–51. See also Anne Chisholm, *Nancy Cunard: A
Biography* (New York: Knopf, 1979); and Nancy Milford, *Zelda: A Biography* (New
York: Harper and Row, 1970).

39. Anderson, *Little Review* 1 (March 1914): 2; Harry Hansen, *Midwest Portraits*
(New York: Harcourt, Brace, 1923), 102; Darne'l, "Martie," 20.

40. Margaret Anderson, "Mrs. Ellis's Failure," *Little Review* 2 (March 1915): 1, 12.

41. For a groundbreaking study of the link between the lesbian and cultural resistance and experimentation, see Terry Castle, *The Apparitional Lesbian: Female
Homosexuality and Modern Culture* (New York: Columbia University Press, 1993).

42. Anderson, "Real-Unreal," 103.

43. See Ellen Kay Trimberger, "Feminism, Men and Modern Love: Greenwich
Village, 1900–1925," in *Powers of Desire: The Politics of Sexuality*, ed. Snitow, Stansell,
and Thompson, 131–52; and Trimberger, ed., *Intimate Warriors: Portraits of a Modern
Marriage, 1899–1944* (New York: Feminist Press, 1981).

44. Anderson, *My Thirty Years' War*, 77–78.

45. Ibid., 4.

46. Ellen Key, *The Woman Movement* (New York: G. P. Putnam's Sons, 1912), 85.

47. Alfred Kreymborg, *A History of American Poetry: Our Singing Strength* (New
York: Tudor, 1934), 440.

48. William Carlos Williams, *I Wanted To Write a Poem: The Autobiography of the
Works of a Poet*, reported and edited by Edith Heal (Boston: Beacon Press, 1958), 33.

49. Anderson, *My Thirty Years' War*, 107. For more on Heap's important role

as editor of, especially, the later years of the *Little Review,* see Susan Noyes Platt, "Mysticism in the Machine Age: Jane Heap and the *Little Review,*" *Twenty/One* 1 (Fall 1989): 18–44.

50. Anderson, *My Thirty Years' War,* 103, 108.

51. Ibid., 54.

52. See Martin Green, *New York 1913: The Armory Show and the Paterson Strike Pageant* (New York: Scribner's, 1988).

53. Margaret Anderson, "The Challenge of Emma Goldman," *Little Review* 1 (May 1914): 5.

54. Emma Goldman, *Living My Life* (Salt Lake City: Gibbs M. Smith, 1931), 530.

55. Anderson, *My Thirty Years' War,* 70.

56. Goldman, *Living My Life,* 531.

57. Anderson, *My Thirty Years' War,* 73.

58. Margaret Anderson, "A Real Magazine," *Little Review* 3 (August 1916): 1.

59. Goldman, *Living My Life,* 531.

60. Goldman, "Tragedy of Woman's Emancipation," 215.

61. See Benstock, *Women of the Left Bank;* Hanscombe and Smyers, *Writing for Their Lives;* and Mary Biggs, "From Harriet Monroe to AQ: Selected Women's Literary Journals, 1912–1972," *13th Moon: A Feminist Literary Magazine* 8, nos. 1–2 (1984): 183–216.

62. Williams, quoted in Dwight Macdonald, "Two Acorns, One Oak," *New Yorker,* January 23, 1954, 92.

63. Margaret Anderson, "The Art of Prose," *Prose* (1971): 9.

64. Anderson, *My Thirty Years' War,* 58.

65. Anderson, "A Real Magazine," 2.

66. Susan Gubar, "'The Blank Page' and the Issues of Female Creativity," in *Writing and Sexual Difference,* ed. Elizabeth Abel (Chicago: University of Chicago Press, 1982), 92.

67. "The Reader Critic," *Little Review* 3 (October 1916): 23.

68. See Scott, Friedman, and Bryer, eds., *Pound/The Little Review.* This collection of Pound's letters to the *Little Review* presents problems for documenting the position of Anderson and Heap since only Pound's letters are presented.

69. Ruthven Todd, "The *Little Review,*" *20th Century Verse* (February 1939): 162.

70. See the Reader-Critic pages of the *Little Review* 4 (1917–18).

71. A.R.S., "The Reader Critic," *Little Review* 4 (August 1917): 23; Margaret Anderson, "What the Public Doesn't Want," *Little Review* 4 (August 1917): 21.

72. Janet Flanner, "Life on a Cloud: Margaret Anderson," in *Janet Flanner's World: Uncollected Writings, 1932–1975,* ed. Irving Drutman (New York: Harcourt, Brace, Jovanovich, 1981), 319.

73. Anderson claims that this letter was typical of hundreds the *Little Review* received. See *My Thirty Years' War,* 212–13.

74. Ibid., 213–14.

75. See Benstock, *Women of the Left Bank,* 377.

76. Jackson Robert Bryer, "Joyce, *Ulysses*, and the *Little Review*," *South Atlantic Quarterly* 66 (Spring 1967): 158.

77. Anderson, *My Thirty Years' War*, 221.

78. Ibid., 222.

79. Margaret Anderson, "*Ulysses* in Court," *Little Review* 7 (January–March 1921): 21–22, 24–25.

80. Many avant-gardists reached that conclusion, but Anderson reached it much earlier than most.

81. Anderson, *My Thirty Years' War*, 239.

82. Platt gives an excellent summary and interpretation of the later issues of the *Little Review* primarily put together by Heap.

83. Form letter, *Little Review* Collection, Fromkin Memorial Archives, University of Wisconsin–Milwaukee.

84. Final Number flyer, *Little Review* Collection.

85. Emma Goldman to Margaret Anderson, April 14, 1928, in the *Little Review* Collection.

86. Anderson, "Editorial," in *The Little Review Anthology*, ed. Margaret Anderson (New York: Horizon Press, 1953), 351.

87. Jane Heap, "Lost: A Renaissance," in ibid., 353.

88. V. F. Calverton, "The Decade of Convictions," *The Bookman* 71 (August 1930): 486–90.

89. Josephson, "The War for Modern Art," 707.

90. Alfred Kazin, "A Life Led as a Work of Art," *New York Times Book Review*, August 16, 1970, 1.

91. Bodenheim, "The Inner Hermit," 63.

3. Home from Bohemia

1. Floyd Dell, *Intellectual Vagabondage* (1926; reprint, Chicago: Ivan R. Dee, 1990), 246.

2. Ibid., 261.

3. See the excellent biography of Dell by Clayton, *Floyd Dell*.

4. Sinclair Lewis, "Literary Portraits: Two," *The Bookman* 53 (May 1921): 245.

5. See Rick Beard and Leslie Berlowitz, eds., *Greenwich Village: Culture and Counterculture* (New Brunswick, N.J.: Rutgers University Press, 1993); and Adele Heller and Lois Rudnick, eds., *1915: The Cultural Moment* (New Brunswick, N.J.: Rutgers University Press, 1991).

6. See Fishbein, *Rebels in Bohemia*.

7. Dell, *Intellectual Vagabondage*, 129.

8. See Djuna Barnes, *New York*, ed. Alyce Barry (Los Angeles: Sun and Moon Press, 1989); and Alyce Barry, ed., *I Could Never Be Lonely Without a Husband: Interviews by Djuna Barnes* (London: Virago, 1987).

9. Edna St. Vincent Millay, "First Fig," *Collected Lyrics* (New York: Harper Colophon, 1981), 95.

10. For the contested meanings of womanhood in urban space, see Christine Stansell, *City of Women: Sex and Class in New York, 1789–1860* (Urbana: University of Illinois Press, 1987); Peiss, *Cheap Amusements;* and Meyerowitz, *Women Adrift.*

11. For Dell's background and career in Chicago and New York, see Clayton, *Floyd Dell,* and Fishbein, *Rebels in Bohemia,* as well as Dell, *Homecoming;* Joseph Freeman, *An American Testament: A Narrative of Rebels and Romantics* (New York: Farrar and Rinehart, 1936); John E. Hart, *Floyd Dell* (New York: Twayne Publishers, 1971); Eric Homberger, *American Writers and Radical Politics, 1900–1939: Equivocal Commitments* (New York: St. Martin's Press, 1986); Henry F. May, *The End of American Innocence: The First Years of Our Own Time, 1912–1917* (Oxford: Oxford University Press, 1959); Judith Nierman, *Floyd Dell: An Annotated Bibliography of Secondary Sources, 1910–1981* (Metuchen, N.J.: Scarecrow Press, 1984); O'Neill, ed., *Echoes of Revolt;* and Steven Watson, *Strange Bedfellows: The First American Avant-Garde* (New York: Abbeville Press, 1991).

12. Dell, "Enter the Woman," in *Looking at Life,* 30.

13. For a compelling treatment of the trope of woman as linked to the past, see Rita Felski, "On Nostalgia: The Prehistoric Woman," in her *Gender of Modernity,* 35–60.

14. Dell, "La Belle Dame sans Merci," in *Looking at Life,* 256. See also Andreas Huyssen, "Mass Culture as Woman," 44–62.

15. Dell, "Feminism for Men," in *Looking at Life,* 19.

16. Ibid., 18.

17. Dell, *Homecoming,* 330.

18. The advertisements and reports on birth control and sex *The Masses* published were, however, subject to the watchful eye of the Society for the Suppression of Vice.

19. Dell, "La Belle Dame sans Merci," 257.

20. For an alternative reading of women's retention of domestic space for cultural production, see Marianne DeKoven, "'Excellent Not a Hull House': Gertrude Stein, Jane Addams, and Feminist-Modernist Political Culture," in *Rereading Modernism: New Directions in Feminist Criticism,* ed. Lisa Rado (New York: Garland, 1994), 321–50.

21. Jane Tompkins has offered the most persuasive argument for the power women wielded through sentimental language. See *Sensational Designs: The Cultural Work of American Fiction, 1790–1860* (New York: Oxford, 1985).

22. See Peiss, *Cheap Amusements;* Meyerowitz, *Women Adrift;* and Ellen Wiley Todd, *The "New Woman" Revised: Painting and Gender Politics on Fourteenth Street* (Berkeley: University of California Press, 1993).

23. On Duncan, see Dell, "Who Said that Beauty Passes Like A Dream?" 48–49; and Dell, "Olive Schreiner and Isadora Duncan," 43. On burlesque, see the excellent cultural history by Robert G. Allen, *Horrible Prettiness: Burlesque and American Culture* (Chapel Hill: University of North Carolina Press, 1991).

24. Dell notes this in *Homecoming* as a way to explain why the conventional paths of courtship were difficult for him even as he observed the dance halls attended by charity girls, and it was a central theme in many of his novels.

25. Floyd Dell, *King Arthur's Socks and Other Village Plays* (New York: Knopf, 1922).

26. Dell, "Burlesquerie," in *Looking at Life*, 58.

27. Ibid., 61.

28. Dell, "Dolls and Abraham Lincoln," in *Looking at Life*, 232, 234.

29. Dell, "Burlesquerie," 62.

30. Dell, "Mona Lisa and the Wheelbarrow," in *Looking at Life*.

31. Clayton, *Floyd Dell*, 138.

32. Floyd Dell, "A Psycho-Analytic Confession," *The Liberator* 3 (April 1920), 15.

33. Ibid., 16.

34. Ibid.

35. Alice Beal Parsons, "Mr. Windle's Wild Oats," *New York Herald Tribune Books*, November 7, 1926, 4.

36. For a fuller analysis of *The Masses'* trials, see Fishbein, *Rebels in Bohemia;* and Hart, *Floyd Dell*, 53–57.

37. Genevieve Taggard, "May Days," in *May Days: An Anthology of Verse from Masses-Liberator*, ed. Taggard (New York: Boni and Liveright, 1925), 12–13.

38. Michael J. Hoffman and Patrick D. Murphy, eds., *Critical Essays on American Modernism* (New York: G. K. Hall, 1992); and Homberger, *American Writers and Radical Politics*.

39. For a general history of women in the 1920s, see Dorothy M. Brown, *Setting a Course: American Women in the 1920s* (Boston: Twayne, 1987). For an intellectual history of women, see Rosalind Rosenberg, *Beyond Separate Spheres: Intellectual Roots of Modern Feminism* (New Haven: Yale University Press, 1982). See also Frederick Lewis Allen's popular history of the era, *Only Yesterday: An Informal History of the 1920s* (1931; reprint, New York: Wiley, 1997).

40. Nancy Cott also argues that modern feminism foundered because it was internally divided between those who sought to protect women and therefore insisted on women's innate "difference" and those who believed that all barriers to equality with men should be torn down. See *The Grounding of Modern Feminism*.

41. See Freda Kirchwey, ed., *Our Changing Morality* (New York: Albert and Charles Boni, 1924); and Pruette, *Women and Leisure*.

42. V. F. Calverton, "The New Society," *The Nation* 122 (May 26, 1926): 585.

43. Douglas Clayton, "Introduction," in Dell, *Intellectual Vagabondage*, i–xiv. Here the themes of modernist opposition to mass culture are expressed in familiar terms: "Put another way, *Intellectual Vagabondage* asked: does the cultural avant-garde genuinely oppose the society it professes to hate, or has it found a way of living with that society while appeasing its own rebellious, disenchanted conscience?" (xiv). Clayton's fine biography of Dell emphasizes the importance of Dell's struggles with "modern love," but focuses on this theme in Dell's life, less so in his ideas.

44. Dell, *Intellectual Vagabondage*, 138.

45. Ibid., 125. In this, Dell's intellectual odyssey articulated the search for a therapeutic ethos among intellectuals. See Lears's *No Place of Grace*.

46. Studies of women as symbols of decadence and mysticism include Bram Dijkstra, *Idols of Perversity: Fantasies of Feminine Evil in Fin-de-siècle Culture* (New York: Oxford University Press, 1986).

47. Dell, *Intellectual Vagabondage,* 128. Subsequent page references appear in the text.

48. See Edmund Wilson, *Axel's Castle: A Study of the Imaginative Literature of 1870–1930* (New York: Scribner's, 1931); Pruette, *Women and Leisure;* Cowley, *Exile's Return;* Harold Stearns, ed., *Civilization in the United States: An Inquiry by Thirty Americans* (New York: Harcourt, Brace, 1922).

49. Dell, *Homecoming,* 361.

50. For discussions of the flapper as the embodiment of modern womanhood, see Paula S. Fass, *The Damned and the Beautiful: American Youth in the 1920s* (New York: Oxford University Press, 1977); John C. Spurlock and Cynthia A. Magistro, eds., *New and Improved: The Transformation of American Women's Emotional Culture* (New York: New York University Press, 1998); and Lynn Dumenil, "The New Woman," in Dumenil, *The Modern Temper: American Culture and Society in the 1920s* (New York: Hill and Wang, 1995), 98–144.

51. Dorothy Day, "Girls and Boys Come Out to Play," *The Liberator* (November 1923): 30.

52. See Ann Ardis, *New Women, New Novels: Feminism and Early Modernism* (New Brunswick, N.J.: Rutgers University Press, 1994).

53. Dell, *Intellectual Vagabondage,* 261.

54. Day, "Girls and Boys Come Out to Play," 30.

55. See Fass, *The Damned and the Beautiful,* as well as Haag, "In Search of 'the Real Thing,'" 547–77.

56. Floyd Dell, *Janet March* (New York: Knopf, 1923), 207–12, 215.

57. Clayton, *Floyd Dell,* 218–21; and Hart, *Floyd Dell,* 93. At least one feminist critic at the time commented wryly on the tenor of the novel. See Florence Guy Seabury, "Stereotypes," in *Our Changing Morality,* ed. Kirchwey, 219–31.

58. "*Little Women* Leads Poll: Novel Rated Ahead of Bible for Influence on High School Pupils," *New York Times,* March 22, 1927, 7; and Joel Myerson and Daniel Shealy, "The Sales of Louisa May Alcott's Books," *Harvard Library Bulletin* 1, no. 1 (1990): 47–86.

59. Alma J. Payne, "Louisa May Alcott: A Bibliographical Essay on Secondary Sources," in *Critical Essays on Louisa May Alcott,* ed. Madeleine B. Stern (Boston: G. K. Hall and Co., 1984), 281.

60. Dell, *Janet March,* 207.

61. See Pruette, *Women and Leisure.*

62. Dell, *Janet March,* 456.

63. The debate between feminists and sexologists was staged in two of the collections edited by the social critics V. F. Calverton and Samuel Schmalhausen: *Sex in Civilization* and *Woman's Coming of Age.*

64. Lorine Pruette, "Why Women Fail," in *Woman's Coming of Age,* ed. Calverton

and Schmalhausen, 243. For an important counterperspective, see William R. Leach, "Transformations in a Culture of Consumption: Women and Department Stores, 1890–1925," *Journal of American History* 71, no. 2 (1984): 319–42.

65. For examples of this sensibility, see Anonymous, "Confessions of an Ex-Feminist," *New Republic* 46 (1926): 218–20; M. B. Bruere, "Feminism's Awkward Age," *Harper's* 150 (1925): 545–51; Diana Freeman, "Feminist's Husband," *New Republic* 52 (1927): 15–16; Lillian Symes, "Still a Man's Game: Reflections of a Slightly Tired Feminist," *Harper's* 158 (1929): 678–86; Worth Tuttle, "Autobiography of an Ex-Feminist," *The Atlantic* 152 (1933): 641–49. See also the autobiographical essays published in *The Nation* in 1926–27 and collected in Showalter, ed., *These Modern Women*.

66. Nancy Evans, "Good-by, Bohemia," *Scribner's Magazine* (June 1931): 646.

67. See Fishbein, *Rebels in Bohemia,* as well as Peter Conn, *The Divided Mind: Ideology and Imagination in America, 1898–1917* (New York: Cambridge University Press, 1983); May, *End of American Innocence;* and Arthur Wertheim, *The New York Little Renaissance: Iconoclasm, Modernism, and Nationalism in American Culture* (New York: New York University Press, 1976).

68. Floyd Dell, "The Fall of Greenwich Village," in his *Love in Greenwich Village* (New York: George H. Doran Co., 1926), 298–99.

69. Floyd Dell, *Moon-Calf* (New York: Knopf, 1920).

70. Dell, "Fall of Greenwich Village," 303.

71. Feminism was thus associated with Victorian prudery, or what Christina Simmons calls the myth of Victorian repression that was created in the 1920s in order to celebrate the modern qualities of the twenties as free, expressive, and healthy. Importantly, this myth had little to do with women's understanding of and attempts to control sexuality in the nineteenth century. See Simmons, "Modern Sexuality and the Myth of Victorian Repression," 17–42.

72. See Alice Beal Parsons, "Man-Made Illusions about Women," in *Woman's Coming of Age,* ed. Calverton and Schmalhausen, 20–34.

73. See Pruette, *Women and Leisure;* La Follette, *Concerning Women;* and Parsons, *Woman's Dilemma.*

74. The mental hygiene movement was a broad consortium of "health" professionals—doctors, psychiatrists, social workers, educators, and sociologists—and it seems to be the flowering of social reform since the movement began in 1908 for the treatment of the insane. The society brought together ideas of mental and physical health to place them in a larger social context. The movement also reflected the institutionalization of psychology and the growing professional status of related fields. As Mary Ross explained in one article, "[M]ental hygiene has been advancing . . . as a science of man in his world, a science which might hope eventually to bring understanding and control of mind and emotions and their interactions in personal and social life as the physical sciences are bringing mastery of more tangible forces." See Ross, "Mental Hygiene Looks at the World," *The Survey* 64 (June 15, 1930): 262–64, 287. I haven't been able to discover Dell's formal connection to this movement, but

Love in the Machine Age: A Psychological Study of the Transition from Patriarchal Society (1930; reprint, New York: Octagon Books, 1973), was celebrated by one of the leaders of the society as one of the best, if not the best, books on mental hygiene. See William A. White, "Review of *Love in the Machine Age*," *Mental Hygiene* 14 (April 1930): 469–72.

75. Richard W. Fox and T. J. Jackson Lears, "Introduction," in *Culture of Consumption*, ed. Fox and Lears (New York: Pantheon Books, 1983), xii.

76. This form of antifeminism was common by the late 1920s and early 1930s. See the collection of representative articles in *Redefining the New Woman, 1920–1963*, ed. with introductions by Angela Howard and Sasha Rana Adams Tarrant (New York: Garland, 1997).

77. This narrows the definition of "sex" from all those issues pertaining to the woman question to the expression of sexuality.

78. Dell, *Love in the Machine Age*, 143. Subsequent page references appear in the text.

79. See Lewis Erenberg, *Steppin' Out: New York Nightlife and the Transformation of American Culture, 1890–1930* (Chicago: University of Chicago Press, 1984).

80. Max Eastman, "Floyd Dell's Double Life," in Eastman, *Art and the Life of Action with Other Essays* (New York: Knopf, 1934), 143.

81. Lorine Pruette, "Happy and Successful Lives," *New York Herald Tribune Books*, April 6, 1930, 6.

82. Ibid., 6.

83. Dell, *Homecoming*, xi.

84. Ibid., 283.

4. In Search of a Usable Past

1. Josephine Herbst, "The Starched Blue Sky of Spain," in *The Starched Blue Sky of Spain* (New York: HarperCollins, 1991), 138.

2. Josephine Herbst, "Spain's Agony: A Period of Exposure," *The Nation* 203 (July 25, 1966): 92.

3. Herbst, "Starched Blue Sky of Spain," 133, 150.

4. Ibid., 131.

5. Much of the information about Herbst's life in this chapter comes from Elinor Langer's biography of her. See *Josephine Herbst* (Boston: Little, Brown, 1983).

6. See Constance Coiner, *Better Red: The Writing and Resistance of Tillie Olsen and Meridel LeSueur* (New York: Oxford University Press, 1995); Michael Denning, *The Cultural Front: The Laboring of American Culture in the Twentieth Century* (London: Verso, 1996); Rabinowitz, *Labor and Desire*; and Nora Ruth Roberts, *Three Radical Women Writers: Class and Gender in Meridel LeSueur, Tillie Olsen, and Josephine Herbst* (New York: Garland Publishing, 1996).

7. Lois Scharf, *To Work and to Wed: Female Employment, Feminism, and the Great Depression* (Westport, Conn.: Greenwood Press, 1980); and Susan Ware, *Beyond Suffrage: Women in the New Deal* (Cambridge: Harvard University Press, 1981).

8. Nancy A. Hewitt, "Reflections from a Departing Editor: Recasting Issues of Marginality," *Gender and History* 4, no. 1 (Spring 1997): 7.

9. Susan Stanford Friedman, "Modernism of the 'Scattered Remnant': Race and Politics in H.D.'s Development," in *Feminist Issues in Literary Scholarship*, ed. Benstock, 218.

10. For an example of this view, see Hugh Kenner, "The Making of the Modernist Canon," *Chicago Review* (Spring 1984): 363–75; for an indictment of the effects of canonization, see Paul Lauter, "Race and Gender in the Shaping of the American Literary Canon: A Case Study from the Twenties," in *Feminist Criticism and Social Change: Sex, Class, and Race in Literature and Culture*, ed. Judith Newton and Deborah Rosenfelt (New York: Methuen, 1985), 19–44.

11. See Alan M. Wald, "Introduction: Marxism and Modernism in the 1930s," in Wald, *The Revolutionary Imagination: The Poetry and Politics of John Wheelright and Sherry Mangan* (Chapel Hill: University of North Carolina Press, 1983); Nelson, *Repression and Recovery*.

12. Josephine Herbst, "A Year of Disgrace," in *The Starched Blue Sky of Spain*, 78.

13. Ibid., 76.

14. Modernist women's writing and art were often associated with their seemingly "natural" bent to convey interiority. See, for example, Paul Rosenfeld, "Georgia O'Keeffe," in Rosenfeld, *Port of New York* (1924; reprint, Urbana: University of Illinois Press, 1966), 199–210. In contrast, Herbst's characters in her early fiction possess almost no interior consciousness at all. Several recent anthologies on gender and modernism challenge essentialist distinctions between men's and women's modernisms. See *Rereading Modernism*, and *Modernism, Gender, and Culture: A Cultural Studies Approach* (New York: Garland, 1997), both edited by Lisa Rado.

15. Josephine Herbst, "The Magicians and Their Apprentices," in *The Starched Blue Sky of Spain*, 33.

16. Herbst, "Year of Disgrace," 69.

17. The argument that modernists created a "myth of Victorian repression to describe and condemn old patterns of sexual behavior and shape new ones" was developed by Christina Simmons in "Modern Sexuality and the Myth of Victorian Repression," in *Passion and Power: Sexuality in History*, ed. Kathy Peiss and Christina Simmons (Philadelphia: Temple University Press, 1989), 157–77.

18. Herbst, "Year of Disgrace," 73.

19. Josephine Herbst, "Ubiquitous Critics and the Author," *Newberry Library Bulletin* 5, no. 1 (1958): 6.

20. Herbst, "Year of Disgrace," 69–70.

21. Josephine Herbst, *Nothing Is Sacred* (New York: Howard-McCann Co., 1928); Herbst, *Money for Love* (New York: Howard-McCann Co., 1929).

22. Josephine Herbst, "Iowa Takes to Literature," *American Mercury* 7 (April 1926): 470.

23. Clifton P. Fadiman, "Small Ways of Small People," *The Nation* 129 (November 29, 1929): 592.

24. Ibid., 592.

25. Ibid.

26. "'Money for Love' and Other Recent Works," *New York Times Book Review*, September 22, 1929, 6.

27. Norah Meade, "Money for Love," *The Bookman* 70 (November 1929): 316.

28. Isidor Schneider, "The Fetish of Simplicity," *The Nation* 132 (February 18, 1931): 184.

29. Josephine Herbst, "Ignorance among the Living Dead," *New Masses* (January 1929): 10.

30. William Troy, "Pathos Is Not Enough," *The Nation* 137 (July 12, 1933): 52.

31. Herbst, "Year of Disgrace," 79. Subsequent page references appear in the text.

32. Denning, *The Cultural Front*, 135.

33. Warren I. Susman, "The Culture of the Thirties," in Susman, *Culture as History: The Transformation of American Society in the Twentieth Century* (New York: Pantheon Books, 1984), 150–83.

34. See Melosh, *Engendering Culture*; Richard Pells, *Radical Visions and American Dreams: Culture and Social Thought in the Depression Years* (New York: Harper and Row, 1973); and William Stott, *Documentary Expression and Thirties America* (New York: Oxford University Press, 1973).

35. Susman, "Culture of the Thirties," 157.

36. Herbst, "Year of Disgrace," 70.

37. Herbst, "Ubiquitous Critics and the Author," 12.

38. Herbst, in "What Is Americanism? A Symposium on Marxism and the American Tradition," *Partisan Review and Anvil* 3 (April 1936): 6.

39. Ibid., 5.

40. Major sources include: Daniel Aaron, *Writers on the Left* (New York: Avon Books, 1961); James B. Gilbert, *Writers and Partisans* (New York: Wiley and Sons, 1968); Eric Homberger, *Equivocal Commitments: American Writers and Radical Politics, 1900–39* (New York: St. Martin's Press, 1986); Alfred Kazin, *On Native Grounds: An Interpretation of Modern American Prose Literature* (New York: Reynal and Hitchcock, 1942); and Stott, *Documentary Expression and Thirties America*.

41. Harvey Swados, in *The American Writer and the Great Depression*, ed. Harvey Swados (Indianapolis: Bobbs-Merrill, 1966), 103.

42. Rose C. Feld, "Miss Herbst's 'Rope of Gold' and Other Recent Works of Fiction," *New York Times Book Review*, March 5, 1939, 6.

43. Richard A. Cordell, "After the Gilded Age," *Saturday Review of Literature* 19 (March 4, 1939): 7.

44. Rebecca Pitts, "The Trexler Trilogy," *New Republic* 98 (March 22, 1939): 202.

45. Edith H. Walton, "Miss Herbst Turns to the Past," *New York Times Book Review*, (May 28, 1933): 6.

46. Pitts, "Trexler Trilogy," 202.

47. Lionel Abel, "A Technician of Mediocrity," *The Nation* 139 (October 31, 1934): 516.

48. Josephine Herbst, *Pity Is Not Enough* (New York: Harcourt, Brace, 1933), 3.

49. Herbst, quoted by Langer in the introduction to *Pity Is Not Enough* (1933; reprint, New York: Warner Books, 1985), x.

50. Herbst, *Pity Is Not Enough* (New York: Harcourt, Brace, 1933), 145, 148–50. Subsequent page references appear in the text.

51. Josephine Herbst, *The Executioner Waits* (New York: Harcourt, Brace, 1934), 312.

52. Josephine Herbst, *Rope of Gold* (New York: Harcourt, Brace, 1939), 47–48, 118.

53. Charlotte Nekola, "Worlds Unseen: Political Women Journalists and the 1930s," in *Writing Red: An Anthology of American Women Writers, 1930–1940*, ed. Charlotte Nekola and Paula Rabinowitz (New York: Feminist Press, 1987), 194.

54. Quoted in Nekola and Rabinowitz, eds., *Writing Red*, 194.

55. Herbst, *Rope of Gold*, 92.

56. Ibid., 363–64.

57. Ibid., 403.

58. Herbst, "Passport to Realengo 18," in *Writing Red*, ed. Nekola and Rabinowitz, 200.

59. Ibid., 199–200.

60. Herbst, "The Enemy," in *Writing Red*, ed. Nekola and Rabinowitz, 96–105.

61. In her biography of Herbst, Elinor Langer also interpreted the polarization of political commitment and romantic love during Herbst's sojourn in Cuba, but Langer's interpretation, while creative, stabilizes the dichotomy anew. Langer assembles Herbst's reporter's diary and her letters to her estranged husband, John Herrmann, and arranges them next to each other in running columns.

62. Herbst, "The Enemy," 97. Subsequent page references appear in the text.

63. Joan W. Scott, "'Experience,'" in *Feminists Theorize the Political*, ed. Judith Butler and Joan W. Scott (New York: Routledge, 1992), 35.

64. Quoted in Langer, *Josephine Herbst*, 316.

65. Nelson, *Repression and Recovery*; and Kalaidjian, *American Culture Between the Wars*.

66. Langer, *Josephine Herbst*, 276.

67. Herbst, "Yesterday's Road," in *The Starched Blue Sky of Spain*, 111.

68. Swados, in *The American Writer and the Great Depression*, ed. Swados, 103.

69. Herbst, "Yesterday's Road," 105.

70. Ibid., 106.

71. Ibid., 108.

72. Herbst's romantic life is not significantly discussed in her memoirs, though she devotes a long, allegorical section of "A Year of Disgrace" to a sailing trip she took with her husband, writer-turned-Communist-organizer John Herrmann. Entirely hidden in Herbst's memoirs were the long-term relationships she had with women. Langer sensitively portrays Herbst's two major relationships with women, an artist, Marion Greenwood, and a poet, Jean Garrigue.

73. She was responding especially to Aaron's *Writers on the Left*.

74. David Madden, *Proletarian Writers of the Thirties* (Carbondale: Southern Illinois University Press, 1968).

75. Herbst, "Yesterday's Road," 125.

76. Herbst, quoted in Madden, *Proletarian Writers of the Thirties*, xv.

77. In addition to Rabinowitz, *Labor and Desire*, and the introductions by Nekola and Rabinowitz in *Writing Red*, see Celia Betsky, "Reconsideration: The Trilogy of Josephine Herbst," *New Republic* 179 (July 8 and July 15, 1978): 45–46; Winifred Farrant Bevilacqua, "An Introduction to Josephine Herbst, Novelist," *Books at Iowa* 25 (1976): 3–20; Ralph F. Bogardus and Fred Hobson, eds., *Literature at the Barricades: The American Writer in the 1930s* (Tuscaloosa: University of Alabama Press, 1982); Robert L. Caserio, "Celibate Sisters-in-Revolution: Towards Reading Sylvia Townsend Warner," in *Engendering Men: The Question of Male Feminist Criticism*, ed. Joseph A. Boone and Michael Cadden (New York: Routledge, 1990), 254–74; Barbara Foley, *Telling the Truth: The Theory and Practice of Documentary Fiction* (Ithaca, N.Y.: Cornell University Press, 1986); Foley, "Women and the Left in the 1930s," *American Literary History* 2 (Spring 1990): 150–69; Candida Ann Lacey, "Striking Fictions: Women Writers and the Making of a Proletarian Realism," *Women's Studies International Forum* 9 (1986): 373–84; Marcus Klein, "Roots of Radicals: Experience in the Thirties," in Madden, *Proletarian Writers of the Thirties*, 134–57; Annis Pratt et al., *Archetypal Patterns in Women's Fiction* (Bloomington: Indiana University Press, 1981); Walter B. Rideout, "Forgotten Images of the Thirties: Josephine Herbst," *Literary Review* 27 (Fall 1983): 28–36; Deborah Rosenfelt, "From the Thirties: Tillie Olsen and the Radical Tradition," *Feminist Studies* 7 (Fall 1981): 371–406; Rosenfelt, "Getting Into the Game: American Women Writers and the Radical Tradition," *Women's Studies International Forum* 9, no. 4 (1986): 363–72.

78. Herbst, quoted in Madden, *Proletarian Writers of the Thirties*, xix, xx.

79. Herbst, "Yesterday's Road," 106.

80. See for example, Herbst, "Spain's Agony: A Period of Exposure," 92. *The Nation* asked Herbst to review Vincent Brome's *The International Brigades* (1966), and instead of writing a review of the book, Herbst wrote the editors a long letter about why she couldn't "properly" review it, because she could not be "completely dispassionate," and because she felt the background necessary for context would only emerge in "pompous" statements. *The Nation* published the letter as a review, with a qualifying contributor's note at the top. The essay, then, is similar to the letter Herbst wrote to David Madden as a mark of her ambivalence as a representative of her generation.

81. Herbst, "Starched Blue Sky of Spain," 134.

82. Herbst wrote in "The Starched Blue Sky of Spain" that she found herself in the middle of such a quandary when she was told in secret that a Spanish intellectual, Robles, who was a professor in the United States, had been shot as a spy. Herbst's quandary was whether she should tell John Dos Passos, who was in Spain searching for Robles, that his friend was dead, which could jeopardize the political position of leftist journalists in Spain, or to stay silent. Robles' death was one of the events leading to Dos Passos' disillusionment with the Left. Herbst carefully balances the moral

questions left by this story—Was Robles a spy? Was he the victim of treachery, or was his murder a mistake?—with her encounter with those struggling to stave off the authoritarian state.

83. Josephine Herbst, "The Ruins of Memory," *The Nation* 182 (April 14, 1956): 302.

84. Herbst, "Starched Blue Sky of Spain," 135. Subsequent page references appear in the text.

85. Hilton Kramer, "Who Was Josephine Herbst?" *New Criterion* (September 1984): 1–14.

86. See Alice A. Jardine, *Gynesis: Configurations of Woman and Modernity* (Ithaca, N.Y.: Cornell University Press, 1985).

87. See Scott, "'Experience.'"

Conclusion

1. Dell, *Homecoming,* 233.

2. "Manifesto: Revolution of the Word," *transition* (June 1929): 13.

3. Rachel Blau DuPlessis, *Writing Beyond the Ending: Narrative Strategies of Twentieth-Century Women Writers* (Bloomington: Indiana University Press, 1985).

4. Herbst, "The Magicians and Their Apprentices," 42.

5. Herbst, *Pity Is Not Enough,* 80.

6. See especially Douglas, *Terrible Honesty,* which is an extension and development of the argument in her earlier *The Feminization of American Culture* (New York: Avon Books, 1977). See also Stanley Coben, *Rebellion Against Victorianism: The Impetus for Cultural Change in 1920s America* (New York: Oxford University Press, 1991).

7. Floyd Dell, "Mona Lisa and the Wheelbarrow," in *Looking at Life,* 11–12.

8. Baker Brownell, "Introduction," in *Civilization and Enjoyment,* ed. Alvin Johnson et al. (New York: D. Van Nostrand, 1929), 5.

9. Duncan, *My Life,* 134.

10. See Walter Benn Michaels, *Our America: Nativism, Modernism, and Pluralism* (Durham, N.C.: Duke University Press, 1995); Susan Manning, *Ecstasy and the Demon: Feminism and Nationalism in the Dances of Mary Wigman* (Berkeley: University of California Press, 1993); and Jean Pickering and Suzanne Kehde, eds., *Narratives of Nostalgia, Gender, and Nationalism* (New York: New York University Press, 1997).

Index

193

Elizabeth Francis teaches American history at the University of Rhode Island and has been a visiting professor in the fields of American civilization, history, and women's studies at Brown University. She wrote the Introduction to a recent edition of *The Starched Blue Sky of Spain and Other Memoirs*, by Josephine Herbst.